MEDIEVAL SCOTLAND

For John and Andrew
and in memory of Hazel

MEDIEVAL SCOTLAND

KINGSHIP AND NATION

ALAN MACQUARRIE

SUTTON PUBLISHING

First published in the United Kingdom in 2004 by
Sutton Publishing Limited · Phoenix Mill
Thrupp · Stroud · Gloucestershire · GL5 2BU

British Library Cataloguing in Publication Data
A catalogue record for this book is available from the British Library.

ISBN 0-7509-2977-4

Typeset in Garamond 3 11.5/14 pt.
Typesetting and origination by
Sutton Publishing Limited.
Printed and bound in England by
J.H. Haynes & Co. Ltd, Sparkford.

Contents

Preface

This work presents an overview of Scottish medieval history from the Roman invasion to the death of James II in a way that attempts to be accessible and non-controversial, while hoping to stimulate the curious to explore the subject more deeply. I hope that this book will help many people to understand Scotland better through a better understanding of our past.

My thanks are due to many colleagues and friends for their help and support while this work has been in progress. I owe a debt to the Department of Adult and Continuing Education at Glasgow University, and to my students there for their many helpful and astute comments. I must thank my son Andrew Macquarrie, whose computer skills have made this task infinitely easier and faster. My colleague Anne Clackson has read the entire manuscript and made many helpful corrections. My wife Hazel read and commented on the first third of the manuscript, and helped to make comprehensible to the general reader many concepts which were difficult enough for a specialist. Sadly, she became seriously ill while this work was in progress, and did not live to see its completion. Her courage in the face of illness has been an inspiration to me.

I alone am responsible for faults and errors which remain despite their best efforts. This book is dedicated with pride to my sons John and Andrew, who helped me through difficult times, and to Hazel's memory.

ALAN MACQUARRIE
University of Strathclyde, Glasgow

Introduction

Medieval Scotland: Kingship and Nation

The Celtic peoples were once dominant across the whole of Europe north of the Alps. By the central Middle Ages, the Scots were the only Celtic people who had established a lasting unified kingdom. Wales and Brittany, subject to the same sort of pressure from a powerful neighbour, retained linguistic distinctness but lost political nationhood; Ireland became a patchwork of petty kingdoms. So why is Scotland's medieval history so different from theirs?

Themes

There are a number of contributory factors to Scottish distinctness which this book will explore. One of these is kingship. In most Celtic nations, very strikingly in Ireland, kingship tends to become fragmented and debased. Heads of quite small clans and kin-groups were entitled to be called *rí*, king. This does not happen in Scotland, where from an early time kingship represented power and prestige. We will seek to explore the origins and development of Scottish kingship, and to explain how the fact of being a self-consciously unified kingdom contributed to Scotland's struggle for freedom in the Middle Ages.

Another factor is national identity. The Scots were a not so much a pure Celtic race as an admixture of Celtic peoples – Gael, Picts and Britons – with strong non-Celtic elements blending in, notably Norse and English. There was perhaps no more hybrid nation in the north-west of Europe. Did this identity, transcending ethnic and linguistic divisions, give Scotland some kind of mongrel robustness?

Another consideration, perhaps a contrast to these, is the fact of regional and local identities and social cohesion. Scots today have a strong sense of attachment to their locality as well as to their nation, and this may always have been the case. Sometimes these local attachments have transcended hierarchical ones, and there is evidence that medieval Scotland was a more open society, with better opportunities for social mobility, than some others. It would be an exaggeration to say that medieval Scotland was egalitarian or democratic; but the striking success of presbyterianism in Scotland has to be explained somehow. Regional and local loyalties may also help to explain how the struggle for identity continued even at times when monarchy and central government were weak.

Like all its medieval neighbours, Scotland was a Christian society. Although English, Gaelic and British elements all went together to make up Scottish Christianity, the resulting Church was a coherent and homogeneous blend. Until the very end of the medieval period, Scotland did not have its own archbishop; but it had a self-consciously national Church, an *Ecclesia Scoticana*, which powerfully preached the virtues of national defence, freedom and patriotism in times of crisis. The Scottish Church has always been notably loyal to Scotland.

Periods

The history of medieval Scotland can be conveniently divided into three periods:

1. Between the end of Roman Britain and the coming of the Vikings, there was a long period of equilibrium between the different races occupying Scotland – Picts, Gael, Britons and Angles. This period saw the conversion of Scotland to Christianity. The shock of the Viking onslaught shattered this balance, and prepared the way for the unification of these disparate peoples, plus the Norse, into a single kingdom under a new and successful dynasty. By the middle of the eleventh century Scotland had recognisably taken on the geographical and ethnic form that it has today.

2. The 'High Middle Ages' was a period of creativity and relative prosperity for Scotland. The descendants of Queen Margaret transformed their Celtic kingdom into a cosmopolitan feudal state within the unity of Western Christendom. Relations with Scotland's most powerful neighbour, England, were for the most part harmonious through the recognition of distinctness and independence, to the advantage of both kingdoms.

3. After 1286, Scotland's history becomes the story of a struggle against successive attempts at conquest and incorporation. The story is one of spectacular triumphs and dismal failures on both sides. The monarchy was at times strong, at other times weak; but always the struggle for national identity was unremitting. There were modest successes as well. Scotland developed distinctiveness in education, architecture and literature, and at the end of the period enjoyed a remarkable cultural renaissance.

Geography

Much early and later history is determined by geographical factors. These determine the nature of an economy and the pattern of trade and settlement. Important factors include the relationship of land and water masses, altitude and climate.

The most obvious point about the area which we now call Scotland is that it occupies the northern third of an island, some 550 miles long and varying in breadth between 300 miles and 50 miles. There is no natural boundary between Scotland and England, but the narrowest point or 'waist' of Britain is formed by the great sea inlets of the Firths of Forth and Clyde, and this isthmus has at times formed an important boundary between political divisions in Britain. It was here that the Roman emperor Antoninus chose to mark the northern frontier of the Roman empire by a solid wall guarded by a network of roads and forts. But the other, more substantial, Roman wall built by Hadrian shows that the line of the Tyne and Solway could also be regarded as a defensible frontier. The present Anglo-Scottish border, having hardly changed since the twelfth century, represents something of a compromise between the two Roman attempts to find a frontier for the island of Britain.

The important point is that, even if it took centuries to establish the Border, Britain always has been divided in two – northern third and southern two thirds – and no serious attempt was made to abandon a political frontier before the eighteenth century. Modern political developments suggest that the Border still has relevance.

This fundamental divide has always existed, and has been determined by a number of factors. The first of these is the shape of Britain, long with a narrow waist; the second is its climate, mild and temperate in the south, cooler and harsher in the north; the third is the quality of land, with fertile plains and broad river valleys in the south, but increasingly broken by ranges of rough mountains further north. In Scotland, much land is over 250 metres above sea level. This is cool and windswept, and unsuited for agriculture, though it provides reasonable rough pasture for cattle, goats and sheep. Such land is best adapted to pastoral farming, not necessarily sedentary, and minimal cultivation mostly of oats on the lower and more sheltered hillsides. The lowlands of the east coast were not *ipso facto* better suited for sedentary agriculture, because the river valleys contained much heavy clay soil which could not be exploited because of the poor technology of draining and ploughing.

This was a land dominated by castles, of which Edinburgh, Dumbarton and Stirling are well-known examples. Natural eminences with artificial fortifications were the bases of Celtic warrior aristocracy. In the later Middle Ages, rocky outcrops crowned with great stone castles continued to be of great strategic importance.

Language

One way by which people are defined is language. Early and medieval Scotland was a land of several languages; some are now extinct or receding, and no language current in Scotland today occupies exactly the same area that it did a thousand years ago. Some explanation is required of the terminology which will be used of these various languages.

All the languages known to have been spoken in medieval Scotland belong to the Indo-European family. The most important group of Indo-European speakers in the European Iron Age were the Celts, who in prehistoric times spread from the Black Sea to the Atlantic seaboard. Within the British Isles, the Celtic languages show a major divergence into Goidelic and Brettonic, now represented by Irish and Scots Gaelic on the one hand and Welsh and (extinct) Cornish on the other. The Britons of the south spoke a Brettonic language akin to Old Welsh. The Dál Riata of the west spoke Old Irish, from which modern Scots Gaelic is descended. The language of the Picts is more problematic, largely because so little of it has survived. It was certainly Celtic, possibly with a closer affinity to continental Celtic (Gaulish) than to Old Welsh. The hypothesis that the Picts preserved in addition a non-Indo-European language for ritual purposes rests on slender evidence and is no longer widely accepted.

But not all the peoples of Dark Age Scotland were Celtic-speakers. The Angles of Northumbria spoke Old English, an Indo-European language of the Germanic branch. The Vikings, irrupting on the scene at the end of the eighth century, also spoke a Germanic language, Old Norse.

The common language of the Christian Church was Latin. Latin was the administrative language of the Western division of the Roman empire, and the liturgical language of western Christianity. In the Middle Ages Latin was the language of law, diplomacy, education and high culture as well as of the Church. It was never, however, a spoken language of the laity.

Latin has many modern descendants, including French. French was the language of the Norman Conquest, and many of the Anglo-Norman knights who settled in Scotland in the twelfth century will have known and spoken French. But French never made significant inroads in Scotland. One Norman-French romance, the *Roman de Fergus*, probably composed in Galloway at the beginning of the thirteenth century, has survived, and there is some evidence that Robert Bruce and his contemporaries were familiar with Norman-French 'courtly' poetry; but French never became the language of court, administration, or Church.

In this work, some compromises over the use of language and spelling of names have been necessary. As far as possible, names are presented in a form that is most likely to be familiar and recognisable. Absolute consistency has not been possible.

Identity

There is a fashionable tendency nowadays to treat Scottish history as an extension of the history of other peoples. Thus English historians writing about Dark Age Scotland treat Scotland as an extension of Northumbria, and Irish historians regard Celtic Scotland as a land that is essentially like Ireland. There are even Welsh historians who argue that Scotland's identity was secured by the British buffer-state of Strathclyde, and that Scottish history is therefore really an extension of Welsh history. Some English historians of the later Middle Ages see Scottish success in the Wars of Independence as a freakish accident, an aberration which delayed the inevitable union of Great Britain by four hundred years. But this is to write 'optative' history, to view the past as one would have liked events to turn out. Above all, it cannot explain why Scotland today is so distinct from the other nations of the British Isles; and the historian has to explain why things turn out as they do.

Many people living in Scotland today, though by no means all, are racially Celtic, linguistically English, and politically British citizens. Yet many also have a consciousness, howsoever vague, of belonging also to something different from these racial, linguistic and political loyalties. It is very difficult to define what that is, and if you ask several Scots what constitutes Scottishness, you will get a variety of answers. National identity is an elusive concept.

This has perhaps always been the case. Yet we can see the development of some kind of national identity from an early time. This is not to view history through the wrong end of the telescope, as it were, to try to explain the past in terms of the present; rather, we must use our past to make sense of the present. It is my hope that this book will help many Scots, and many others, to understand Scotland better.

CHAPTER 1

The Romans in Scotland and their Legacy

Although archaeology can throw light on prehistoric societies, the Celts are the first peoples documented by classical writers. History tells us nothing of the Stone Age and Bronze Age inhabitants of Scotland, or of the builders of the unique type of fortification known as brochs, found mostly in the Northern and Western Isles and the north and north-west mainland. It is not until the people of northern Britain came into contact with classical writers that they emerge into history, and even then they are largely seen through the eyes of their enemies.

Ptolemy's Geographia

The starting point for any discussion must be the *Geographia* of the early second-century Greek scholar Ptolemy.[1] In his map of north Britain he names a number of rivers and islands which can be identified, and others whose identification is less certain. He also makes northern Britain the home of a number of tribes. It is clear that we should view these tribes as kin-groups presided over and exploited by warrior aristocracies in competition with one another, occasionally forming alliances against powerful enemies. The name of the *Caledonii* is given prominence in the central Highlands, possibly indicating that some other tribes were subordinated to them.

Much of Ptolemy's information about the British tribes came from accounts of the campaigns of Agricola, the first Roman general to invade what is now Scotland. Julius Caesar had carried out exploratory raids into Britain in 55 and 54 BC, and Claudius had carried out a full-scale invasion and established Britain as a Roman province in AD 43 and the years following. By AD 78 two major revolts of British tribes had been suppressed and the frontier extended as far north as the Tyne–Solway line. There were major Roman bases at York and Chester to service the army. The stage was set for the campaigns of Agricola.[2]

Agricola

Julius Agricola was fortunate in having for his son-in-law the historian Tacitus, who wrote a vivid account of his life and campaigns. Before his posting as governor of

Falkirk is more confused. Inchtuthil in Strathmore was intended as a major legionary stronghold to check the power of the *Caledonii*, and the line of marching camps indicates the route which ultimately led to the battlefield at *Mons Graupius*. This hill, which has by a misreading given its name to the Grampian Mountains, has not been certainly identified.

Among his achievements, Agricola sent his navy on a circumnavigation of Scotland, thus proving for the first time that Britain was an island. His troops sailed round the *Orcades* (Orkney Islands) and saw *Thule*, probably Fair Isle, in the distance. Tacitus does not mention the Western Isles at all, but Ptolemy's *Geographia* names several of them in the *Oceanus Deucaledonius*, the 'Ocean of the two *Caledonii*'.

Even had Agricola not been recalled in 84, it is doubtful how much more success he could have expected. His campaigns were not a defeat for Roman arms, but they ensured that Scotland would never be part of the Roman empire. It was decided to retain the Forth–Clyde frontier, with only Inchtuthil as a major outpost beyond. Within a few years this fort too was abandoned, carefully dismantled with more than a million iron nails buried to keep them from the enemy. Some ten years later there is evidence of a major rebellion by the tribes of southern Scotland in which the forts at Newstead, Dalswinton and Glenlochar were burned, and evidence too of a Roman withdrawl to the Tyne–Solway line. In about 120 the emperor Hadrian decided upon a solid stone wall at this point, with a great ditch and mile-castles evenly spaced. It seemed as if the conquest of Scotland had been permanently abandoned.

The Antonine Wall

But about twenty years later the Agricolan frontier was recommissioned by the emperor Antoninus Pius, and a new wall was built on the Forth–Clyde isthmus.[3] The Antonine Wall consisted of a footing of dry stones covered by a turf rampart surmounted by a timber parapet, with a large ditch in front. The wall ran 40 Roman miles from Bridgeness on the Forth to Old Kilpatrick on the Clyde and was guarded by forts at an average distance of a little over two miles. For the most part it marches across the brow of low north-facing hills dominating the valleys of the Kelvin and Carron. The objective seems to have been to control the tribes whose territories straddled the Wall, and to give the Romans access to the farmlands beyond.

The Late Roman Empire and North Britain

The Antonine Wall seems not to have succeeded in its objective. There is little documentary evidence, but archaeology points to the abandonment of the northern

Opposite: anti-clockwise from top, the Antonine Wall:
Bridgeness Distance Slab, Bo'ness. *(Historic Scotland)*
Croy Hill. *(Historic Scotland)*
Ditch, Watling Lodge. *(Historic Scotland)*
Stone base of rampart, New Kilpatrick. *(Historic Scotland)*

wall *c.* 155, with one or more brief reoccupations later in the second century. By 197 the historian Dio Cassius described how the Roman governor had to buy peace from a tribe called the *Maeatae*, who were being aided in rebellion by the *Caledonii*.[4] A decade later the Romans were making progress against their confederation, but not fast enough for the emperor Septimius Severus. In 208 Severus arrived in Britain, carrying out an extensive campaign in Scotland in the following year, and marching so far north that he saw the midsummer sun at night; but he could not bring the *Caledonii* to battle. By the time he died at York in 211, Severus had fought in Scotland more extensively than anyone since Agricola; but his son Caracalla decided to recommission the Hadrianic frontier. Thereafter the northern frontier of the Roman empire was at peace for almost 100 years.

One name not mentioned until the very end of the third century, although it becomes common thereafter, is that of the *Picti*, Picts. A writer in 297 mentioned the achievements of Julius Caesar, who conquered Britain when 'the nation of Britons was still uncivilised and used to fighting only Picts and Irish, both still half-naked enemies'. A clue to the identity of these Picts is found in a poem of 310, which refers in passing to 'the forests and swamps of the *Caledonii* and other Picts, neighbouring Ireland or far-distant *Thule*'. The name *Picti* appears to mean 'painted people', but by the fourth century it had become common for all the people dwelling beyond the Antonine Wall.

A writer in the 360s states that the Picts were divided into two tribes, *Dicalydonae* and *Verturiones*. *Dicalydonae* clearly incorporates the name *Caledonii*. The *Verturiones* presumably were Picts living between the *Caledonii* and the Roman walls. Although the name no longer survives, for many centuries there was a district of Scotland, including Strathearn and Gowrie, called *Fortrenn*, and this is probably connected with *Verturiones*. It may be that the pressure exerted by the Romans contributed to a degree of unification of the Picts into these two big groupings.

The peaceful relations between Roman Britain and the Pictish tribes beyond the frontier which prevailed during the third century did not long survive into the fourth. In 306 the emperor Constantius and his son Constantine (later the first Christian emperor) responded to renewed outbreaks of trouble in north Britain by crossing the Wall and marching as far as the Tay; but they again withdrew to the Hadrianic frontier, retaining some fortified outposts beyond. In the 360s the Picts were again attacking the Roman province, and from this time the situation never seems to have been totally restored. In the 380s the northern frontier was stripped of troops by the ambitious general Magnus Maximus in his bid for the imperial throne. By *c.* 400 Hadrian's Wall had been abandoned. The last Roman attempt to hold back Pictish incursions into north Britain was by the general Stilicho in 400–2, who returned from the campaign with his legion 'which curbs the fierce Scot, and while slaughtering the Pict scans the devices tattooed on his lifeless form'.

Thereafter Constantine III made another attempt to seize the imperial throne by withdrawing British troops and leaving the frontier exposed, in 407–11; in 410 the province of Britain was instructed to undertake its own defence, as all available imperial troops were required in other places. In the winter of 406/7 hordes of barbarians had swept into Gaul. That province was in an unsettled state for much of the fifth century; Britain must very quickly have become isolated from Roman civilisation. Archaeology suggests a rapid deterioration in British culture, with coinage for trafficking having gone out of use by c. 430. Britain passed into the hands of local 'tyrants' who carved up the imperial province and ruled tribal areas from hilltop fortresses.

Northern Britain after the Roman Withdrawal

There is great obscurity about Britain after the Roman withdrawal, and its degree of continuity with the old province. Germanus bishop of Auxerre came to Britain c. 429 and was met by a sophisticated and Romanised aristocracy led by a man 'of tribunician power'.[5] About ten years later he revisited Britain and was again preaching to the British aristocracy when a report of a raid by Picts and Saxons reached them. The contrast between the relative peace of Germanus' first visit and the unsettled conditions of his second suggests changed times.

One British tyrant, called Vortigern in later sources, is said to have called in Saxon mercenaries to repel Picts and Scots, and found that these Germanic warriors stayed to carve out settlements for themselves in eastern England. In c. 446 the remnant of the Roman province appealed to the Roman general Aetius for help against the Saxons; but he was too preoccupied with Goths and Huns in Gaul.

It is in this obscure age, perhaps around the year 500, that moves the shadowy figure of Arthur, 'leader of battles', who fought against the Saxons and held up their progress for a time. Who he was is uncertain, and so is his sphere of action; a number of northern places seem to commemorate him, but it is not clear that he was a northerner. Arthur is so obscure and surrounded by legend that it is difficult to perceive him as a historical figure at all.

Finds of pottery, coins and precious metals do not suggest a profound influence by the Romans on the tribes beyond the Wall. But the tribes enumerated by Ptolemy between the two walls, the *Novantae*, *Selgovae*, *Votadini* and *Damnonii*, would be expected to have had the closest contacts and to have felt the greatest influence. Beyond them, influence on the *Verturiones*, *Maeatae* and *Caledonii* appears to have been slight.

The best archaeological evidence for Roman contact comes from Traprain Law in East Lothian, a tribal fortress of the *Votadini*.[6] Here, within the enclosure of a Dark Age hillfort has been found a hoard of Roman silver objects – plates, cups, cutlery, bowls, flagons, and the like – which had been broken up and flattened and then hidden in a shallow pit. Coin finds among the hoard date it to c. 425. Among the objects were some with Christian symbols. Because the objects are portable and appear to have been in preparation for being melted down, they hardly represent evidence for the tastes and religious beliefs of a Votadinian prince of the early fifth century. The burial and abandonment of the hoard are suggestive of troubled times.

The abandonment of Traprain suggests that the *Votadini* were under pressure by the mid-fifth century, less than half a century after the Roman withdrawal. Further west, a tribe called the *Damnonii* formed themselves into a powerful war-band under a dynasty of tyrants ruling from Dumbarton Rock. It was probably this semi-Romanised, semi-Christianised band that St Patrick described as allies of Scots and renegade Picts, 'a foreign race which does not know God'.

Those who claimed to be the heirs of the Roman province of Britain were gradually driven back into the mountains and marginal regions of Britain, Cornwall, Wales and southern Scotland. Southern and eastern England was settled in the fifth and sixth centuries by Germanic peoples – Angles, Saxons and Jutes. North of the Antonine Wall were the Picts, still in Patrick's time a foreign, heathen and renegade race. In the west, Scots from Ireland were raiding and settling; *c.* 500 a Gaelic dynasty from County Antrim seized power in Argyll. The Scots, the people who were ultimately to give their name to the country, were among the last to settle permanently in Scotland.

Britons, Scots, Picts and Angles – these, according to the historian Bede, were the four races who inhabited the island of Britain; by 500 they had all arrived and in the following centuries were to work out their destinies in competition and cooperation.

Silver tableware from the Traprain Law Hoard. *(National Museums of Scotland)*

CHAPTER 2

Early Kingdoms and Peoples

THE SCOTS OF THE WEST: A WARRIOR KINGDOM?

In AD 1249, the boy king Alexander III was installed as king of Scots at Scone. The ceremony began in the abbey church, where the king heard mass and was consecrated by the bishop of St Andrews. Then he was led outside to the 'moot-hill' of Scone, on which had been set the ancient enthronement stone of the Scots. The earl of Fife led Alexander to the stone and set him upon it; homage was paid to him, and he swore an oath to defend his people and rule justly. Then, the last act of all, a Gaelic *seanchaidh* stepped forward and proclaimed the new king's ancestors: 'Here is Alexander king of *Alba*, son of Alexander, son of William, son of Henry, son of David, son of Malcolm, son of Duncan, son of Bethoc, daughter of Malcolm, son of Kenneth, son of Malcolm, son of Donald, son of Constantine, son of Kenneth, son of Alpin, son of Eochaid, son of Áed Finn, son of Eochaid, son of Eochaid, son of Domangart, son of Domnall Brecc, son of Eochaid Buide, son of Áedán, son of Gabrán, son of Domangart, son of Fergus Mór, son of Erc.' The *seanchaidh* did not stop there; he could go back many generations to Goidel or Gaythelos, founder of the Gael, husband of Scota, daughter of Pharaoh king of Egypt.[1]

Of course, the pedigree has no historical validity for most of its length, and the tacking on of biblical figures is an obvious fabrication for a race that had only been converted to Christianity during the fifth century. But it shows the tremendous pride in ancestry which was a hallmark of early Gaelic kingship.

The Dál Riata

Fergus Mór is said to have been the first of the people of the Dál Riata to have held sway in part of Britain, and to have died in Britain *c.* 501. The Dál Riata were a small Irish tribe inhabiting the coastal regions of County Antrim, within sight of Islay and Kintyre. Gael had probably been settling in these areas for some time before AD 500, and there were probably Gaelic settlements elsewhere in south-west Scotland as well.

The reasons for Gaelic settlement in Kintyre and surrounds are not difficult to find. The fifth century witnessed the rise in Ireland of a powerful new dynasty, the Uí Néill. Their expansion must have put great pressure on existing northern kin-groups. One of these, the Dál Riata, sought their fortunes in Scotland.

Sources

Historical sources for the late fifth and early sixth centuries are sparse and unreliable, and all dates must be treated as to some extent approximate.[2] Annals were not at first kept contemporaneously, but were entered retrospectively in the margins of Easter tables in monasteries. The Dál Riata are the subject of a group of annal entries which contain information about Picts, Britons and Angles as well, but their main concentration is on the Scots. They contain information about kings, their battles and followers, and also about the monastery of Iona, which was almost certainly the place of compilation. So there was an Iona Chronicle, a contemporary document in the seventh century and remaining so until the middle of the eighth.

We are also fortunate in possessing for the Dál Riata a genealogical tract and military survey called *Senchus Fer nAlban*, 'Lore of the Men of Scotland'. This falls into two parts, the first a genealogy of the descendants of Fergus Mór in Scotland, the second a survey of the 'houses' of the Dál Riata and their assessment for military purposes. The Dál Riata were divided into three tribes, called after Gabrán, grandson of Fergus Mór, and after Loarn and Oengus, supposedly brothers of Fergus. The *Senchus* states that the tribe of Oengus occupied Islay, and by inference the tribe of Loarn occupied Lorn and adjacent islands (Kerrera, Lismore, Mull, Coll and Tiree), and the mainland areas of Morvern and Ardnamurchan. The tribe of Gabrán, by elimination, occupied Kintyre and Knapdale.

Each tribe is divided into houses, which were units of exploitation based on the cultivation requirements of a single extended family. Usually these are grouped in multiples of five (5s, 10s, 20s, 30s, etc.). An idea of the size of the Gaelic 'house' is provided by the historian Bede, who states that the island of Iona was not large, being about five households. Each group of houses was required to provide a certain number of armed men for mobilisation in time of war, plus two galleys per twenty houses in a sea expedition. The *Senchus* shows a society of systematic aristocratic exploitation geared for war, with groups of peasant households under the sway of aristocrats, paying them tribute so that they and their sons, retainers and foster-sons could go on plundering raids and military campaigns.

At the head of these aristocrats were the leaders of their kin – the principal families of the Dál Riata. Within these families succession did not normally pass from father to son, but usually by alternation between brothers and cousins or other aristocrats within a certain degree of kinship with the king, so that the chosen king was always an adult male. Thus Domangart, son of Fergus Mór, was succeeded by his two sons in turn, Comgall and Gabrán, Gabrán was succeeded by Comgall's son Conall, and he by Gabrán's son Áedán; thereafter the succession was vested in the descendants of Áedán, sometimes by alternation among descendants of his different sons, sometimes by succession of brothers, until with the rise of the tribe of Loarn in the late seventh century members of that kin-group enter a system of alternation with the tribe of Gabrán. It may sound orderly, but the system legitimised the ambitions of any aristocrat within a certain degree of kinship, and made at times for internal disputes, bloodshed

The Inauguration of King Alexander III, 1249, from a fifteenth-century manuscript. A *seanchaidh* kneels before the boy king and proclaims his genealogy in Gaelic. *(The Master and Fellows of Corpus Christi College, Cambridge.)*

and survival of the fittest. The result was that kings were ambitious, tough and militaristic; but damaging internal disputes could weaken the kingdom. Military failure usually resulted in death, overthrow, exile, or forcible retirement into a monastery.

The best-known monk-aristocrat from this society is St Columba. His *Life* was written by Adomnán abbot of Iona (d. 704). The *Life* has much important evidence about secular politics of the period 563–97 and later; for although Columba is portrayed throughout as a devout and conscientious churchman, he also appears as an important councillor of king Áedán son of Gabrán, in contact with neighbouring aristocrats and the kings of the Picts and Britons. Much of what Adomnán says can be accepted as historically accurate.

The Early Kings of the Dál Riata

The earliest kings of the Dál Riata are no more than names. Conall son of Comgall (*c*. 560–74) is the first king to be more than this. When Columba sailed to mainland Britain in 563, he was welcomed by Conall, accommodated for a time at his court (perhaps at Dunadd), and given by him the island of Iona for the site of his monastery. One military exploit is credited to Conall, a campaign in the Hebrides in company with the king of the southern Uí Néill of Meath, in 568.

His death *c*. 574 was followed by a disputed succession. There was a battle in Kintyre *c*. 574, in which Conall's son Donnchad and 'many allies of the sons of Gabrán' were killed. The successful competitor was Áedán son of Gabrán, who may earlier have carved out for himself a lordship on the upper Forth. His first move as king was to associate himself with Columba and the legitimacy of Christian inauguration. But Adomnán implies that Columba was at first reluctant to inaugurate Áedán, preferring his brother:

> He saw one night, in a mental trance, an angel of the Lord who had been sent to him, having in his hand a book of glass of the ordination of kings. And when the saint had received it from the hand of the angel, at the angel's command he began to read. But when he refused to ordain Áedán as king, as it was commanded in the book, because he had more love for his brother Eoganán, the angel quickly stretched out his hand and struck the saint with a scourge. . . . 'Know surely that I am sent to you from God with the book of glass so that, as you have read in it, you will ordain Áedán as king. If you refuse to obey this command, I will strike you again.' . . . The saint submitted to the Lord's word. He sailed to the island of Iona, and there, as he had been bidden, he ordained Áedán as king, who arrived about the same time. . . . And laying his hand upon Áedán's head he ordained and blessed him.[3]

This is the first recorded example of a Gaelic king being inaugurated with Christian rituals, and it may have gone some way towards legitimising Áedán's position.

Opposite: Dunadd: Inauguration stone on the summit, showing carved footprint. *(Historic Scotland)*

Áedán son of Gabrán

Áedán is the best documented, and probably the most successful, of the kings of the Dál Riata. A later source states that 'Áedán son of Gabrán seized *Alba* by force'. The annals attribute a number of battles to him, most of them victories. In about 580, he mounted an expedition to the Orkneys. About two years later, he fought a campaign against *Mano*, probably a territory around the headwaters of the Firth of Forth. Adomnán mentions a battle against the *Miathi*, probably the same campaign, which Áedán won with heavy losses. Áedán won another victory at the Battle of *Lethreid* (unidentified, possibly in Strathclyde) *c.* 590. One of his rare setbacks was a battle in Mearns, *c.* 598. His last great battle was fought against the Angles of Northumbria and their king Æthelfrith in 602 or 603 at an unidentified place called *Degsastan*; English and Scottish accounts of this battle differ, with both sides claiming victory with heavy losses on both sides. As well as his campaigns against Picts, Britons and Angles, Áedán also was active in Ireland. At some point in his reign, counselled by St Columba, he met the king of the northern Uí Néill at a *rígdál* or 'assembly of kings' to discuss the relationship of the Dál Riata in Ireland and Scotland with the kings of the northern Uí Néill.

Áedán's Successors

When Áedán died *c.* 608 he was succeeded (as prophesied by Columba) by his son Eochaid Buide, who was also called king of the Picts. During his reign there is no sequence of successful campaigns to match his father's. He seems to have allowed some of his authority over the Dál Riata, probably in Ireland, to devolve on his son Connad Cerr, who was killed along with other grandsons of Áedán in battle in Ireland in 629.

Eochaid's son and successor Domnall Brecc fought a series of battles; but with a single exception at the beginning of his reign, he was always on the losing side. In 642 he was defeated and killed in the Battle of Strathcarron (near Falkirk) by Ywain king of Strathclyde. The defeats and death of Domnall Brecc reversed the successes of his grandfather Áedán; commenting on these disasters, an abbot of Iona remarked *c.* 660: 'since that time [the Dál Riata] have been held down by foreigners; which causes the heart to sigh with grief'.[4]

Sources for the subsequent period are much more sparse. For nearly half a century after the death of Domnall Brecc, the kingship of the Dál Riata continued with the tribe of Gabrán, while at the same time the power of the tribe of Loarn seems to have been increasing. In *c.* 678 the tribe of Loarn under their leader Ferchar Fota ('the tall') was defeated by the Britons of Strathclyde; but this is perhaps symptomatic of their rise, for Ferchar Fota figures prominently in the annals thereafter. He was recognised as king of the Dál Riata by the time of his death *c.* 697. Thereafter three of his sons held the kingship. Selbach (*c.* 701–23 and 727–30) was perhaps the most successful of these; he fought several battles against the Britons of Strathclyde, and at one point intended to end his life in monastic retirement. But he was faced by internal disputes as well, both from the tribe of Gabrán and within his own tribe of Loarn. In spite of his proposed retirement, he is found fighting at the head of a war-band again in 727, and may have returned to power before his death in 730.

The Dál Riata also faced external threats. The second quarter of the eighth century is dominated by the towering figure of Onuist son of Uurguist, king of the Picts. In 736 Onuist invaded the lands of the Dál Riata, took Dunadd, and 'bound with chains two sons of Selbach'; an attempt by his nephew Muredach to assert his position was defeated soon after. The tribe of Loarn was virtually wiped out, and the Picts ruled supreme in Dalriadic territory.

Some interpretations of the subsequent period suggest that the Dál Riata were in a state of subjection to the Picts from this time until the rise of Kenneth son of Alpin a century later. But these do not account for the poorly documented but significant reign of Áed Finn son of Eochaid (c. 748–78). He appears to have been of the tribe of Gabrán, reviving the fortunes of that house after the dominance of the tribe of Loarn. Unfortunately, of his actions we know little. By 768 he fought a battle against the Picts; the result is unknown, but apparently Áed was the aggressor. Late writers imply that there was a series of campaigns between Áed Finn and the Picts.[5] He died c. 778 and was succeeded by his brother Fergus son of Eochaid; such a succession implies the restoration of the old system of succession among the tribe of Gabrán.

After the death of his successor Domnall c. 805, there is a series of short reigns and confused succession for much of the first half of the ninth century. The fortunes of the Gael of the west, temporarily revived by Áed Finn, were once again imperilled. Not until the rise of Kenneth son of Alpin in the 840s were these fortunes revived.

THE PICTS: A DARK AGE ENIGMA, AD 500–800

The Picts seem now to have been wiped out, and their language so wholly destroyed, that now it seems a fable when mention of them is made in the writings of the ancients. And to whom will it not suggest the love of heavenly things and the dread of earthly things, when he considers that not only their kings and princes and people have perished, but even their whole stock, their language and the recollection of them have failed altogether? And if the rest were no wonder, yet it seems marvellous concerning the language, which from the beginning of languages God established as one among the rest.[6]

Thus commented a twelfth-century English historian on the obliteration of Pictish as a spoken language; it had disappeared completely before he wrote.

Who Were the Picts?

The Picts have always been regarded as a mysterious and enigmatic people. There are no extant Pictish chronicles, poems or religious manuscripts such as the other ancient peoples of Britain have left, no lives of Pictish saints or verses about Pictish heroes.

All that survives, glorified under the title of the *Pictish Chronicle*, is an origin-story and king list with names of kings and their patronymics and reign-lengths. This list survives in two main versions, one of which has spellings of names showing Gaelic influence, but the other showing many strange forms which must reflect the Pictish language.[7]

The Picts are mentioned in other sources, and so are not a complete blank to us. The Irish annals have many references to Picts, particularly in the period 670–740. Adomnán's *Life of Columba*, written *c.* 700, has much information about Columba's dealings with the Picts, and incidentally their relations with the Dál Riata. Bede in his *Ecclesiastical History*, composed *c.* 730, names the Picts as one of the four peoples occupying Great Britain, and has some information about their conversion to Christianity, with occasional glimpses of political structure and customs.[8]

These sources locate the Picts as a people in Scotland, living north of the Antonine Wall in the east and north. Non-literary evidence, such as archaeological finds and place-names, fills out this picture. In archaeological terms, we can plot the distribution of brochs, souterrains and vitrified forts; we can look at the spread of other certainly Pictish archaeological sites; and most significantly, we can look at the pattern of Pictish symbol stones, by far the most important and considerable remains of the Picts. These stones are of different sizes and styles and are fashioned by different techniques, but have in common that they bear unique symbolism found in Pictland and nowhere else. This is partly apparently abstract, as in such symbols as the crescent and V-rod and double-disc; partly representative of identifiable objects, like the mirror and comb; and partly zoomorphic, as in the fine representations of horses, bulls, birds, fish, stags and serpents, but also of mythical beasts and monsters. The area of distribution of the stones helps us to define the area of Pictland.

Likewise, in place-names we have an element which is unique to a certain area of central, eastern and north-east Scotland. In these areas are found places which incorporate the word *pett*, now Pit-, as in Pitlochry, Pittenweem, etc., which seems to mean a settlement or township.[9]

It has been suggested that some Pictish social or governmental institutions survived into a later period. In later centuries there are references to an official called the thane, and his jurisdiction over a thanage. Almost all thanages are found in an area which corresponds to the distribution of uniquely Pictish archaeological and place-name elements. Likewise the oldest Scottish earldoms are also mostly found in the east and north. So a case can be made for earldoms and thanages being in origin Pictish institutions. Eleventh-century documents from north-east Scotland mention local office-holders called *mormaer* ('great steward') and *toisech* ('leader'), and there is a temptation to connect earls and thanes with these.[10]

Pictish Symbol Stones

We have seen that the word 'Pict' first appears in AD 297, when it was used to distinguish the people of northern Britain from the British tribes within the Roman province and from the Irish. Subsequently, it was used to mean all northern tribes

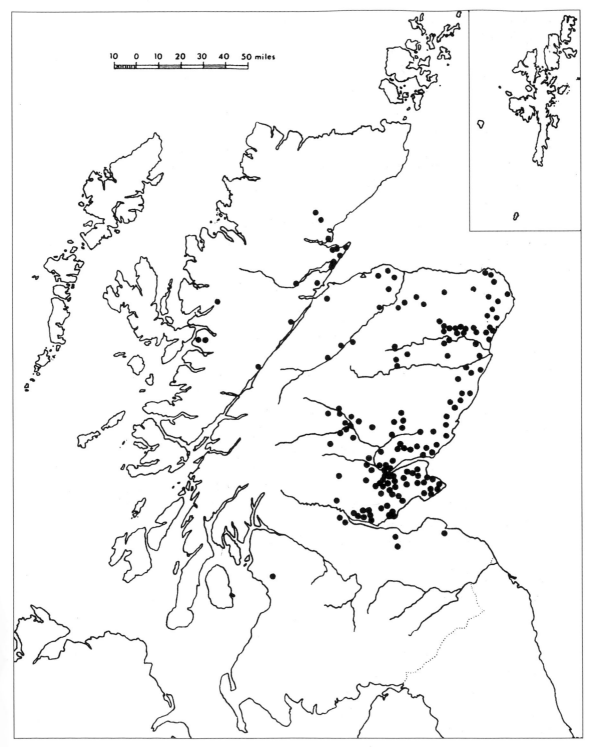

Place names containing 'pit'. *(W.F.H. Nicolaisen; by permission of the Trustees of the Historical Atlas of Scotland)*

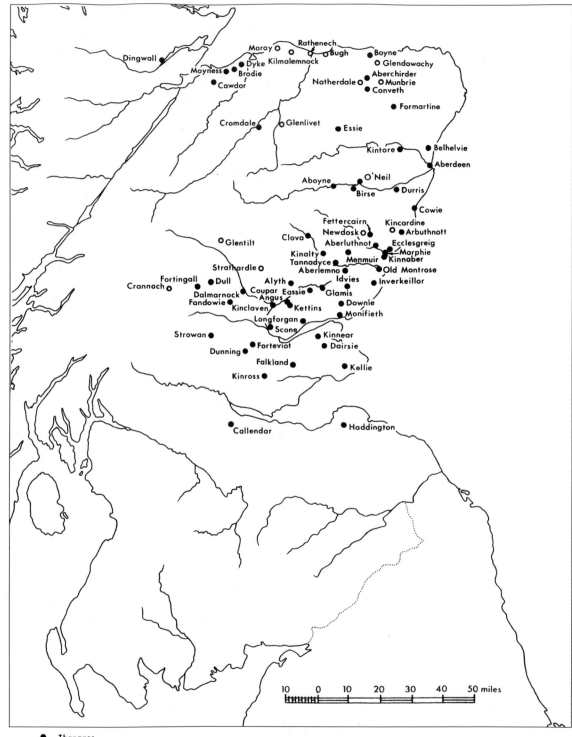

Thanages. *(Richard Muir; by permission of the Trustees of the Historical Atlas of Scotland)*

beyond the Roman frontier. The name appears to mean 'painted people', 'pictured ones', a description which almost certainly refers to the well-recorded practice of tattooing among the peoples of Britain; Isidore of Seville, *c.* AD 600, states that the Picts are so-called because their bodies bear designs made by subcutaneous pricking with needles. The Picts seem to have called themselves by the Celtic name *Priteni*.

Could the tattoos with which they adorned their bodies be the same images as they carved on their stones? There is no universal agreement on this point. It has been argued that the earlier symbol-stones occur with greater frequency than coincidence would allow in or near later burial grounds, and are likely to be funerary monuments. Other suggestions are that the stones are boundary markers or proclamations of marriages or alliances.[11]

It is clear that the symbols represent a system of statements intelligible to the society which caused the monuments to be set up; but the symbolism is no longer intelligible to us. The stones themselves fall into three classes which represent a chronological sequence. The earliest, or Class I, stones are rough-hewn boulders or undressed slabs with a few symbols incised on one face. A development from this is the second phase, Class II, which consists of shaped and dressed stones with carving in relief: usually a Christian cross on one side and symbols, or a mixture of symbols and scenes from life, on the other. The latest group, Class III, consists of stones with a cross on one face and naturalistic carving on the other, but none of the characteristic symbols; it is usually assumed that these come after the Pictish period, and it may be doubted whether it is correct to call them 'Pictish' at all.[12]

The symbols hardly ever appear singly, but usually in groups of two, three, or (more rarely) more. The pairings and groupings appear to have some significance; for example, it is rare to find more than one zoomorphic figure on a stone. Some symbols appear very frequently, such as the 'crescent and V-rod', others seldom or once only. There is sometimes superimposition; the crescent symbol sometimes appears alone, but much more frequently with a V-rod superimposed; likewise the double disc with connecting bar ('Pictish spectacles') often appears with a superimposed Z-rod, and sometimes zoomorphic images have a Z-rod superimposed.

The relative dating of the stones can be reasonably established; but do we have any absolute chronological framework in which to set them? There is an approximate final date limit in the extinction of the Pictish dynasty *c.* 850, at the hands of Kenneth son of Alpin. Although we should probably not assume that the carving of Pictish symbols stopped abruptly in 850, we may guess that relatively few of the Class II stones date from much later. There are close parallels between the artwork of the best Class II stones and the early free-standing crosses on Iona and elsewhere in Argyll, which probably date from before 807. Class II stones then belong mostly to the eighth century, with the latest continuing into the middle of the ninth century. It has been suggested that the great churchyard stone at Aberlemno, stylistically early among the Class II stones, commemorates the Pictish victory at the Battle of Dunnichen in 685.

Class I stones are also difficult to date. A relative date is provided by the Class II stones; if it is accepted that these run from the late seventh to the mid-ninth century, then the bulk of Class I stones must be earlier. There are almost no symbol stones in Argyll, so presumably at the time when the Dál Riata settled, *c*. 500, the Picts had not yet begun the practice of setting up symbol stones.

The bulk of Class I stones are found in the north, around the Moray Firth and in the Great Glen, and in the valleys of the Spey, Don and Urie. By contrast, the bulk of Class II stones are found further south, especially in Angus and Mearns and the valleys of the Tay and Earn. Bridei son of Mailcon was a powerful Pictish king north of the Mounth, with an important royal centre near the River Ness; his reign should probably be placed *c*. 556–86. Later, the sources lay greater stress on the kingship of Fortrenn, i.e. Strathearn and Gowrie. So there may be grounds for thinking that the Class I stones date from a time when Pictish hegemony was held by northern kings. The main centres of Pictish power and patronage may have shifted south to a kingship based in Fortrenn, giving rise to the great bulk of the Class II stones in Strathearn, Gowrie and Angus, probably datable to between the end of the seventh and the middle of the ninth centuries.[13]

A very small number of stones has inscriptions as well as symbols. These are mostly in Irish ogams, a script produced by setting marks at diagonal or right angles to a central line and assigning letter values to different groups of marks. Sadly, the ogams can be transliterated to make phonetic sense, but are not easily intelligible. Personal names appear on some of the inscriptions, and some Gaelic loan-words. It used to be suggested that the Celtic Picts took over a non-Indo-European language from an earlier people and continued its use for ritual purposes; but it is more likely that the inscriptions are difficult to read because of scribal mistakes and weathering. The hypothesis of a non-Celtic Pictish language is based on slender evidence and is no longer widely accepted.[14]

Matrilineal Succession?

One odd feature which has been attributed to Pictish society was the custom of matrilineal succession. The evidence for this is not nearly so conclusive as was once believed. Bede, writing *c*. 730, knew of a strange custom of succession to the Pictish kingship through female descent and lineage, but he stated that this was practised 'when the matter comes into doubt', and he quotes an origin-legend to explain it. This stated that when the Picts came to Ireland first they had no women of their own, so they asked the Irish to give them wives, and the Irish agreed, on condition that they settle in Scotland and always choose their kings through the female line. A Gaelic poem of the eleventh century, recording the same origin-legend, states that the Picts were sworn always to choose their kings through female lineage.[15]

The Pictish king list is the only historical document that the Picts have left us about themselves. From Bridei son of Mailcon to Bridei, predecessor of Kenneth son of Alpin, it contains the names of thirty kings, covering nearly three centuries.

Pictish Class I Stones. *Top left:* Aberlemno roadside stone, Angus. (*Historic Scotland*). *Top right:* Easterton of Roseisle, Moray. (*Historic Scotland*). *Bottom:* Birsay, Orkney, showing a group of Pictish warriors.

Pictish Class II Stone: Maiden Stone, Chapel of Garioch, Aberdeenshire. *(Historic Scotland)*

Pictish Class III Stone: Meigle, Angus. Daniel in the Lions' Den is at the centre. *(Historic Scotland)*

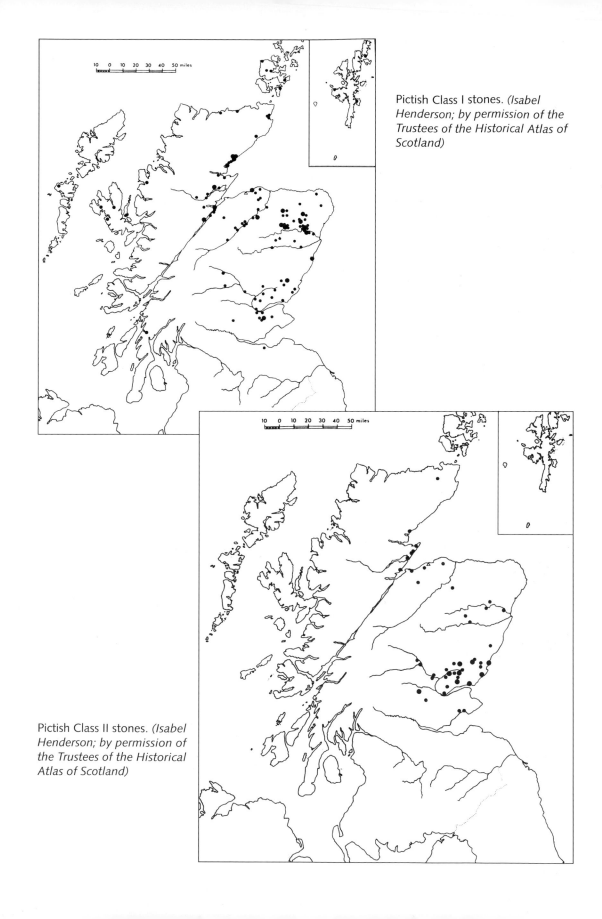

Pictish Class I stones. *(Isabel Henderson; by permission of the Trustees of the Historical Atlas of Scotland)*

Pictish Class II stones. *(Isabel Henderson; by permission of the Trustees of the Historical Atlas of Scotland)*

THE PICTISH KING LIST

King	Probable Dates	King	Probable Dates
Galam Cennalaph 1 yr, and		Onuist son of Uurguist, 30 yrs	729–61
with Bridei for 1 yr	578–80	Bridei son of Uurguist, 2 yrs	761–3
Bridei son of Mailcon, 30 yrs	554–84	Ciniod son of Uuredech, 12 yrs	763–75
Gartnait son of Domelch, 11 yrs	585–97	Elpin son of Uuroid, 3½ yrs	776–80
Necton grandson of Uerb, 20 yrs	597–620	Drest son of Talorgen, 4 or 5 yrs	780–5/6
Ciniod son of Lutrin, 19 yrs	612–31	Talorgen son of Onuist, 2½ yrs	786–9
Gartnait son of Uid, 4 yrs	631–5	Canaul son of Tarlan, 5 yrs	784–9
Bridei son of Uid, 5 yrs	635–41	Castatin son of Uurguist, 35 yrs	789–820
Talorc his brother, 12 yrs	641–53	Onuist son of Uurguist, 12 yrs	820–34
Talorc son of Enfret, 4 yrs	653–7	Drest son of Castantin and Talorgen	
Gartnait son of Donuel, 6½ yrs	657–64	son of Uuthoil, 3 yrs together	834–7
Drest his brother, 7 yrs	664–71	Uuen son of Onuist, 3 yrs	837–9
Bridei son of Bili, 21 yrs	671–92	Uurad son of Bargoit, 3 yrs	839–42
Taran son of Enfidich, 4 yrs	692–6	Bridei [son of Uurad], 1 yr	842
Bridei son of Deilei, 11 yrs	696–706	[Cinaed son of Uurad, 1 yr]	842–3
Necton son of Derilei, 15 yrs	706–21,	[Bridei son of Uuchel, 2 yrs]	843–5
	728–9	[Drest son of Uurad, 3 yrs]	845–9
Drest and Elpin together, 5 yrs	721–8		

(The last three names are not in the 'Pictish' MS, and are taken from the 'Gaelic' version of the list.)

Of these thirty kings only two, and none before the ninth century, can be even arguably the son of a person who had previously been king. But if paternity was not apparently a determining factor, other relationships were important. Six of the kings succeeded a brother. A number of fathers of kings can be demonstrated to have come from outside Pictland; some fathers of Pictish kings are certainly or probably identifiable as outsiders, and others have names which do not appear to be Pictish. Could there have been an element of exogamy in Pictish royal lineage? At least 20 per cent of the kings appear to have had non-Pictish fathers. The question must remain open, for there is not really enough evidence for certainty.

Arguments against the matrilineal thesis are based on the contention that Pictish kingship worked like the provincial kingships of Ireland, where kingship revolved among a group of tribes. This argument does not, however, explain why so many of the kings succeeded brothers, or had fathers who were definitely or probably not Pictish.

On the other hand, the king list identifies kings by their paternity; clearly, fathers were important. And the problem remains of what Bede meant when he stated that the Picts chose their kings from the female line 'when the matter is in doubt'. There is no parallel to female succession among any Celtic or Indo-European people. Even if some sort of matrilineal system operated among the Picts, its precise workings are not clear. The matrilineal hypothesis is by no means as secure as it once was; but it may be too early to write it off altogether.

There is no hint either of matriarchy or presence of women in prominent political roles, even if the imposing female figure on the Hilton of Cadboll stone may imply social importance for Pictish women. Neither Adomnán nor Bede names an important Pictish woman; Adomnán, considerate towards women himself, implies that Gaelic women were badly treated when they fell into Pictish hands.[16]

Early Pictish Kings: Bridei Son of Mailcon and His Successors

When Columba visited the court of Bridei son of Mailcon, he found a powerful king holding hostages of the sub-king of the Orkneys ruling from a fortress near the banks of the River Ness with strong gates and a great hall; the most likely site is Craig Phatric beside Inverness. Columba may have been visiting Bridei on a political mission from Áedán son of Gabrán, to whom he acted as adviser between 574 and 597. Columba preached and converted some individuals at Urquhart and on Skye, but although he won the respect of King Bridei it does not appear that he baptised him. Áedán's only known expedition to northern Pictland was an attack on the Orkneys c. 580, and we know this to have been an area of Bridei's influence. For much of the period between then and c. 670, we know little except names and reign-lengths of kings, most of which were short.

The Battle of Dunnichen, 685

About 678 the kingship fell to Bridei son of Bili king of Strathclyde. Bridei may have restored the fortunes of the Pictish kingdom after previous troubles. He was victor in the Battle of Dunnichen in 685, when King Ecgfrith of Northumbria 'rashly took an army to ravage the kingdom of the Picts. . . . The enemy feigned flight and lured the king into some narrow passes in the midst of inaccessible mountains; there he was killed on 20 May with the greater part of the forces he had taken with him.' English sources call this the Battle of Nechtansmere, the Irish annals call the place *Dún Nechtain*, Nechton's fort, now Dunnichen in Angus. Bede describes the Picts recovering territory as far as the Firth of Forth, and the Scots and Britons of Strathclyde also recovering ground which they had lost to the Angles. We should probably see Dunnichen as a major turning-point in northern history.

The battle confirmed Bridei's position as the most powerful ruler in the north, a position which Pictish kings were to hold for most of the next century. When he learned of Bridei's death in 693, Adomnán abbot of Iona is quoted as saying:

> Many wonders performs the King who was born of Mary,
> . . . [giving] death to Bridei, son of Bili;
> 'Tis strange that, after he has been king of the north,
> A hollow stump of withered oak is about the son of the king of Dumbarton.[17]

The Sons of Derelei and Onuist Son of Uurguist

A succession dispute seems to have followed, with his immediate successor Taran being driven from the kingship and sent into exile in Ireland by the sons of Derelei. The first of these, Bridei, won a victory over the Angles in 698, which was reversed by an Anglian victory in 711 over Bridei's brother Nechton. It may have been this defeat that decided Nechton to seek friendlier relations with Northumbria, particularly in church matters. Nechton's assertion of supremacy in church matters is shown by his enforcement of Roman custom at Iona, and expulsion of Columban monks from Pictish territories; it is clear that Pictish kings could enforce their will in the lands of the Dál Riata.

But despite these signs of power, and the warm commendations of Bede, Nechton's reign did not end happily. He went into monastic retirement in 724, probably not voluntarily, as two years later he was imprisoned by his successor. A contest then emerged in which the formidable Onuist son of Uurguist was the eventual victor. In the early 730s he stamped out the remaining opposition to his rule in Pictland; in the later 730s he attacked the Dál Riata, destroyed all the main fortresses and killed all those of royal stock whom he could get hold of, and 'overthrew' the kingdom in 741. Then he turned his attentions to the Britons of Strathclyde, fighting an indecisive engagement against them in 744, and being soundly defeated in 750; his brother Talorgen and many of his men were killed, and the Irish annals record 'the decline of the power of Onuist'.

But the Irish writer's hopes were premature. Onuist made an alliance with Eadberht of Northumbria, and marched jointly with him against Dumbarton, which surrendered to them on 1 August 756. The kingdom of Dumbarton disappears from historical records for almost a century. But the campaign of 756 had terrible consequences for Eadberht and his army; within ten days of the surrender of Dumbarton, while he was on his homeward march, his army was attacked and destroyed at *Ouania* (the Avon, either that in Lanarkshire or in West Lothian) by unnamed assailants. There is the suspicion of treachery by Onuist; by the time of his death Northumbrian sources had turned hostile to him: 'In the year 761 died Onuist king of the Picts, who from the beginning of his reign even to the very end continued as a tyrannical slaughterer, perpetrating bloody crimes'.

In spite of this, Onuist seems to have sought the legitimacy of Christian kingship. During his reign we hear for the first time of the monastery of *Cennrigmonadh*, later St Andrews, and its foundation legend credits him as the founder. The St Andrews sarcophagus, with its superb royal figure cast in the role of King David, probably belongs stylistically to the second half of the eighth century. It is speculation, but tempting to see this royal portrait as a memorial to Onuist son of Uurguist himself.

After Onuist's eventful and long reign, our sources become sparser. The names of Pictish kings are recorded, but little else is known about them. There are suggestions that Onuist's successors were less powerful; the Dál Riata seem to have recovered ground under Áed Finn, and have carried aggression into Pictland; and there is a suggestion of a division within the Pictish kingdom, with a reference to a 'king of the Picts on this side of the Mounth'.

In 793 the Viking raids began, but at first these were for the most part directed against the western seaboard. The Picts should have been better positioned to withstand Viking pressure than their western neighbours. How it came about that it was the Scots who emerged victorious from the confusion, while the Picts disappeared virtually without trace, is a very difficult question. In this, as in so much else, the Picts are Scotland's Dark Age enigma.

THE BRITONS, AD 500–800: LARGELY IGNORED

We have seen that Dark Age Scotland contained four peoples, Picts, Scots, Britons and Angles. Although the Picts are regarded as the most enigmatic, it may be the Britons about whom least is known. The Britons have not fared well at the hands of contemporary and modern writers. From the kingdom of Strathclyde with its citadel at Dumbarton Rock, all that survive are pedigrees of northern kings and annalistic entries preserved in compilations which in their present form are not earlier than the ninth century. Saints' *Lives*, even later in date, show signs of early British *strata*, but they are not easy to disentangle or interpret. Heroic poems, especially the *Gododdin*, name many northern heroes, but usually tell us only their names. Welsh 'triads' name northerners, but mostly in cryptic fashion. The Britons are mentioned in the Irish annals and by Bede, but he was curiously hostile to them. Even recently the Britons of southern Scotland have attracted relatively little attention.

The Tribes between the Roman Walls

Ptolemy names several tribes in southern Scotland, between the Solway and the Forth–Clyde isthmus, and it must be from them that the Scottish Britons, the 'Men of the North', were descended. How far they were ever Romanised by their contact with the Roman empire is difficult to assess, and depends on slender archaeological and literary evidence, much of the latter being from a later period. Of Ptolemy's tribes, we can safely assign four to the area between the Roman walls: the *Votadini* in Lothian; the *Damnonii* in Strathclyde; the *Selgovae* in the Southern Uplands; and the *Novantae* in Galloway. Of these peoples, only the *Votadini* have a name which survives in Dark Age records: for they were known later as the *Gododdin*, a tribe with important centres at Traprain Law and Edinburgh Rock. The Scots knew them too, for they referred to Berwick Law as 'the notable peak of *Fothadan*', a Gaelicisation of *Gododdin*.[18]

The name of the *Damnonii* did not survive, but the kingdom of Strathclyde with its fortress on Dumbarton Rock did. The extent of this kingdom is obscure and probably fluctuated; it probably extended up the Clyde as far as Beattock, and at times beyond; it would have included Strathgryfe and probably Cunninghame, but it is not certain whether it included Kyle. In Glen Falloch near the north end of Loch Lomond is a stone called *Clach nam Bretann*, the 'stone of the Britons', which marked the northern boundary of their kingdom.[19]

Edinburgh Rock: a hill-fort of the Gododdin. *(Historic Scotland)*

The *Selgovae* also did not survive, and there is doubt about the extent of their lands. There is little doubt, however, that the *Novantae* occupied Galloway.

There were other northern British kingdoms as well, presumably inhabited by descendants of the *Brigantes* mentioned by classical writers. The British kingdom of Rheged is usually reckoned to have been centred on Carlisle, but its exact location has been questioned. There was a British kingdom called Elmet, probably originally extending into the Vale of York, but later confined to the Pennines. The northern province of English Northumbria was known by the British name Bernicia, perhaps the name of a lost kingdom in Northumberland and County Durham.

By the middle of the fifth century the former Roman province of Britain was under pressure from all sides. The withdrawal of the Roman legions had left it vulnerable to attacks from the Picts to the north and the Irish to the west. The sixth-century writer Gildas gives a fantastic account of the incursions of the Picts and Scots against Hadrian's Wall:

As the Romans went back home, there eagerly emerged . . . the foul hordes of Scots and Picts, like dark throngs of worms who wriggle out of narrow fissures in the rock when the sun is high and the weather grows warm. . . . A force was stationed on the high towers to oppose them, but it was too lazy to fight, and too unwieldy to flee; the men were foolish and frightened, and they sat about day and night, rotting away in their folly. Meanwhile there was no respite from the barbed spears flung by their naked opponents, which tore our wretched countrymen from the walls and dashed them to the ground. Untimely death was in fact an advantage to those who were thus snatched away; for their quick end saved them from the miserable fate which awaited their brothers and children.[20]

But the greater threat came from the Angles and Saxons in the south and east. Gildas states that they were originally called in as mercenaries by a 'superior tyrant' (possibly called Vortigern) but stayed as unwelcome settlers. We know of some resistance to the Saxons, but in all this obscure process the overriding pattern is the one described by Gildas: 'The barbarians drive us to the sea; the sea drives us back upon the barbarians; between them we find two kinds of death; we are either slain or drowned'.

The character of post-Roman British society emerges in the few literary sources which we have from this period. St Patrick in the fifth century speaks of Roman Britain as having important personages with Roman civic titles, living in towns, and owning country estates and slaves of both sexes. Among these were deacons and priests who were allowed to marry. But Patrick's picture of fifth-century Britain also contains ruthless tyrants surrounded by war-bands, who launch plundering raids from their hillforts; although nominally Christian, they mock priests who rebuke them, and require to be excommunicated for their crimes, and godly men are warned not to receive their alms.[21]

Writing perhaps about half a century after Patrick, Gildas rebukes the British kings of Wales and south-west England in tones which reflect the same problems.

> Kings has Britain, but they are tyrants; she has judges, but they are wicked. They often plunder and terrorise the innocent; they defend and protect the guilty and thieves; they have many wives – whores and adulteresses; they constantly swear false oaths; they make vows, but at once they tell lies; they wage unjust civil wars; . . . they exalt their military companions, bloody, proud and murderous men, adulterers and enemies of God. . . . They hang around the altars swearing oaths, then soon scorn them as though they were dirty stones.[22]

In the case of one tyrant named by Gildas, we are lucky enough to have surviving his tombstone, where he bears the Roman title *protector*, while a descendant of another entered religion and became a famous saint. Evidently there was more to these Welsh tyrants, and perhaps to their Scottish cousins also, than Gildas was prepared to admit.

Y Gododdin

But by far the best and most vivid record we have of British heroic society, composed perhaps about fifty years after Gildas was writing, is the extraordinary poem *Y Gododdin*.[23] This describes an expedition of the war-band of Gododdin from their fortress at *Etyn*, Edinburgh Rock, to fight against the Angles at a place called *Catraeth*. *Catraeth* has been identified with Catterick in Yorkshire, but it is equally possible that it was the lost name of some place nearer to the borders of Bernicia and Gododdin.

There is a vivid picture of warriors drinking mead, boasting and feasting, receiving the largesse of Mynyddog, king of the Gododdin, and finally going out to be slaughtered almost to a man in a heroic but catastrophic struggle against the 'barbarians'. A few verses suffice to give a flavour of this elegy for fallen heroes.

> The men went to Catraeth, swift was their host,
> the pale mead was their feast and it was their poison;
> three hundred fighting men according to plan,
> and after the jubilation [of battle] there was silence.
> Though they should go to churches to do penance,
> the inescapable tryst with death overtook them.
>
> The men hastened forth, they were feasted together
> for a year over the mead; great were their boasts.
> How sad to tell of them, what insatiable longing!
> Cruel was their resting-place, no mother's son succoured them.
> How long was the grief for them and the yearning,
> after the fiery men from the land of wine-feasting!
> For the spirited men, Gwlyged of Gododdin
> contrived the famous feast of Mynyddog,
> costly when paid for at the battle at Catraeth.
>
> Ceredig the beloved chieftain, a furious champion in battle,
> the gold-filigreed champion of the battle-field,
> with broken spears in splinters and a bold mighty sword-stroke.
> Like a man he used to stand his ground among spears;
> before the grief of burial, before the suffering,
> he used to defend his post. . . .
> May he have a welcome among the host [of heaven],
> in perfect union with the Trinity.

What this poem conveys is the demise of the Gododdin or *Votadini* in the face of Anglian pressure from Northumbria. It is usually dated *c.* 600, with a number of interpolations of different dates. Despite the destruction of their war-band at *Catraeth*, the Gododdin continued to occupy Edinburgh Rock until the annals record the 'siege of Etin' in 638.[24]

Another north British kingdom, Rheged, also disappeared in the seventh century. This kingdom was later celebrated in Welsh heroic poetry, but is historically very obscure. It may have included Carlisle and the Solway basin. In the 580s it was ruled by Urien, who drew together a great confederation of north British rulers to attack the Angles on Lindisfarne *c.* 588–95; but the assault failed when Urien's relative Morgan murdered him. Urien Rheged was succeeded by his son Ywain, who also figures as a hero of Welsh heroic verse of a later age; but soon after that the line of kings fails. The collapse of Rheged may have come during the reign of Ecgfrith of Northumbria, 670–85.

The Kings of Dumbarton

We should perhaps, then, expect to find the tyrants of the *Damnonii* at Dumbarton Rock clinging grimly to their position in the face of imminent extinction in the early seventh century. But this is far from the case. Instead, the British kings at Dumbarton were holding their own against outside pressure, and often showed striking signs of aggression.

The first king of Dumbarton for whom there is independent confirmation is Rhydderch Hael son of Tudwal. The earliest source which mentions Rhydderch is Adomnán's *Life of Columba*, which tells a story of Columba's prophecy 'concerning king Roderc son of Tothail, reigning in the Rock of the Clyde':

> At one time this king . . . sent to him a secret message, seeking to know whether he would be slain by his enemies or not. . . . Thereupon the saint foretold: 'He shall never be given up into the hand of his enemies, but shall die in his own house, upon his pillow.' And this prophecy of the saint was completely fulfilled, for according to his word Roderc died a peaceful death in his own house.[25]

Columba may have reassured Rhydderch that Áedán son of Gabrán did not intend to attack him, but their relations were not always so friendly: a Welsh 'triad' describes how 'Áedán the traitor went into *Ail Cluit* [Dumbarton] to the court of Rhydderch Hael; after [his plundering] there remained neither food nor drink, nor any living thing'. Áedán's plundering of Strathclyde later became the subject of an Irish heroic tale.[26] Rhydderch is also named as one of the British kings who allied with Urien Rheged against the Angles of Bernicia. He is also named in a collection of old Welsh genealogies which call him son of Tudwal and great-grandson of Dyfnwal Hen, an important ancestor-figure in many northern pedigrees.

Another source to mention Rhydderch is the twelfth-century *Life of St Kentigern*.[27] Although it contains accretions and much that is demonstrably inaccurate, the *Life* may contain an early *stratum*. It claims that the death of King Rederech took place within a year of Kentigern's own. A set of Old Welsh annals places the death of Kentigern *c.* 614. The date of Rhydderch's death was probably not too much earlier or later than this.

The next king of Dumbarton seems to have been Nwython, a grandson or great-grandson of Dyfnwal Hen. It is chronologically possible that this Nwython is identical with the Nechton who appears in the Pictish king list, and who is also mentioned in the Irish annals, where his death is recorded in 621. It is a possibility that one man may have been king of Dumbarton and of Fortrenn between *c.* 614 and 621; this might explain why the 'grandson of Nwython' was fighting against the Dál Riata in Strathcarron in 642. Nwython's son Bili may be the Belin whose death is recorded in the Welsh annals in 627.[28]

His son Ywain (or Owen) was one of the most successful war leaders of the men of Strathclyde, defeating and killing Domnall Brecc, king of the Dál Riata, at the Battle of Strathcarron in 642. The Britons' victory in this battle was celebrated in a heroic poem, of which a fragment survives interpolated into *Y Gododdin*:

> I saw an array, they came from Kintyre,
> And splendidly they attacked around the conflagration.
> I saw the accustomed muster hastening to the town,
> And the men of the grandson of Nwython had arisen.
> I saw men in array, they came with the battle-shout;
> And the head of Dyfnwal Frych [Domnall Brecc], ravens gnawed it.[29]

His victory at Strathcarron must have made Ywain master of southern Scotland as far as the Firth of Forth. During the same period, there are hints of succession disputes and civil wars among the Picts; when the Picts finally emerged under a strong ruler, it was Bridei son of Bili, 'son of the king of Dumbarton'. Bili, of course, was also the father of Ywain, so Bridei and Ywain must have been at least half-brothers. The whole impression is one of close relations between Picts and Britons during much of the seventh century.

Down to the middle of the eighth century, the Irish annals present a picture of an orderly succession to the kingship of Dumbarton for the descendants of Ywain, in agreement with the Old Welsh genealogy of his family. Some of the reigns are strikingly long, often a sign of stability in Dark Age dynastic politics. But during the 740s the Britons of Strathclyde came to face a new and ultimately very damaging threat: the growing power of Onuist son of Uurguist, king of the Picts.

We have seen that Onuist emerged at the top only after a protracted and bloody power struggle in the late 720s, and even after he had defeated all his main rivals there were still rumblings of unrest into the 730s. In the late 730s he was strong enough to attack the Dál Riata, whose kingdom was overrun and subjugated by 741. Only then did he turn his attention to his other neighbour to the west, the British kingdom of Strathclyde. That it took so long for him to subdue Strathclyde must be a tribute to the continuing power and durability of the British kingdom. The first engagement came in 744, when a battle is recorded between Picts and Britons. In 750 Onuist sent his brother Talorgen with a large army into Strathclyde, to fight a battle at *Mygedawc* (probably Mugdock); the result was an overwhelming defeat for the Picts, with Talorgen killed and his army almost destroyed. As a result of this battle, the Irish annals recorded the 'waning of the power of Onuist' in 750.

But internal events within Strathclyde gave Onuist a second chance. Tewdwr, king of Dumbarton since 722, died in 752. His immediate successor was Rotri (Rhodri), who died in 754 and was succeeded by Tewdwr's son Dyfnwal. Probably there was a succession dispute between Rhodri and Dyfnwal, in which Rhodri was ousted and killed after a short reign. This would have left Strathclyde internally weakened and vulnerable to a fresh attack from the ever-predatory Onuist. The attack came in 756, when Onuist allied himself with Eadberht of Northumbria, and the two marched at the head of an army to besiege Dumbarton. The Britons were compelled to accept

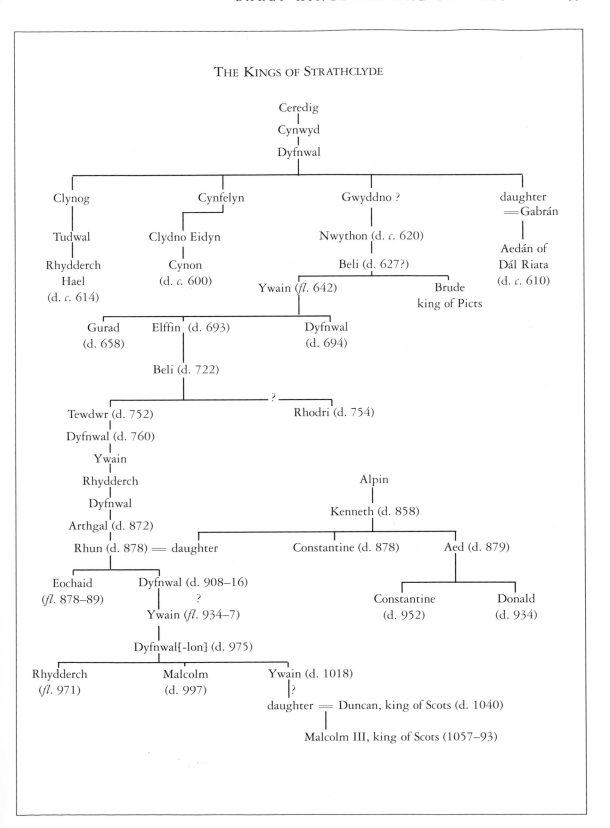

THE KINGS OF STRATHCLYDE

terms of surrender on 1 August. But Eadberht's victory was short-lived. Ten days later, on his homeward march, he was ambushed at *Ouania* and almost his whole army destroyed.

As a result of his defeat in 756, Dyfnwal son of Tewdwr went into exile. He is last heard of fighting in a battle against the 'Saxons' at Hereford, on the Welsh marches, in 760.

After his death, the kingdom of Strathclyde disappears from historical record for three-quarters of a century. No battles involving Britons are recorded again until the 820s, and the deaths of Strathclyde kings are not entered in Irish, Welsh or English annals. The eclipse of the kingdom seems to have been complete, with the only record surviving being that of the names of Dyfnwal's successors in the Welsh genealogies. Clearly, the British dynasty did continue a shadowy existence before re-emerging almost a century later, but for the time being Strathclyde seems to have gone the way of the kingdom of the Dál Riata, and been effectively annexed to Onuist's Pictish empire. Its eclipse is mysterious, and a reminder of just how little we really know about the British kingdom of Dumbarton. But the kingdom of Strathclyde does emerge later from this obscurity, and its dynasty of kings continued into the eleventh century: one of the most remarkably long-lived dynasties in all of Dark Age Britain. They do not deserve to have been largely ignored.

THE ANGLES OF NORTHUMBRIA: A NATION OF SCHOLARS AND HEROES?

The last of the peoples who went together to make up ancient historical Scotland were the Angles. Not perhaps last chronologically, because their settlement in the British mainland must have been roughly contemporary with that of the Irish Scots; but never regarded as of greatest importance for Scottish history, because the frontier of Scotland, when it came to be delineated in the mid-twelfth century, included only a small area which had been occupied continuously by Angles.

But the Angles are important for a number of reasons. It is their speech and culture which eventually became dominant in Scotland, spreading from a small heartland in the south-east to overrun the very much larger area of Celtic speech. Much of our knowledge of Scottish history in this period comes from Anglian writers, most notably the great scholar Bede. And many centuries later the legal and political institutions which the Angles brought into England came to dominate the British Isles.

The English Invasions

The earliest history of the Germanic kingdoms in Britain is known only in the vaguest outline. But there is no reason to disbelieve Gildas's statement that large-scale Anglo-Saxon settlement began *c*. 450 at the invitation of British rulers who sought mercenaries to fight the Picts and Irish; that the soldiers outstayed their welcome and

settled over a large area of south-east England, wresting new lands from their paymasters; that after about fifty years of contraction the British fought back in a series of campaigns, and there was peace between the Britons and the invaders for some fifty years, until c. 550; and that thereafter the Anglo-Saxon advance was renewed, until by c. 600 there were Germanic kingdoms stretching from Dorset to Lothian.

Northumbria

It is the Anglian kingdom of Northumbria which impinged on what later became Scotland. According to traditional accounts, Ida, the first king of the Northumbrians, founded Bamburgh c. 547, and united the provinces of Bernicia and Deira under his rule; thereafter the kings of Northumbria traced their ancestry to him, and ultimately to Woden. Bernicia, an Anglicised form of a British name of uncertain meaning, was the northern province, stretching roughly from the Tees to the Firth of Forth; Deira lay to the south, covering most of Yorkshire north of the Humber.

As one would expect, the earliest records we have for Northumbria are of wars against the Britons. The *Historia Brittonum* describes how British kings, led by Urien Rheged, attacked Bernicia, c. 588–95; the kingdom of Bernicia survived because of infighting among the Britons. This is a good illustration of how vulnerable these Anglian kingdoms were in their infancy. A few years later, c. 600, we have seen how the war-band of the Gododdin rode from Edinburgh Rock to attack the heathen Angles of Northumbria, and be slaughtered by them, at a place called *Catraeth*.[30]

Another great battle was fought by the Northumbrians at this time, also at a place which is difficult to identify. Their king Æthelfrith was challenged to battle by Áedán son of Gabrán, king of the Dál Riata, who had in the 580s and '90s made himself master of much of central Scotland. The two armies met in 602 or 603 at *Degsastan*, and the result of the battle was differently reported in the histories of the two sides. Both sides claimed victory while acknowledging heavy losses; so probably we should believe that the battle was indecisive and involved heavy casualties on both sides. Degsastan has not been satisfactorily identified. One statement by Bede can be relied on, however: 'From that time no king of the Irish in Britain has dared to make war on the English race to this day [731]'. Northumbria had become the most formidable force in the north.

Æthelfrith's most devastating attentions were reserved for the Britons of Wales. A few years after the indecisive carnage at *Degsastan* he defeated Gwynedd, probably the most powerful British kingdom at the time, at Chester. He well deserved Bede's description:

He might indeed be compared with Saul who was once king of Israel . . . for no ruler or king had subjected more land to the English race or settled it, having first either exterminated or conquered the natives.[31]

The death of Æthelfrith in 617, fighting against the king of East Anglia, brought no respite to the Britons of the North. He was succeeded by a Deiran prince, Edwin, who had himself been an exile under Æthelfrith and whose first act was to expel Æthelfrith's seven sons from Northumbria. Two of them at least, Eanfrith and Oswald, fled north and found refuge among the Picts and Scots. Eanfrith married a Pictish princess, who bore him a son who was given the Pictish name Talorcen, who was king of Picts 653–57. Oswald studied at Iona and later showed favour to Columban monks when he was able to return to Northumbria.

Edwin was the first Northumbrian king who was regarded as holder of the *imperium Britanniae*, supreme rule over all the English in Britain, although it is not clear what this involved. His first campaign was against the British kingdom of Elmet, by now bottled up in the Pennines. He expelled the last native king, whose death is recorded soon after. He then crossed the Pennines and fought a series of campaigns against Cadwallon of Gwynedd. He had some successes, because he was able to add Anglesea and Man to his domains (implying the overrunning of much of Gwynedd), and *c.* 632 besieged Cadwallon. But Cadwallon allied himself with King Penda of Mercia, a heathen Anglian kingdom covering much of the Midlands, and the two of them slew Edwin at a great battle at Hatfield Chase in 633.

Edwin had been the first Northumbrian king to embrace Christianity; he was baptised by Bishop Paulinus of York in 627. British tradition records that Edwin's baptismal sponsor was Rhun son of Urien, king of Rheged. Bede has nothing to say about this, and he maintains that the Britons refused to preach the gospel to their English neighbours; but the story is probably to be accepted. A granddaughter of Rhun was married to Oswy, a later king of Northumbria.

Edwin's death in 633 was followed by another wholesale change in the upper political layer in Northumbria. Penda and Cadwallon ravaged the kingdom, forcing Bishop Paulinus and the queen to withdraw; the sons of Æthelfrith returned and fought among themselves; Bernicia and Deira seem to have been divided; and there was a resurgence of paganism. Order was restored by Oswald, one of Æthelfrith's younger sons, a year after Edwin's death. In a great battle near Hexham he defeated and slew Cadwallon of Gwynedd, drove out the Britons, and made himself master of all Northumbria. Bede accounted him one of the holders of British *imperium*, so he must have quickly restored the fortunes of Northumbria, though he was still not strong enough to challenge Mercia.

One of his early acts was to reintroduce Christianity into his kingdom. But he did not send to Canterbury or to any other of the Anglo-Saxon kingdoms which had been converted by Roman missionaries in the years since 597; instead he sent for missionaries to the northern lands where he had spent his exile, where Christianity had been established for much longer. For a generation the successors of Columba at Iona had strong influence in the most powerful of the English kingdoms. Thus Oswald established cultural links between Northumbria, Ireland and Scotland which were to have a profound impact on all three lands.

But Oswald had to do more than import Irish monks to earn his imperial title. He appears to have intervened in the affairs of the South Saxons, confirming their royal charters; and he had influence in Kent. To Adomnán, some fifty years later, he was 'emperor of all Britain'. His most important act as far as Scotland was concerned was the final extinction of the kingdom of the Gododdin. Bede has nothing to say about this, recording only that he ruled within 'the same bounds' as his predecessor Edwin; but the Irish annals record the 'siege of Etin' c. 638. Northumbria now stretched to the Firth of Forth, and had a frontier with Pictland.

King Oswy

The removal of a buffer state between the Picts and Northumbria was important. Earlier, Northumbrian royal exiles had been able to take refuge among the Picts, and one of them, Eanfrith, had married into the Pictish royal house and fathered a king of Picts. These good relations were now to change, especially after the death of Oswald (slain in battle by Penda of Mercia) in 641. Oswald's successor was perhaps the most powerful of the kings of Northumbria, under whom the kingdom reached its greatest extent, and the last Northumbrian to hold the *imperium*. He was Oswy, famous for his part in the Synod of Whitby, reputed a pious Christian by Bede, but clearly ruthless in his elimination of rivals at home and his expansion abroad.

One of Oswy's greatest successes came in 654, when he was at last strong enough to defeat and kill Penda of Mercia, the last heathen Anglian king. This victory, and the subsequent conversion of Mercia to Christianity, left Oswy free to concentrate on northward expansion into Pictish territory. Bede states that Oswy 'made tributary even the tribes of Picts and Scots who inhabit the northern part of Britain', but says little about the processes by which this was done. There are no records of great battles in which he defeated the Picts, either in English or Irish sources; and when he established an Anglian bishop for the Picts, his episcopal seat was at Abercorn, south of the Forth, rather than in Pictland itself.

The best-known event of Oswy's reign was the Synod of Whitby in 664. It has been suggested that underlying the synod was not so much a desire for catholic unity as a dispute between Oswy and his son Alhfrith, who disappears from record soon after. Also, if Oswy was extending his influence into Pictland and Dál Riata, he may have been glad to seize an opportunity to reduce the influence of Iona and promote churchmen of his own. His Anglian bishop at Abercorn would have been free from the jurisdiction of Iona, whereas all the monasteries of Pictland (says Bede) were subject to the rule of its abbot. By establishing a territorial bishop for the Picts on the fringe of Pictish territory he was able to reduce the influence of the Dál Riata, and to increase his own.

One of the undocumented successes of Oswy's reign was the elimination of the kingdom of Rheged. How this came about is unknown, but it must have happened about this time. In the same way that the fall of Gododdin c. 638 had brought Northumbria into direct contact with the Picts of Fortrenn, so the fall of Rheged gave Northumbria a common frontier with the Britons of Dumbarton. There seemed to be no end to Northumbrian expansion.

Northumbria after Oswy

Whatever reservations we may have about Bede's portrait of Oswy, we can be sure that he was a very powerful and successful king; he is unusual in that he died peacefully in his bed after a reign of twenty-eight years. His son and successor Ecgfrith was less successful, though he started his reign from a more secure base than any of his predecessors. But the power of Mercia soon began to recover after the death of Penda, and in 679 there was open war between Mercia and Northumbria, and Ecgfrith's brother Ælfwine was defeated and killed in a battle on the Trent. Theodore, archbishop of Canterbury, made peace between the two kingdoms to prevent further bloodshed.

Ecgfrith's renewed troubles in the south may have tempted the Picts to resist Northumbrian demands for tribute, and led Ecgfrith to launch a major expedition into Pictland in May 685, resulting in his defeat and death at Dunnichen. The battle guaranteed the independence of the Pictish kingdom and halted the seemingly inexorable Northumbrian advance into central and eastern Scotland.

Dunnichen, according to Bede, initiated the waning of Northumbria. It allowed for more cordial relations between Northumbria and some of its northern neighbours; Adomnán, abbot of Iona, visited Northumbria twice, in 686 and 688, the first time to negotiate the release of Irish captives taken on a raid in 684, the second time to observe the practices of the Church in Northumbria and to dedicate to King Aldfrith his new book, *A Description of the Holy Places*.[32]

A desultory state of hostilities, however, continued between Northumbria and Pictland; battles are recorded in 697 and 711. Relations improved soon after, for by 715 the Pictish king Nechton son of Derilei wrote to Osred of Northumbria asking for information on ecclesiastical matters. By the time the *Historia Ecclesiastica* was written (731), Bede was able to speak of 'a treaty of peace' between the Picts and Angles, and how 'the Scots who live in Britain are content with their own territories and devise no plots or treachery against the English'.

This was the situation of Northumbria and its northern neighbours in 731. Probably after Dunnichen the Pentland (*Pict-land*) Hills south of Edinburgh represented the boundary between Picts and Angles; Anglian place-names are very much more numerous to the east. But in the west the Anglian frontier seems to have been shifting. After Dunnichen 'a part of the Britons regained their liberty', says Bede; perhaps an extension of control by the Strathclyde Britons into former Rheged territory on the Solway. When Bede wrote that by 731 '[The Britons] are partly their own masters, yet they have also been brought partly under the rule of the English', he was probably referring to renewed Northumbrian expansion into the Solway basin. Shortly before 730, Galloway had been annexed by the Angles, and an Anglian bishopric established at Whithorn; the first bishop, Pehthelm, was a friend of Bede. The Anglian crosses at Bewcastle and Ruthwell, plus the evidence for an Anglian monastery at Hoddom, are signs of cultural advance in the eighth century in this area, which must have been paralleled in political terms. In 750 King Eadberht of

The Ruthwell Cross,
near Dumfries: Anglian
culture in south-west
Scotland,
eighth century.
(Historic Scotland)

Northumbria 'added the plain of Kyle and other lands to his kingdom'. This expansion came at a time when Pictish power was at its height, under Onuist son of Uurguist, and there was no prospect of Northumbrian advance in that direction. Indeed, Onuist seems at one time to have had an alliance with King Æthelbald of Mercia, thus encircling Northumbria. By 756 Onuist had entered into an alliance with Eadberht of Northumbria with a view to dismembering Strathclyde and dividing it between them, but the alliance ended after the defeat of the Britons when Onuist treacherously turned on his erstwhile allies. When recording Onuist's death in 761, a continuator of Bede's *Historia* bitterly denounced him as a 'tyrannical slaughterer' and 'perpetrator of bloody crimes'.[33]

The attack on Dumbarton in 756, with its disastrous aftermath, was the last Northumbrian attempt at northward expansion. Attempts to expand into Pictish territory had ceased long before. The Angles were able to hold on to the Solway basin, for a series of bishops at Whithorn continued to be recorded. But Northumbria was no longer the dominant force in English politics; Mercia superseded Northumbria as the most powerful Anglian kingdom. The second half of the eighth century is a rather obscure period in Northumbrian history; the laconic sources suggest a picture of much royal in-fighting during the later eighth century, with kings having short reigns and meeting violent ends at the hands of their successors. Northumbria no longer posed an expansionist threat to its northern neighbours, and was to fall an easy victim to the Viking whirlwind which struck from 793 onwards.

Were the Angles of Northumbria 'a nation of scholars and heroes'? The answer depends on whether one believes Bede. His formidable scholarship, unrivalled in contemporary northern Europe, was an amalgam of Roman and Irish learning. Northumbria's reputation as a haven for scholars rests chiefly on him; his monastery was able to amass such a good library that he was never tempted to leave Northumbria, and made himself into a great scholar in a remote corner of northern Europe.

As for heroes, they are mostly Bede's heroes. Northumbrian kings look much like the kings of any other nation in the heroic age. Territorial expansion, tribute and protection, the spoils of war and the glory of battle, were the stuff of Anglian kings just as they were of all the neighbouring societies. Their good fortune was to have the pen of Bede to record the process.

CHAPTER 3

The Coming of Christianity

EARLY SAINTS: PATRICK, NINIAN AND KENTIGERN

One of the most significant factors in shaping early Scottish society was religion, and more specifically the religious system introduced by the Roman empire – Christianity. This was, in origin, one of a number of oriental mystery cults which spread through the Mediterranean world in the early centuries of our era, and which contended with, and sometimes co-existed with, classical paganism. Christianity was by far the most successful cult of its kind long before the emperor Constantine's victory at the Milvian Bridge in 312.

Christianity in Roman Britain

The situation in Britain, the imperial province furthest from the Mediterranean heartland, is very difficult to assess. Some early Christian writers speak of Christianity in Britain. The martyrdom of St Alban, a Roman army officer, at an uncertain date in the third century, is attested by a number of later writers. In the fourth century the picture becomes clearer. In 314 three British bishops and lesser clergy attended the Council of Arles; clearly a church hierarchy was already established in Britain. British clergy attended the councils of Nicaea (325), Sardica (342) and Rimini (359).

Archaeology provides some clues to fill out this picture. In Roman villas, mosaics have been found which could plausibly be interpreted as having a Christian element. The cumulative evidence indicates 'an educated and wealthy Christian society in the Romano-British countryside in the second half of the fourth century'.[1]

Evidence from Roman towns, and from the more militarised northern zone, is thinner. But most of the fourth-century emperors encouraged Christianity among the army, and the two British usurpers of the period, Magnus Maximus (383–8) and Constantine III (407–11), commanded the garrisons on the Wall and were Christian themselves. A few Christian symbols have been found at military sites in northern England, and items from the Traprain Law hoard shows that the fifth-century *Votadini* were in contact with Christianity, though it is not clear how this treasure was acquired.

The Galloway Inscriptions

In the fifth century, northern evidence for Christianity becomes more continuous, but not necessarily easier to interpret. There is an impressive group of fifth- and sixth-century Christian inscribed stones in Galloway, the territory of Ptolemy's *Novantae*. The earliest is probably the 'Latinus stone' from Whithorn, from the middle or second half of the fifth century: 'We praise Thee, O Lord. Latinus, 35 years of age, and his daughter, four years of age. The descendants of Barrova[n]dus made this monument'. This stone has a curiously provincial, Celtic, quality; it misquotes the opening of the early Christian hymn *Te Deum Laudamus*, 'We praise Thee, O God'; there are some missing letters and grammatical mistakes. The inscription shows the Celtic concern for ancestry by noting that Latinus was a descendant of Barrovandus.

Probably slightly later are the stones at Kirkmadrine in the Rhinns of Galloway; one reads: 'Here lie the holy and outstanding priests, namely, Viventius and Mavorius'. Another stone commemorates two people, one of them called Florentius. A third stone from the Rhinns of Galloway, now lost, commemorated a deacon called Ventidius. Another stone from Whithorn proclaims 'The Place of the apostle Peter'; this is probably slightly later in date, but suggests continuing links with Rome. This Galloway group of early Christian stones is proof of Christianity in that area, certainly by the late fifth and sixth centuries.[2] It is with this area that we associate St Ninian, the 'apostle of the Picts'.

Elsewhere in southern Scotland, the Christian symbols among the Traprain Law hoard have been mentioned, as has the fact that it is not clear whether this hoard was plunder, payment, or an accumulation of treasures by peaceful means. The poem *Y Gododdin* contains a few passing references to Christianity: 'The poet prays that various warriors may go to heaven. . . . A hero lays gold upon the altar; another takes communion; another would more gladly go to battle and be killed than to a wedding-feast or the altar; and the army is said to have gone to churches to do penance. However, apart from a couple of biblical names among the warriors, that is about all, and . . . God himself is nowhere mentioned.'[3]

Early Christian stones of the post-Roman period have been found in upper Tweeddale, including one commemorating 'Neitanus the priest' at Peebles; another stone from the same place, now lost, reportedly marked 'The Place of bishop Nicholas'. At Yarrowkirk is a stone bearing an inscription in debased Latin capitals, part of which is difficult to read, but which appears to end: 'Here lie in the tomb the two sons of Liberalus'. These stones indicate Christianity in that area at a date not much later than that indicated in Galloway. Further north, but again not too much later in date, is the Catstane at Kirkliston, with an inscription: 'In this tomb lies Vetta son of Victus'. This lies in a burial ground of long cists, which probably indicates Christian burial practices. Similar cemeteries, probably sixth- or seventh-century, have been found at Lundin Links, St Andrews and near Dundee.[4]

Patrick: a Unique Voice

A very important source of information for Christianity in fifth-century Britain is found in the two letters of St Patrick. Our certain knowledge about St Patrick derives entirely from what he tells us about himself in his letters, and limited inference.[5]

He is British, he tells us, with a family living in Britain; he came from the *vicus* of *Bannavem Taburniae*, where his father Calpornius was a deacon, and his grandfather Potitus a presbyter; his father was also a *decurio* or civic official, owner of a *villula* or estate, and owner also of slaves of both sexes. When he was nearly sixteen, Patrick was captured by Irish raiders and carried into slavery in Ireland; there he spent six years herding flocks, some of the time at a place called *Silva Vocluti*, the forest of Foclut, 'beside the western sea'. As a result of a vision, Patrick ran away from his master, travelled on foot some 200 miles to a seaport, where he obtained passage on a ship which took him away from Ireland. The sea journey lasted three days and brought Patrick to a land which he does not name, where he walked for twenty-eight days before he came to human habitation. This land was probably not Britain, since Patrick immediately goes on to say 'A few years later I was in Britain with my family'. Northern Gaul is most likely.

Once back in Britain, now in his twenties, Patrick was reunited with his family, who begged him never to leave them again. But in a vision he heard the voices of the Irish begging him to come and walk with them; he determined to work as a Christian missionary among the people who had once enslaved him. So he trained for the priesthood and, shortly before being ordained, he confessed to a friend a sin which he had committed when he was about fifteen. The nature of his sin is not stated, but it did not disqualify him for the diaconate. Nor, in the eyes of his friend and confessor, did it disqualify him for the episcopate, for the same friend told him that he should be made bishop. Subsequently he was consecrated bishop and sent to Ireland. He must have been at least thirty, the minimum age for consecration.

Judging by his description, his missionary years in Ireland were many and successful, though fraught with dangers. He baptised many converts and ordained clergy; some of his converts became monks and nuns. He travelled round the country with a retinue of the sons of kings and visited the courts of kings, making payments to them and to the brehon lawyers. On at least two occasions he was imprisoned, and he states that his life was in danger twelve times. Clearly he made many friends in Ireland, including powerful men who were able to negotiate his release from captivity on one occasion, and he mentions converting one lady of noble birth, who subsequently became a nun against her parents' wishes. On one occasion a large group of newly baptised converts was attacked, some killed and some enslaved, by the war-band of a ruler called Coroticus; Patrick exerted himself to have the captives released and their goods restored.

After about thirty years of his ministry in Ireland, however, Patrick was faced by another threat. He was attacked by a group of his *seniores*, presumably bishops. It is clear that his trial took place in Britain, in Patrick's absence. Patrick learned from some brethren that his old friend and spiritual adviser would speak in his defence, but instead the man betrayed him by revealing in public the sin which Patrick had confessed to him thirty years before. As a result his defence was rejected and his name stripped of honour. The principal accusation against Patrick seems to have been that he accepted bribes for performing baptisms and ordinations, accusations which he refuted. He refused to leave Ireland and abandon his converts, asserting that he had not gone there voluntarily but by the will of God, and that his episcopate was conferred on him by God. The letter reads like an explanation of why Patrick has refused a recall by his superiors and has chosen instead to remain in Ireland.

Patrick speaks to us across the centuries as a unique voice from fifth-century Britain: personal, passionate, and profoundly human.

But our interest is Patrick's relevance for the development of Christianity in northern Britain. There was a tyrant of the *Damnonii* of Strathclyde in the late fifth century named Ceredig; by the eighth century he had become identified with Patrick's Coroticus. The identification has been questioned, but there seems little reason to doubt it; Coroticus was certainly a northerner, since he was an ally of the Picts. Patrick writes as though Coroticus and his war-band considered themselves to be Christians; his denunciation of them as 'fellow-citizens of demons' rather than Romans and Christians, would otherwise have no point.

Patrick writes of a Church with bishops, priests and deacons, clerics, monks and virgins. He mentions a gathering or synod of senior bishops who attempted to depose and recall him. Patrick belonged to a missionary Church. He himself was chosen as a missionary bishop among the northern Irish because his captivity had familiarised him with the language, customs and terrain of Ireland.

Ninian

We know much less about Ninian than we do about St Patrick. The earliest mention of him comes in a passage in Bede's *Historia Ecclesiastica*:

> The southern Picts, who have their dwellings on this side of the mountains, had, so they claim, given up the error of idolatry long before [Columba's time], and received the faith of truth, through the preaching to them of Bishop Nynia, a reverend and holy man of British race, who was regularly educated at Rome in the faith and mysteries of the truth. His episcopal see, renowned for its church dedicated to the holy Bishop Martin, where his body rests with those of many saints, now belongs to the English race. This place . . . is commonly called 'At the White House' [Whithorn], because he built there a church of stone, in a manner unknown to the Britons.[6]

This does not name Ninian as the founder or first bishop of Whithorn, but says only that he built a stone church there where he was buried. It does not give any clue as to when he lived, except to say that it was 'a long time before' the coming of Columba in 563. Bede did not have dates for Ninian, and was deliberately vague.

Bede appears to have known of Ninian from two distinct sources: he had a letter from the Picts themselves in which they outlined their account of their conversion (hence the words 'so they claim' (*ut perhibent*) in the above passage); and he had information from the English occupants of Whithorn about the saints buried at the church there. Bede's interest in Ninian arises mainly because he was interested in the conversion of the Picts, and sought to set Columba's achievements in context. His interest in Whithorn as the site of Ninian's burial is secondary.[7]

Contemporaries of Bede who knew about Whithorn appear to have had less knowledge about Ninian. In about 735, an English bishop in Germany wrote to the bishop of Whithorn on a point of canon law; his letter enclosed gifts for the church of Whithorn, but made no mention of the saint who was buried there. This contrasts with a letter to the monks of Whithorn from the Latin scholar Alcuin *c.* 790, in which he enclosed gifts specifically for the shrine of its famous patron St Ninian.[8]

The next written source for St Ninian's career is an eighth-century Latin poem, *Miracula Nyniae Episcopi*, which was composed at Whithorn at the time of Anglian occupation (from *c.* 730), showing Celtic influence. It has a few details which are not in Bede, including the statement that Ninian was exiled by a local tyrant called Tudwal, who was then struck blind and restored to health by Ninian's prayers. He performs a number of miracles and more occur at his tomb after his death.[9]

The name of the local tyrant is presumably meant to refer to Tudwal, father of Rhydderch Hael, king of Dumbarton (d. *c.* 614). But we should not hang much weight on this identification. Medieval saints' lives frequently make their heroes contemporaries of people who lived at a very different time; and Tudwal may have been introduced simply to associate Ninian with a king who was known to be earlier than Columba.

A third source is the twelfth-century *Life of Ninian* attributed to Ailred of Rievaulx, which applies to Ninian all the conventions of medieval saints' lives, and is of no independent value. It is to this source that we owe the modern spelling of Ninian's name, with final 'n'.[10]

There is a good deal of credibility in Bede's story about St Ninian. Archaeology and place-name evidence show that there was a British-based mission to the Picts. The spread of place-names incorporating the element *eccles-*, indicating early churches founded under British influence, extends as far as the Mounth but not beyond; exactly the area described by Bede. The oriented long-cist burial-grounds in Fife and near Dundee, datable to the sixth and seventh centuries, have been mentioned. An objection might be that Gildas *c.* 540 describes the British Church as decadent, hardly able to conduct missions to strange heathen lands. But Gildas admits that there were 'a very few good pastors', and he corresponded with one of them, a missionary in Ireland called Vinnio (a name Gaelicised as Finnian). Possibly Ninian was his contemporary.[11]

Kentigern: Lord of the Dogs

There is a third British saint whose name is connected with this period and area: St Kentigern of Glasgow. His career is very obscure indeed, and our knowledge about him is restricted to a single brief entry in a set of later Welsh annals recording his death (*c.* 614), a reference in a Welsh 'triad', and a body of later saints' lives. One of these, written *c.* 1180, claimed that Kentigern was a contemporary of a king called Rhydderch, whose name is spelt in an early form, and it knew that this king had a royal manor at Partick near Glasgow. It states that Rhydderch died less than a year after Kentigern himself, and that king could not have died too much earlier or later than *c.* 614.[12]

The name Kentigern has a curious history. The earliest surviving form is *Conthigirnus*, from the aristocratic British name *Con tigern*, 'lord of hounds'. In later British it becomes *Kyndyern*, which was corrupted in Gaelic to *Ceanntighearn*. A twelfth-century writer was told by Gaelic speakers that Kentigern meant 'chief lord'. But the association of Kentigern with dogs was not forgotten, for he was accorded the pet-name *Mo(n)Chú*, 'my little dog'. It is by this name, Mungo, that he is still remembered in Glasgow.

Taken together, the archaeological and epigraphic evidence, and what we know of the careers of Patrick, Ninian and Kentigern, suggest that the post-Roman Church in Britain in the fifth, sixth and early seventh centuries was flourishing and expansionist, rather than decadent or introverted. But, like the British kingdoms themselves, it was to be eclipsed by more dynamic forces from south and north. One of these was the missionary Church introduced into southern England by St Augustine and Roman monks in 597; also important, if ultimately less successful, was the vigorous and highly individual blend of Christianity introduced from Ireland in the sixth century, which we most closely associate with the name of Columba.

EARLY SAINTS: COLUMBA AND THE ACHIEVEMENT OF IONA

We have seen that Christianity in Scotland had a long history before the coming of St Columba in 563. But early Scottish Christianity is most firmly associated with the founder and first abbot of the monastery of Iona. There were other Gaelic saints contemporary with him who visited Scotland, most notably St Donnan, founder of the monastery of Eigg, and St Brendan of Clonfert, who founded a monastery at Ailech. How did it happen that Ireland, outside the Roman empire, became such a centre for missionary activity?

The process is a very obscure one. We have the documents of Patrick's mission, and a single reference to St Palladius, consecrated and sent by the pope to the 'Irish believing in Christ' in 431. We know of Vinnio and other British missionaries active in Ireland *c.* 540. For the most part, however, the processes by which Ireland became a Christian land in the fifth and sixth centuries are lost to us; but these processes may explain the warm welcome which Columba received when he came to the court of Conall son of Comgall, king of the Dál Riata, in 563.

Most of our knowledge about St Columba comes from the *Life* written by Adomnán, abbot of Iona, *c.* 700, a century after the saint's death. Additional information is provided by Bede, and by the collections of Irish annals, which seem to embody material compiled at Iona down to the mid-eighth century. Adomnán had access to at least one earlier *Life* of Columba, and to oral tradition preserved among the monks of Iona from the 620s.[13]

Columba's Early Career

Columba or Colum Cille, 'the dove of the church', was a monastic name, taken at the time of entry into religion rather than given at his birth in 521. His father was an aristocrat of the tribe of Conall who ruled over much of County Donegal. At an early age Columba was fostered to a priest, and in youth studied under some of the greatest ecclesiastical teachers in Ireland at the time, including Vinnio.

It is uncertain whether he began his career as a founder of monasteries before he came to Scotland. Bede states that the Columban monastery of Durrow (County Offaly) was founded before Columba left Ireland, but Adomnán implies that it was being built after Columba had settled in Iona. Neither Bede nor Adomnán speak of a monastery at Derry, but Adomnán mentions it several times as a port for embarkation to Iona, and there was later a Columban monastery there. Since Iona 'held the pre-eminence' over all other Columban foundations, it was probably the earliest.

Iona Abbey, showing the eighth- to ninth-century crosses and buildings from the tenth to fifteenth centuries and modern restoration. *(Alan Macquarrie)*

The western *machair* and beach on Iona. *(Alan Macquarrie)*

Little is known about Columba's career in Ireland. A turning-point in his life seems to have come in the year 561, the year of the Battle of Cúil Dreimne, fought between branches of the royal house of the Uí Néill of which Columba's own family was part. Columba was held responsible for instigating the battle and the bloodshed involved. The details of the battle and its causes are very obscure; but it seems to have resulted in considerable unpopularity for Columba, for in the following year (562) he was excommunicated by a synod of Irish clergy. Although his excommunication was not long-lasting, and Columba was defended by St Brendan of Birr, it was probably this event which made him decide to leave Ireland. So in 563, accompanied by twelve companions, he sailed away from Ireland to the court of Conall son of Comgall, king of the Dál Riata in Scotland.

Adomnán states that on Columba's first arrival in Britain he resided with King Conall, and the Irish annals state that it was Conall who gave Iona to him for the foundation of his monastery. Iona was probably established as Columba's home and monastic centre soon after his arrival in Scotland.

Columba, Royal Counsellor

Adomnán has little to say about Columba's relationship with Conall after his initial residence at court. Perhaps these early years in Scotland were spent in work at Iona and on the foundation of other island monasteries in the southern Hebrides. It was while staying at one of these, the island of 'Hinba' (unidentified – possibly Oronsay), that Columba learned of the death of Conall in 574. An angel instructed him in a vision to consecrate Áedán son of Gabrán as Conall's successor, and Columba did so at a ceremony of laying-on of hands at Iona. Subsequently, Columba and Áedán co-operated closely on a number of occasions. Áedán took Columba with him to a meeting with the king of the northern Uí Néill at Druim Cett in northern Ireland, at which Columba acted as his adviser in matters concerning the relationship of the two kings. Before embarking on a campaign against a Pictish tribe, probably in 582, Áedán consulted Columba about the succession to the kingship in the event of his death. Columba, as well as advising Áedán which of his sons would outlive him, lent him the aid of his prayers in battle.

The expansion of Áedán's kingdom may have affected Columba's relationship with other kings in Scotland at the time. He made at least one visit to the court of Bridei, king of the northern Picts, who had a royal fortress near the River Ness, probably Craig Phatric. Although at first the king barred the gates against him, Columba won his admiration and respect. Columba baptised the general of the army of the *Geona*, presumably a Pictish tribe in Skye, after preaching to him through an interpreter, and he baptised other Picts in and around the Great Glen; but Adomnán does not speak of a large-scale conversion of Picts, and probably no large-scale conversion took place until later. Adomnán also describes how Columba received a secret message from Rhydderch, king of the Britons at Dumbarton, whom he assured that he would die peacefully in his bed. Columba also had dealings with kings and aristocrats in Ireland after his coming to Scotland.

In addition to describing Columba's dealings with the aristocracy of his day, Adomnán speaks of the monastic life of Iona, its buildings and its monks. None of the timber buildings of Columba's time survives, but traces of a substantial perimeter earthwork can still be seen. Within this there would have been a church and large monastic common-room, individual cells for Columba himself and some of his senior monks, and various other buildings such as a scriptorium where the copying of manuscripts took place; beyond the perimeter were stables and farm buildings. There were shepherds' huts on the western *machair* of the island, and perhaps a boathouse at the narrowest point of the Sound of Iona to facilitate the ferrying of visitors across from Mull. These visitors included kings and their messengers, ecclesiastical pilgrims, penitents and sick persons seeking medical and spiritual cures. Although Columba came to Iona seeking solitude for his 'pilgrimage', the impression is that the island was quite a busy place, with a regular stream of visitors coming and going amid the constant activity of the abbot and his monks.

The Death of Columba

The longest chapter of Adomnán's *Life of Columba* is the description of the saint's death. In the month of May 597, some weeks after Easter, Columba was taken in a cart to visit the monks who were at work in the western parts of the island. He told them that his end was drawing near, and blessed them and the island; then his cart was brought back to the monastic enclosure. On the following Sunday, he saw a vision of angels while celebrating mass in the monastic church. On the Saturday after that, he and his servant Diarmait went out for a short walk, but Columba's age (he was about seventy-six) prevented him going further than the nearest farm buildings; these he blessed, while he told Diarmait that he expected to die that same night. On the way back to the monastery he sat down to rest, at a point which was later commemorated by a cross set in a mill-stone which still stood in Adomnán's time. While he sat resting, he was approached by one of the monastery's horses, 'an obedient servant who was accustomed to carry the milk-vessels between the cow-pasture and the monastery', which placed its head in the saint's bosom and seemed to weep, as if it knew that its master was soon to be taken from it. Columba would not allow Diarmait to drive the horse away; rather he allowed it to nuzzle against him, before 'he blessed his servant the horse, as it turned sadly away from him'. Then he climbed a small hill and gave his monastery his last blessing: 'On this place, small and mean though it be, not only the kings of the Scots with their peoples, but also the rulers of barbarous and foreign nations with their subjects, will bestow great and especial honour'. Then he returned to his writing hut to continue the copying of a psalter on which he had been working. He continued this activity up until the time of vespers, the office which initiated the Lord's day; after attending vespers in the church, he retired to his own lodging to sleep. When the bell rang for the midnight office, Columba hurried to the church ahead of the monks, and they, coming in carrying lamps to light the dark church, found him collapsed and dying in front of the altar. He raised his hand feebly in a last benediction, and expired. The date of his death was Sunday 9 June 597.

An assessment of Columba's life and career is not easy. Adomnán is more concerned to demonstrate Columba's power and God's favour towards him than to present the events of his life in chronological order or assess his secular influence and importance. There can be no doubt that Columba did have secular influence, as a high-born aristocrat who moved easily in the company of kings and princes; but it would be misguided to view him as a clerical manipulator of secular politics. He was equally concerned with the spiritual well-being of his monks and the pilgrims and penitents who visited him. There are stories of kindness to animals, an unusual trait in a society of rural subsistence. It is also hinted by Adomnán that sick people came to Iona seeking remedies for physical ailments, and there are constant references in the *Life* to the copying of books, especially the Bible. The monastic life at Iona also involved manual labour, in the fields and on building projects, though Columba was concerned that his monks should not be overburdened. Finally, there are references to the regular monastic offices, including vespers and the midnight office, and the celebration of mass on Sundays and holy days. Wednesday was observed as a fast day at Iona, but this could be relaxed if there were visitors. It is not certain how far Columba practised personal austerities: Adomnán states that he slept on the bare rock, but he was constantly attended by his servant Diarmait, and was served at mealtimes by his monks.

It is difficult to get any closer to Columba. No poem or manuscript certainly by him has survived. Subsequent tradition and hagiography have obscured him as much as they have revealed him, and tell us as much about the later reputation of Iona as they do about Columba himself. But there can be no doubt that Iona's reputation was built on a firm foundation of piety and scholarship, and that foundation was laid by Columba himself. He was an active and vigorous churchman who travelled widely and worked hard among his contemporaries, both lay and clerical. The reasons for his departure from Ireland are now obscure, but it is not certain that they constituted a voluntary withdrawal from home and family; certainly he revisited both later. On the other hand, he was not a clerical kingmaker; the extent of his influence over his aristocratic contemporaries has probably been exaggerated. This is not, however, Adomnán's doing; he was concerned above all to set out his great predecessor's spiritual power and sanctity.

Other Saints, Gaelic and Otherwise

Columba's career contrasts with that of his younger contemporary, St Donnan of Eigg. Donnan appears to have carried out missionary work among the Picts of the west coast and Western Isles north of Ardnamurchan before he was martyred with 150 monks in 617.[14]

There were other less well-documented missionaries as well. St Brendan of Clonfert is said to have founded a monastery at Ailech, probably Eileach an Naoimh in the Garvellachs. St Blane of Kingarth on Bute founded a church which had a long history as an episcopal centre. St Fillan (Gaelic Faolán, 'wolf-cub') was active in Breadalbane. St Kessog by tradition came from Munster and evangelised the lands around Loch Lomond. Over fifty years after the tragic end of Donnan's mission to the islands of the north-west, St Maelrubha from Bangor founded the church of Applecross and renewed missionary activity in Skye and the north-west Highlands.

Very few of the heroes of the 'Age of Saints' can be dated with any precision. St Serf is the subject of a twelfth-century *Life* which locates his miracles and churches in Clackmannanshire and west Fife, but one cannot be confident about when he was active, or even where he came from. He may have been Pictish, given an exotic career by later writers who were unfamiliar with his unusual name. The same thing may have happened to St Ethernan of the Isle of May, whose originally Pictish name was corrupted to Adrian.[15]

For all the uncertainty which surrounds many Scottish saints, there can be no doubt that within a century of Columba's death Christianity was widespread throughout Scotland, and was the accepted faith of all kings and aristocracies. This was not wholly the achievement of Iona; but Columba and his successors played the greatest part.

The Gaelic Church

The form of church organisation, and to some extent the ethos, of Irish Christianity are distinctive in certain respects. But it is misleading to speak of 'the Celtic Church' as if it were other than a fully integrated part of Western Christendom. The Irish Church was totally orthodox in its system of belief and unswervingly loyal to the papacy. Its eccentricities were no greater than those of, say, Spain or North Africa. But it does seem to have had certain liturgical and organisational peculiarities, and to have retained an outmoded method for calculating the date of Easter, long after this had been abandoned elsewhere.

Structurally, the main peculiarity was the development of great families of monasteries all subject to the jurisdiction of the abbot of a senior monastery, who was regarded as the successor of the founder. Iona had a family of dependent monasteries in Ireland and Britain, presided over by the 'successor of Columba'. Other great Irish houses also had dependent houses. In such a situation, the role of the bishop is not always clear. Some great churches had bishops, but in some churches the abbots who were in charge of administration and jurisdiction were presbyters. Bede describes this unusual arrangement at Iona:

> This island always has for its ruler an abbot who is a presbyter, to whose authority the whole province, including even bishops, must be subject; by an unusual arrangement following the example of their first teacher, who was not a bishop but a presbyter and monk.[16]

Adomnán tells a curious story about a bishop's visit to Iona:

> There came to the saint from the province of Munster a stranger who . . . kept himself humbly out of sight, so that none should know that he was a bishop. But this could not be hidden from the saint. For the next Sunday, requested by the saint to consecrate the body of Christ according to custom, he summoned the saint, so that they as two presbyters might break the Lord's bread together. Then the saint, coming to the altar, suddenly looked upon his face, and spoke to him thus: 'Christ bless you, brother! Break this bread alone, according to the episcopal rite. Now we know that you are a bishop; why have you tried to conceal yourself up to now, so that the respect due from us to you has not been paid?'[17]

It is clear that bishops were accorded special respect; they would also have carried out ordinations and consecrations of new bishops. An early collection of canon law, in the compilation of which Iona played an important part, stresses the importance of the bishop as having a role parallel to that of a tribal king in secular society.[18] Bede described the situation at Iona as unusual, and so it must have seemed to a widely read Northumbrian; but the arrangement at Iona may not have been common in Ireland either.

Another adaptation to Irish custom was the druidical tonsure for monks. But this was perhaps a relatively minor bone of contention. Far more serious was the 'paschal controversy', or argument over the correct date for the celebration of the Easter festival.

CHRISTIANITY IN SCOTLAND AFTER THE AGE OF SAINTS

We have seen how Columba first came to Scotland, the background from which he came and the conditions he came to, and we have charted his rise to power and influence. In looking at the uses his successors made of that influence, our best source is the great historian of early Christianity in the British Isles, the Northumbrian Bede.

Bede

In popular imagination, Bede is sometimes regarded as the enemy and critic of Celtic practice, because he chronicles the triumph of 'Roman' or 'Catholic' practice over ancient local traditions. But this is misleading for several reasons. For one thing, the controversy of his day between local traditions and centralised uniformity was not a primitive version of the Catholic/Protestant divide which affects post-Reformation Christianity. There was no debate about doctrine, which is the central difference between the 'Catholic' and 'reformed' Churches; there was no dispute over papal authority, which remained loose even after Gregory the Great sent missionaries to England in 597. Irish monks were every bit as 'Catholic' as English bishops.

Bede does criticise the Church in Celtic lands for adhering to conservative practices in matters of the computation of the date of Easter; but he had a personal interest in calendrical calculations, and they were less important to some others. Bede speaks with warm approval of Celtic saints Columba, Aidan, Cuthbert and Adomnán. In summarising Columba's career, he comments:

> . . . we know this for certain about him, that he left successors distinguished for their great abstinence, their love of God, and their observance of monastic discipline. . . . they diligently practised such works of religion and chastity as they were able to learn from the words of the prophets, evangelists and apostles.[19]

Bede himself was a product of a mixed tradition, founded by the Celtic monks of Lindisfarne and reformed by the English monks of Wearmouth and Jarrow.

For us, Bede is above all a historian. He collected and analysed sources, which he usually acknowledged, and presented them to his readers in a unified and elegant Latin style. He had his prejudices, but on the whole was not unfair. His greatest achievement was to create a unified scheme of chronology so that events could be dated accurately; to this end he took over the calculation of the *Annus Domini*, calculated by a Syrian monk, and developed it into the standard chronological scheme which is still in use today.

For all his learning and his use of varied sources, Bede was not widely travelled; he never left Northumbria. He was born near Jarrow *c.* 673 and entered the monastery of Wearmouth as a child in 680. In the following year he moved to Jarrow where he studied under Abbot Ceolfrith. A story in the *Life* of Ceolfrith describes how during an attack of plague at Jarrow many of the monks were dead or dying, and the only people left to sing the offices were the abbot and one small boy, but they did this together day after day. The unnamed boy must have been Bede himself.

Bede spent the rest of his life at Jarrow building up a library of great depth and variety. In the *Ecclesiastical History* he quotes extensively from the Bible, English writers, papal letters, classical writers and church fathers. He had a copy of Adomnán's *Holy Places*, presented by the author to King Aldfrith in 688. For information about Kent, he wrote to the church of Canterbury, and received copies of documents from their archives in reply; these he lodged in his own collection. With such a library, he did not need to travel extensively; sadly, the collection which he assembled was destroyed by the Vikings. Bede did visit Lindisfarne in connection with the *Life of Cuthbert* which the monks there commissioned; he also travelled to York, but he never crossed the Humber.

Bede was a voluminous writer. In the *Ecclesiastical History* he lists the many scriptural commentaries and homilies which he wrote, saints' *Lives*, the 'History of the Abbots' of Wearmouth and Jarrow, the *Ecclesiastical History* itself, a martyrology (list of saints), books of poetry, treatises on chronology, orthography, the art of metre, and 'the nature of things'. He also wrote other books, including his edition of Adomnán's *Holy Places*, which he does not list. He describes his life in these words: 'I have spent all my life in this monastery, applying myself entirely to the study of the scriptures; and amid the discipline of the rule and the daily task of singing in the church, it has always been my delight to learn or to teach or to write.'[20] There is something about this which is very close to the values and traditions of Iona.

The Conversion of Northumbria

Perhaps the greatest achievement of Iona in the generation following Columba's death was the conversion of Northumbria. This is described by Bede at some length. The Roman mission of 597 had sent a bishop, Paulinus, to York; but his success was limited and he was driven out with most of his followers when King Edwin was killed in 633. In the following year his kinsman Oswald reversed the situation and recovered the Northumbrian throne. But rather than inviting the Roman missionaries to return, Oswald turned instead to his friend Abbot Ségéne of Iona (abbot 623–52), who had sheltered him during his exile. When Oswald returned in triumph to Northumbria in 634, he invited Ségéne to send him a bishop from Iona, and the man chosen, Aidan, established a monastery on Lindisfarne, a tidal island of similar size to Iona, within easy reach of the royal fortress of Bamburgh. Upon his death the Iona monks sent a successor bishop, Finán, and then another, Colmán. The Church in Northumbria, stretching from the Humber to the Forth, looked for inspiration to Iona for thirty years, 634–64, until the Easter controversy altered their relationship.

The Easter Controversy

Bede's writings amply illustrate relations between Celtic and English Christians, and more particularly the Paschal controversy, the most serious conflict to engulf the Church in Britain in the seventh century. The dispute arose because Easter is a feast whose date is calculated according to very complex rules, involving harmonisation of the solar year (it must be after the vernal equinox), the lunar month (it falls after a certain day of the month), and the artificial weekly cycle (it must be on a Sunday). 'In those days,' writes Bede, 'there arose a great and active controversy about the keeping of Easter.' To resolve this, Oswy summoned a great synod to assemble at the church of Whitby in 664. 'King Oswy began by declaring that it was fitting that those who serve one God should observe one rule of life and not differ in the celebration of the heavenly sacraments, seeing that they all hoped for one kingdom in heaven.'

At the root of the conflict at Whitby may have been tension between King Oswy of Northumbria and his son Alhfrith, sub-king of Deira. There is some evidence that Alhfrith had been trying to stir up trouble against his father, and certainly he disappears from public affairs after 664.

Colmán of Lindisfarne appealed to the authority of St Columba for the establishment of the rules for celebrating Easter, but Wilfrid of Ripon, spokesman for the Roman party, appealed to Peter. Bede makes up very long speeches for them, packed with technical detail. A more contemporary writer gives a more concise and dramatic account:

> At the end of Wilfrid's speech Oswy asked them, with a smile, 'Tell me, which is greater in the kingdom of heaven, Columba, or the apostle Peter?' Then the whole synod replied with one voice and one accord, 'The Lord himself settled this question when he declared: Thou art Peter and upon this rock I will build my church, and the gates of hell shall not prevail against it; and I will give thee the keys of the kingdom of heaven. . . .' Then the king added, showing his wisdom: 'He is the keeper of the doors and the keys. . . . As long as I live I will abide by his every decision.'[21]

Bede gives a slightly different version; he carefully omits reference to King Oswy's smile and gives him a more pious speech: 'Since he is the doorkeeper I will not contradict him; but I intend to obey his commands . . . otherwise when I come to the gates of the kingdom of heaven there may be none to open them.'

Most of the Celtic monks chose to hold to their old ways and depart. The reason for this can be illustrated by a letter from an important churchman from the south Midlands of Ireland to the abbot of Iona and others *c*. 633. It was written after an Irish synod had appealed to Rome for guidance on the question and been instructed to adopt the Alexandrian computation. Whom ought we to follow, the writer asks,

> The Hebrews, Greeks, Latins and Egyptians, who are united in their observance of the principal solemnities? Or an insignificant group of British and Irish, who are almost at the ends of the earth, as one might say, but a pimple on the face of the earth? . . . What thought more perverse can there be about Mother Church, than if we say, Rome is wrong; Jerusalem is wrong; Alexandria is wrong; Antioch is wrong; the Irish and the British alone know what is right?[22]

Ségéne of Iona, probably the most powerful and influential churchman in the British Isles, was unmoved; what was good enough for Columba was good enough for him. It is significant, however, that the churchmen of central and southern Ireland should have felt the need to appeal to Iona on this issue. Even the broad-minded Adomnán, who fifty years later accepted the Catholic Easter under the influence of Ceolfrith of Jarrow, continued to reside at Iona after he had failed to convince his brethren (Bede states the contrary, but wrongly). Not until 716 did Iona accept the dating of the Catholic Easter, after the whole of Ireland had gone over, leaving only a few isolated areas in Wales.[23]

The Aftermath of the Paschal Controversy

Although the Synod of Whitby did reduce the influence of Iona in Northumbria, it did not end contact between Ireland, Scotland and the north of England. The career of Cuthbert is an example of continuing contact and influence. He began as a monk of Old Melrose, a house of the *familia* of St Columba, in 651. This monastery was Anglo-Irish in tone: it lay within Bernicia, and the abbot, Eata, was an Englishman, but the prior, Boisil, was an Irishman. In this respect the mixture resembled that at Lindisfarne itself. Eata and Cuthbert moved for a time to a new foundation at Ripon, but withdrew to Melrose when King Alhfrith insisted on the observance of the Roman Easter. After the Synod of Whitby, Melrose accepted the Northumbrian decision, and Eata became bishop of Lindisfarne in succession to Colmán. Cuthbert went with him as prior. After about ten years, in 676, he withdrew from communal life to become a hermit on Farne Island. Early in 685 he was summoned from his hermitage, though unwilling, to be bishop of Hexham, but he soon exchanged this for his beloved Lindisfarne. After two years he resigned the bishopric and retired to Farne Island, where he died soon after (20 March 687). It was said that his only reason for accepting the bishopric was that Boisil, prior of Melrose, had prophesied to him that he would become a bishop; and so he accepted the post.[24]

Boisil was also instrumental, this time from the grave, in the conversion of Iona to the Catholic Easter. Bede records that an Englishman called Egbert lived for many years in Ireland, where he became a monk and planned to conduct a mission to the Frisians and other Germanic tribes. But one of the brothers told him that Boisil had appeared to him in a vision prophesying that Egbert would not make the journey but rather would go to Iona to correct the errors of the monks of St Columba; and this Egbert did.

Bede mentions other Englishmen who lived as monks in Ireland, including one Wihtbert, who eventually did preach to the Frisians. But their king Radbod rejected baptism when he was told that all his ancestors were in hell and that if he were baptised he would be parted from them. Wihtbert eventually returned to Ireland and the solitary life which he loved.

The careers of men like Aidan and Colmán before Whitby, and Boisil (commemorated in St Boswells, near Melrose), Cuthbert and Egbert later, show the extent of contact between Ireland, Scotland and Northumbria. It would not be true to say that the Synod of Whitby changed nothing; in one sense the relationship was never quite the same, because Iona was no longer the dominant partner. But in some respects, as for instance the art of the great biblical manuscripts of this period – the Lindisfarne and Echternach Gospels, the Book of Kells – there is still cross-fertilisation between Ireland, Scotland and Northumbria. It was the Vikings who destroyed this, as so much else.

Christianity among the Picts

We have seen that Columba visited Skye and travelled to the Inverness region on at least one occasion. Sadly, but not surprisingly, the conversion of the Picts is much less well documented than that of the Northumbrians. Bede says that Columba converted the northern Picts; Adomnán only mentions a few scattered baptisms, however, and crucially not that of Bridei son of Mailcon himself. However, by the time of Nechton son of Derilei (king 706–26 and 728–9) it is clear that the Picts were in effect a Christian people, who 'rejoiced to submit to the new-found guidance of Peter, the prince of the apostles, and to be placed under his protection.'[25] The extent of Christianity by this time is also implied by Adomnán and later writers. In Pictish art, the cross is absent on the earliest Pictish stones, but had come to be widely used on Pictish monuments of the late seventh and eighth centuries and later. In a way, the spread of Christian symbols on Pictish stones provides the most eloquent 'documents' of Iona's expanding influence among the Picts in the two centuries following Columba's death.

CHAPTER 4

The Making of Scotland

THE VIKINGS IN SCOTLAND: THE FIRST HELL'S ANGELS?

Throughout earlier centuries, the sources record frequent battles, slaughters, murders, burnings and sieges, but from the 790s they begin to record a new phenomenon:

794   Devastation of all the Isles of Britain by the Gentiles.
795   Burning of Rathlin by the Gentiles; and Skye was pillaged and devastated.
795   Devastation of Iona, and Inishmurray and Inishbofin.
796   The Gentiles in Ireland.
798   The Gentiles made great incursions both in Ireland and Scotland.
798   The western Isles and Ulster were plundered by the *Lochlannaich*.
802   Iona was burned by the Gentiles.
806   The community of Iona was slain by the Gentiles, namely 68 [monks].
825   The martyrdom of Blathmac son of Flann by the Gentiles in Iona.[1]

The men who perpetrated these outrages were described variously as gentiles, foreigners (*gall*), or *Lochlannaich*, Scandinavians. They are known to us as the Vikings.[2]

The Earliest Vikings

The Viking raids began suddenly and without warning (unless one counts the 'terrible portents seen over Northumbria . . . exceptional flashes of lightning, and fiery dragons seen flying in the air' in 793, shortly before 'the harrying of the heathen miserably destroyed God's church in Lindisfarne by rapine and slaughter'); the perpetrators seemed at first to have come from nowhere, and were only slowly identified as Scandinavians. Above all, the raids were the work of heathens who showed no respect for church property, but looted monasteries with especial enthusiasm because they were storehouses of treasure guarded by defenceless monks. The raids continued with little appreciable abatement for some eighty years, and by the end of that time the political map of Scotland, indeed of the whole British Isles and much of Europe, had changed irrevocably. One Irish historian has spoken of 'the passing of the old order' in that country,[3] and there is no doubt that in Scotland the delicate equilibrium of Scots, Picts, Britons and Angles which had existed for 300 years also passed away.

Later Norse sagas interpret the first Viking exodus as a response by free men to the increasing tyranny and centralisation exercised by Norwegian kings. But this explanation is unsatisfactory. It may help to explain the colonisation of Iceland from *c.* 870, but Ireland, Scotland and the Isles were already full of Vikings. It is doubtful whether a king can have exercised such wide authority to have driven out enough free-born aristocrats to account for the Viking phenomenon. Archaeology does suggest that the population of Scandinavia had been steadily rising before 800; holdings of farmland had become increasingly divided and subdivided.

By the early 790s a technology of shipbuilding had been developed which was superior to anything known in more southerly waters. The Vikings' navigational skills may not have exceeded those of the Irish monks who had sailed their skin-clad coracles to the Northern Isles, the Faeroes and Iceland during the eighth century, but their ships were faster, more seaworthy and more reliable. In the first raids, it was the element of speed and surprise which gave the Vikings their advantage.

Irish annals and Anglo-Saxon chronicles say a great deal about piratical raids on churches, and present a picture of marauding freebooters seizing moveable wealth and returning whence they came. But they were written in monasteries by the outraged victims of such raids, and might represent only one aspect of the Vikings' activity. The sagas stress the hunt for land as well as for treasure. The enthusiasm with which Iceland was settled so quickly after its discovery *c.* 870, and simultaneous abandonment of raids in Ireland, confirms this. One saga describes how a Viking warlord fell foul of his king and decided to emigrate: 'he said that he thought he would go to Scotland; the land was good there and he knew it well, having raided there many times in his youth'.

Some writers have argued that if we perceive the Vikings as misunderstood long-haired tourists – as it were, the first Hell's Angels – who were really only in search of an honest living, we should dismiss most of the lurid accusations brought against them. There can be no question that the Vikings used force, both to seize good pasture-land at St Ninian's Isle in Shetland, forcing the local family to conceal their treasures under the floor of their little church and flee, and also to loot Iona, as they did repeatedly from 794. But the impression given by monastic chroniclers is that they perpetrated acts of extreme cruelty and barbarity. The German monk Walafrid Strabo chronicled the following atrocity perpetrated on Iona in 825:

> The violent accursed host came rushing through the open buildings, threatening cruel perils to the blessed men; and after slaying with mad savagery the rest of the company, they approached the holy father [Blathmac] to compel him to give up the precious metals wherein lie the holy bones of St Columba. . . . Then he spoke to the barbarians in such words: 'I know nothing at all of the gold you seek. . . . Barbarian, draw thy sword, grasp the hilt, and slay; gracious God, to thy aid I commend me humbly.' Therefore the pious sacrifice was torn limb from limb. . . . Thus he became a martyr for Christ's name, and he rests there, and there many miracles appear by his holy merits.[4]

Silver items from St Ninian's Isle Treasure, Shetland. Pictish silver concealed from Vikings, late 8th century. (*National Museums of Scotland*)

The Norse sagas do little to dispel this view when they chronicle the violence inflicted by Vikings on each other. One saga tells of a battle in Orkney:

> Then they came thither, and found there Halfdan Longleg, and they took him captive. . . . Then Earl Einar went to Halfdan, and carved on him an eagle on his back, in such a way that he cut with his sword along the backbone to the inwards, and cut all the ribs right down to his loins, and drew out there the lungs; and that was the death of Halfdan.[5]

This ceremony of the 'blood-eagle' sacrifice to Odin is held up as the final proof of the extremity of Viking cruelty. This cannot be dismissed simply as the exaggeration of terrified monks who sought to blacken the name of newcomers who refused to abide by the old rules. In a violent age, the Vikings were extremely violent; they practised striking cruelties against each other, against their enemies, and against innocent non-combatants who got in their way. Adomnán's 'Law of the Innocents', promulgated in Ireland in 697, had offered protection to women and other non-combatants in time of war.[6] But the Vikings had no respect for church property or innocent women and children.

Viking Settlement in Scotland

The extent of Viking settlement in Scotland must be judged by archaeological and place-name evidence. Norse place-names are thickest in Shetland and Orkney, becoming progressively thinner through Caithness, Sutherland, Lewis, Skye, the southern Isles and Argyll. Names indicating primary settlement are more northerly, clustered near the coast, and largely absent from the Scottish mainland, while names indicating secondary penetration are found further south and further inland. The earliest names seem to follow the sea-route of Viking ships going to plunder the wealth of Ireland.[7]

Place-names show an absence of Viking settlement in east and central Scotland south of the Moray Firth. The distribution of Viking graves confirms this picture: there are hardly any in Pictland, in contrast with the dozens in the Western and Northern Isles, Caithness and Sutherland. Perhaps Viking settlers sought lands which were like the land they had left; and we know on linguistic and archaeological grounds that these Scottish settlers of Scotland came mostly from the fjords of western Norway. Northern and western Scotland, a maze of archipelagos and deep, steep-sided sea lochs, was like Norway in miniature.

The Early Raids

The first phase of Viking raiding began in 793 and lasted for nearly fifty years. It consisted of small and highly mobile groups of warriors in small fleets of ships plundering defenceless sites for moveable wealth. In 793 Lindisfarne in Northumbria was the first target to be attacked. In the following years a Viking fleet plundered in the Hebrides, and in 795 came the first recorded attack on Iona, raiding Rathlin and as far as Inishbofin in County Mayo. In 796 a Viking fleet landed on mainland Ireland for the first time. In 798 the Hebrides and Ulster were extensively plundered, and in 802 and 806 Iona was again ravaged. On the last occasion the monks must have put up some resistance, for sixty-eight of them were slaughtered. These repeated attacks had already convinced the monks of Iona that the new and terrifying phenomenon would not go away, and in 804 they had acquired a site at Kells in the plain of Meath. The events of 806 persuaded the community to build at Kells, and in 807 work was begun on the new monastery there. This was completed by 813, and part of the community of St Columba took up permanent residence at Kells. In that year Abbot Cellach, who had supervised the move, resigned his abbacy and travelled sadly back to Iona, where he died in the following year. Iona was not abandoned; some relics of Columba were kept there in a valuable shrine until about 849, and it was to learn the whereabouts of this shrine that the Vikings tortured and killed Blathmac in 825. 'St Matthew's Cross' on Iona belongs stylistically to the ninth century.

The community retained on Iona may eventually have been reduced to something like 'the abbot and 15 elders' who were slain by later Vikings in 986. Clearly Iona became only a shadow of its former glory, and the library amassed by Columba and his successors was destroyed. Its greatest treasures, including the Book of Kells, were taken to Ireland. The loss of Iona as Scotland's cultural headquarters was of incalculable significance. We have no Scottish illuminated manuscripts between the eighth-century Book of Kells and the vastly inferior Book of Deer from the tenth century. Scotland seems to have become something of a cultural desert. The Viking attacks on Lindisfarne, beginning in 793, contributed to the same phenomenon. Dependent monasteries like Melrose, Abercorn and Abernethy were left leaderless.

Large Armies and Extensive Campaigns

From c. 840 we see a new phase of Viking activity. Armies became larger and their campaigns more ambitious. Instead of terrorising defenceless monks, they began to engage the land armies of local rulers. In 839 a Viking fleet sailed up the River Bann in Ulster and on to Lough Neagh. In the same year an army marched across Scotland into Fortrenn where they defeated the army of the Picts under Uuen son of Onuist, killing the king with many of his nobles 'almost without number'. Two years later, in 841, the first permanent Viking town in the British Isles was founded at Dublin. The Viking army was led by a fearsome warrior called Thurgeis. Having defeated the Picts in 839, he 'overthrew' Northumbria in 844, and Vikings from Dublin looted Iona c. 845. In the first of a series of successes against the Vikings, a confederation of Irish kings defeated and captured Thurgeis in 845, and executed him by drowning.[8]

The precautions taken by the victims of the first raids had driven the Vikings to new measures: larger armies which could raid inland and, if necessary, fight against local land armies. This involved greater risks, and for the first time we hear of Vikings suffering defeats. Another new phenomenon is that of Norse kings attempting to

An evangelist from the Book of Kells, eighth century, probably from Iona. *(The Board of Trinity College Dublin)*

An evangelist from the Book of Deer, tenth century. Cambridge University Library MS Ii.6.32
f.29v. *(By permission of the Syndics of Cambridge University Library)*

intervene in Viking affairs and sending their own retainers to control and exploit Viking activity. Another new feature from *c.* 850 is a division among the Vikings themselves. From this period the Irish annals speak of 'black gentiles' and 'white foreigners', and soon after they speak of 'foreign Gael' (*Gall-Gaidil*) as well. The 'white foreigners' were Norwegians; the 'black gentiles' were Danes. The *Gall-Gaidil* must have been Hebrideans of mixed race, who gave the southern Hebrides their curiously mixed place-names. These *Gall-Gaidil*, who are first recorded fighting in Ireland in 856, must at some time have colonised and given their name to Galloway. Place-names in south-west Scotland indicate Norse settlement there, but with some distinctions from that of the Hebrides: for example, names like Kirkcudbright, Kirkbean, etc., have the Norse form *Kirk-* followed by the name of a saint in Celtic word order.[9]

The irruption of the Danes in the 850s added an important new dimension. We have seen a trend towards larger Viking fleets in Ireland and Scotland from *c.* 840; but even these were small by comparison with the 350 Danish ships which sailed up the Thames in 851. In 855 the Danish host wintered in England for the first time. Thereafter the Anglo-Saxon Chronicle records a series of disasters for all the English kingdoms; Northumbria, Mercia, East Anglia and Kent all succumbed to Viking attack in the 860s. York became a Viking city like Dublin, and the men of Kent paid Danegeld, protection money in return for peace. Of the English kingdoms, only Wessex under Alfred (870–99) survived the Danish onslaught; Alfred consolidated his own kingdom of Wessex, added west Mercia and Kent to it, reached a treaty with the Danes dividing England between them, and even persuaded King Guthrum of East Anglia to accept baptism.

North and east England were settled by Danes, as place-name evidence shows, and much energy from the 860s onwards was spent trying to hold together a loose empire stretching from York to Dublin. The first 'king' of Dublin was Olaf Conung son of Godfrey, who came to Dublin in 853 with his brother Ivar. They campaigned against the *Gall-Gaidil* in Ireland in the 850s, and in the 860s raided in Scotland. In 870 Olaf and Ivar carried out one of their most ambitious campaigns: a four-month siege of Dumbarton with the objective of the total destruction and annexation of the kingdom of Strathclyde. They returned to Dublin in triumph with a great number of prisoners, including King Arthgal of Dumbarton. In 872 Arthgal was put to death 'by counsel of Constantine son of Kenneth, king of Scots', perhaps meaning that Constantine refused to ransom him. Constantine's daughter was married to Arthgal's son Rhun, and it appears that after Arthgal's death Constantine could have expected to be the effective ruler of Strathclyde, with Rhun as a puppet-king.[10]

The Norse in Scotland: the Later Phase

The year following the death of Arthgal, 873, saw the beginning of the '40 years' rest' in Ireland, when that island was relatively free from Viking attack. This period was that of the colonisation of newly discovered Iceland. Some of the new settlers came from the Northern and Western Isles of Scotland. Some of them were

Christians, although it is clear that within a generation Christianity had died out in Iceland.

Although Ireland enjoyed a '40 years' rest' from 873 to 915, Scotland was less fortunate. The Danes defeated an army of 'Picts' at Dollar in 875 and raided as far as Atholl; two years later a Danish army defeated and killed Constantine son of Kenneth. In the 890s the Scots defeated Danish raiders. Other Vikings fought and slew a Scottish *mormaer* called Maelbrigde, but suffered losses in the process; and they attacked and destroyed Dunottar. In 903 a Norse army, probably from Dublin, looted Dunkeld, but in the following year it was destroyed in Strathearn.

Throughout the tenth century Viking raids remained a menace, but they were never repeated on the scale of the great Danish armies which overran England in the 860s. A new equilibrium was established to replace the old, with the dynasties of Wessex and Fortrenn emerging from the storm to divide Britain between them. Later Viking raids were more limited. There was a raid on Iona in 986–7, where Vikings slew the abbot and monks, but were themselves later rounded up; 140 were hanged and others sold into slavery. As the tenth century progressed Viking raids, particularly on churches, became increasingly less common, until these became a throwback to a past age. Two factors contributed to this change in attitude: the establishment of permanent lordships in these areas, and the adoption of Christianity.

Norse Lordships in the British Isles

In Orkney the picture is fairly clear; an earldom was established under the descendants of Turf Einar, with a line of jarls ruling over Shetland, Orkney, Caithness and Sutherland as far as the Oykel. There was frequent war between the jarls and the Scottish crown and the *mormaer* of Moray; jarl Sigurd the Stout fought against Finnlaech *mormaer* of Moray in the 990s. Sigurd's son, Thorfinn the Mighty, has been called the last of the Vikings, but he was a Christian and he acknowledged that he held Caithness and Sutherland of the king of Scots.

In the Western Isles the picture is less clear. There was a line of kings of Man, including Godfrey Harold's son, who was slain by the Gael of Argyll in 989; the kingship of Man lasted into the eleventh century, and must have held sway over many of the *Gall-Gaidil* of the Western Isles. But there was also a line of rulers in the southern Hebrides descended from Godfrey son of Fergus, an aristocrat from County Armagh, who is described as lord of *Innse Gall* ('Islands of the foreigners') at his death in 853. In the twelfth century his descendant Somerled struggled to recover his inheritance. So perhaps there was in the Western Isles a struggle between the kings of Man and the descendants of Godfrey.

There were other lines of *Gall-Gaidil* chiefs in Galloway and the northern Hebrides: there was a jarl Gilli in the Hebrides in 1014 who was Sigurd the Stout's brother-in-law; later in the eleventh century there was a Suibne son of Kenneth lord of Galloway, who was ruler over the *Gall-Gaidil* there. All these dynasties are poorly documented and obscure.

Christianity among the Norse

It is clear that the first Vikings were heathen, and their lack of respect for churchmen and church property was one of the features which shocked their victims. The sagas date the conversion of the Vikings to Christianity to 995:

> Then King Olaf [Trigvy's son] sailed to the [Orkney] Islands with his army and put into harbour there. . . . And when the king knew that earl [Sigurd] lay there already, he had the earl called to speak with him. But when the earl came to speak with the king, they had spoken but a little while when the king said that the earl must have himself baptised and all the people of his land, or as an alternative he should die on the spot; and the king said he would go with fire and burning through the islands, and devastate the land, unless the people were baptised. And since the earl was thus pressed, he chose to take baptism.[11]

But there are indications that Christianity had begun to infiltrate the Western Isles already. There are many examples of islands called Pabbay or Papa in the Western and Northern Isles, a name which means 'hermit's isle' or 'priest's isle'; this indicates a measure of co-existence between heathen conquerors and Christian hermits. Some of

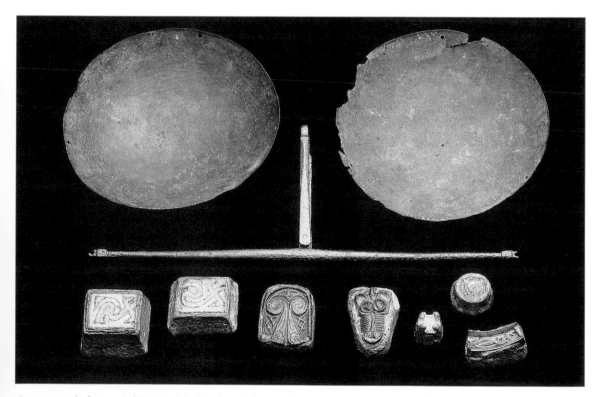

Grave-goods from a Viking Burial, Kiloran, Colonsay. The grave also contained Christian symbols. *(National Museums of Scotland)*

Cille Bharra, Barra: Stone with cross and runic inscription (front, left; back, right), possibly eleventh century. *(National Museums of Scotland)*

the colonists of Iceland were Christians, though Christianity died out there within a generation. The finding of grave-goods in Viking graves indicates paganism; but there is one example from Colonsay of a grave with grave-goods and a sacrificed horse, but also stones incised with a cross. Coin finds date this grave soon after 854.[12]

In the late ninth and tenth centuries pagan graves with grave-goods become rarer. This is evidence of Christianity modifying the funerary practices of the Vikings long before the conversion of Olaf Trigvy's son in the 990s; Norse place-names in *kirk-* and the use of existing Christian cemeteries for Viking burials point in the same direction. An undated, possibly eleventh-century, stone from Cille Bharra, Barra, has a cross on one side and on the other a runic inscription: 'After Thorgerth, Steinar's daughter, this cross was raised'.[13]

The effects of the adoption of Christianity by the Vikings are difficult to assess. For Iona and other churches it meant a cessation of plundering raids. But the damage to Scotland's culture had already been done. The Vikings themselves may have become to some extent 'civilised', abandoning human and animal sacrifice; still violent, of course, but perhaps moderated by Christianity. After the traumas of the ninth century, life in Scotland settled down to a new equilibrium.

THE UNIFICATION OF SCOTLAND: THE NINTH CENTURY

From 794 onwards, the shock of the Viking attacks upset the delicate political equilibrium of Dark Age Scotland. Scots, Picts, Britons and Angles had co-existed and competed for 300 years; they had sought territorial expansion without seeking to eliminate other races or kingdoms. But in the ninth century the kingdoms of Angles and Picts were destroyed, that of the Britons narrowly escaped the same fate, and the kingdom of the Scots shifted its centre from west to east. The end product, in the dynasty established by Kenneth son of Alpin *c.* 849, was a unified kingship of Scotland.

'King of the North'

But how new was the concept and reality of a kingship of Scotland? Bede speaks of Bridei son of Mailcon as a 'very powerful king of the Picts', ruling from a fortress on the River Ness. He may be one of the last in a line of powerful northern kings, a line one is tempted to see as stretching back to the power of the ancient *Caledonii*.

Later powerful Scottish kings seem to have concentrated their energies further south. Áedán son of Gabrán of the Dál Riata is said to have 'seized *Alba* by force', and to have ruled 'in Fortrenn'. His son Eochaid Buide is called 'king of Picts' at his death *c.* 630, though he does not figure in the Pictish king list. Ywain of Strathclyde must have made himself master of much of southern Scotland by his victory over the Dál Riata in Strathcarron in 642. Next, Oswy of Northumbria is said to have made the Picts and Scots 'tributary' to him. His son and successor Ecgfrith may have found it difficult to enforce his superiority over Scotland, and was defeated and killed at Dunnichen in 685 during a punitive raid against the Picts.

The victor in this battle, Bridei son of Bili king of Picts, was called 'king of the north' in a verse attributed to Adomnán; so he too may well have had authority outside his own kingdom. The same is true of two of his successors as kings of Picts: Nechton son of Derilei certainly had some power over the Dál Riata when he enforced the Catholic Easter at Iona in 715, and Onuist son of Uurguist destroyed the Dál Riata and the Britons of Strathclyde, and seemingly ambushed the Angles at a time when they were his allies. From 685 onwards, it appears that southern Pictish kings 'of Fortrenn' had a wider authority over much of central Scotland. But the poorly documented reign of Áed Finn of the Dál Riata (c. 748–78) involved campaigns against the Picts, who were clearly not getting it all their own way.

In this list of powerful kings we may be able to piece together some kind of notional over-kingship of the North. It could be suggested that this passed from northern 'Caledonian' Pictish kings first to the Dál Riata under Áedán and his immediate successor, then to the Britons, Angles of Northumbria at the height of their power, and back to southern Pictish kings with a powerbase in Strathearn, Gowrie and Angus. This area, known as Fortrenn, constitutes the heartland of east-central Scotland, and its control was vital for any overlordship. Thus Áedán was regarded as king 'of Fortrenn'; the great British victory in Strathcarron in 642 and the Pictish victory at Dunnichen in 685 must have given the victors control over the same area, and thereafter Pictish kings were rulers of Fortrenn. At later times inauguration at Scone was regarded as important, accompanied by ancient ritual using the 'Stone of Destiny' set upon the 'Hill of Belief'. So it could be argued that there was some kind of notional over-kingship of the North. If so, this may explain the success of Kenneth son of Alpin and his dynasty, at a time when the Viking raids were eliminating most of his rivals for the position of over-king and enabling him and his dynasty to make it a more concrete reality than before.

The Northern Kingdoms in the Early Ninth Century

There is a speculative element in this interpretation, and it is not the only possible one for this period. An examination of the king lists and annals for the early ninth century shows in all the kingdoms a different pattern from before. For the Britons of Strathclyde, we have only a genealogy of the kings, and after 756 the kingdom and its rulers are largely absent from external sources for nearly a century. The Dumbarton dynasty did survive and revive later, but for much of this time they controlled only a small area of territory around Dumbarton and were not a threat to their neighbours. We know nothing of the kings except their names; not even their dates or reign-lengths survive.

Northumbria is better documented owing to the Anglo-Saxon Chronicle, but the kingdom's history is hardly any brighter. Notices consist of accounts of short reigns and the violent overthrow of kings, competing dynasties and few kings dying natural deaths or being succeeded by a son or other blood relative. This pattern continued for about a century until the final destruction of Northumbrian kingship by the Danes in the 860s.

As for the Scots of the Dál Riata, there is confusion and disagreement among the different versions of their king list, and no version is totally reconcilable with the sparse records in the Irish annals. Áed Finn died in 778 and was succeeded by his brother Fergus, representing a return to the customary succession among brothers and cousins which had prevailed for most of the sixth and seventh centuries. When Fergus died in 781, the king list records a Domnall 'son of Constantine' with a reign of twenty-four years (781–805). Domnall was succeeded by a son of Áed Finn, Eochaid 'the Venomous', with a reign of thirty years (? 804–34). His son was Alpin, and his son was Kenneth. This may sound fairly straightforward; but the other versions of the king list and the account of the Irish annals present a much more confused and confusing picture. The annals record the death of a Donncorci 'king of the Dál Riata' in 792, who is otherwise unknown. They also name other kings who are difficult to fit into any pedigree, and who seem to belong to rival dynasties. So the situation is far from clear.

There are signs of greater closeness between the kingship of the Picts and that of the Dál Riata. From 789 to 839, a period of fifty years, the kingship of Picts was held by sons and grandsons of Fergus brother of Áed Finn and himself king of the Dál Riata from 778 to 781. One of them, Castatin or Constantine, may be the 'Custantin filius Fircus' who is commemorated on an inscription on the Dupplin Cross near Forteviot.[14] Constantine, his brother Onuist (Oengus) and nephew Uuen (Eoganán) also appear in the Dalriadic king lists. Another person who is named in Dalriadic king lists, Áed son of Boanta,

The Dupplin Cross, Forteviot, Perthshire. The stone bears an inscription commemorating Constantine, son of Fergus, d. 820. *(Historic Scotland)*

is named by the Irish annals as one of the nobles who fell fighting beside Eoganán against the Vikings in 839. So here is evidence of a new trend in relations between the two kingdoms. Kenneth son of Alpin was not the first man to hold the kingship of both Picts and Scots.

The Union of Picts and Scots

The Viking raids were the most obvious factor drawing, or pushing, Picts and Scots closer together in the ninth century. Meanwhile, the Gaelic nobleman Alpin and his son Kenneth were able to establish a powerbase in the west which was eventually to lead Kenneth to the kingship of Fortrenn. In 836 the annals record that 'Godfrey son of Fergus, a lord of the Airgialla [a group of tribes living to the west and south of Lough Neagh] went over to Scotland to reinforce the Dál Riata at the bidding of Kenneth son of Alpin'.

In 839 'a battle was fought by the gentiles against the men of Fortrenn, and in it fell Eoganán son of Oengus, and Bran son of Oengus, and Áed son of Boanta; and others fell almost without number'. A later English chronicler wrote: 'Danish pirates had occupied the shores, and with the greatest slaughter had destroyed the Picts who defended their land'. Clearly this battle was a major catastrophe for the Picts. The massacre of followers was not a feature of Celtic warfare, where battles usually stopped as soon as the defeated king was killed; but it was a practice of the Danes and other Vikings, and was, of course, much more destructive for kingdoms. After the slaughter the Danes withdrew.[15]

The kingship of the Picts was taken by Uurad son of Bargoit. Meanwhile in the west the annals record the rise of Alpin, a son of Eochaid the Venomous. He is said to have become king in 839 and to have died fighting in Galloway two years later; presumably his opponents in Galloway were Norwegians or Hebridean *Gall-Gaidil*. He was succeeded by his son Kenneth, according to both annals and king lists. Mortality among eligible adult males both in Pictland and among the Dál Riata had been very high during the 830s, and Kenneth may have had few rivals for the kingship of the Dál Riata. Among the Picts, there is again a suggestion that the number of eligible candidates for kingship was narrow; the Uurad who succeeded in 839 died three years later, and was succeeded by three sons (a previously unknown pattern), Bridei, Cináed and Drest, plus the unrelated Bridei son of Fochel, during the 840s. These all had very short reigns.

The various accounts of Kenneth's reign are sparse and could be interpreted in different ways. The most likely interpretation is that he became king of Scots *c.* 842, fought a series of campaigns in Pictland over the next few years, ending in his triumph and the elimination of all possible Pictish rivals by 849. He reigned as king of Fortrenn until his death at Forteviot in *c.* 858, raiding extensively in Lothian during his later years. Although his successes were due largely to his military ability, Kenneth was anxious to secure Christian legitimacy for his dynasty, and it is for this reason that 'in the seventh year of his reign [*c.* 849] he transported the relics of

St Columba to a church which he had built', probably the church founded by Constantine son of Fergus (d. *c.* 820) at Dunkeld.[16]

Kenneth died of cancer *c.* 858 in his bed in the 'great palace' of Forteviot, of which a magnificent ceremonial entrance arch has survived, and was succeeded, by the traditional Gaelic custom, by his brother Domnall or Donald. Donald reigned for four years, and 'in his time the Gael with their king made the rights and laws of the kingdom [called] the laws of Áed son of Eochaid, in Forteviot'. Áed Finn was remembered as a lawgiver, and Donald son of Alpin was remembered for importing his legal system into Pictland – a sign of the imposition of Gaelic culture on the Picts. Like his brother Kenneth, Donald was buried in Iona.

His successor was his nephew Constantine son of Kenneth, another sign of Gaelic succession customs at work. Constantine faced threats from the Scandinavians which his father had managed to avoid; in 864 a Viking army invaded Fortrenn and devastated it, taking hostages and levying taxes; 'and taxes were given to them for a long time afterwards'.

The Disappearance of the Picts

Later writers speak of 'the destruction of the Picts', and wondered if the Pictish race were simply a myth of the past. Some later accounts of the events of 849 are clear fabrications, like the fantastic story told by the twelfth-century Welshman Giraldus Cambrensis:

> The Scots betook themselves to their customary and, as it were, innate treacheries, in which they excel all other nations. They brought together as to a banquet all the nobles of the Picts, and taking advantage of their excessive drunkenness and gluttony, they noted their opportunity and drew out the bolts which held up the boards; and the Picts fell into the hollows of the benches on which they were sitting, caught in a strange trap up to the knees, so that they could not get up; and the Scots immediately slaughtered them all.

We know of the existence of an Irish heroic tale, now lost, *Braflang Scoine*, 'The Treachery of Scone', which may have been Giraldus' source.[17]

Medieval writers had to find explanations for the disappearance of the Picts, and so have we. We cannot, of course, imagine ninth-century kings indulging in Nazi-style genocide, attempting the total extirpation of a race; they had not the resources or, for that matter, the will. Much of the Pictish nobility must have fallen in the disastrous battle against the Danes in 839, and Kenneth must have eliminated more during his campaigns of the 840s; the deaths of short-lived Pictish kings in 842, 842, 843, 845 and 849 presumably represent a series of victories for Kenneth in which rivals were eliminated.

There is really very little evidence as to how a transition from a Pictish to a Gaelic aristocracy took place. The Norse sagas record the names of Scottish *mormaer* or earls in the tenth and eleventh centuries who all seem to have Gaelic names; the Gaelic notes of land grants copied into the Book of Deer in the eleventh and twelfth centuries contain many names of aristocrats of north and north-east Scotland of that and earlier periods, but most are Gaelic names, with only a few which are identifiably Pictish. These notes, written in the vernacular language of Buchan in the eleventh century, show no traces of Pictish influence.[18] The powerful family of earls or *mormaer* of Moray traced its ancestry to the tribe of Loarn. It seems that at the same time that Kenneth son of Alpin of the tribe of Gabrán was pushing into Fortrenn and establishing his dynasty as kings there, a family from the more northerly tribe of Loarn was pushing up the Great Glen and establishing itself as ruler of the Pictish province of Moray; another example of a Dalriadic family moving east into Pictish territory.[19]

Why had the Pictish language totally disappeared by the eleventh century at latest? To find an explanation, one must resort to generalisations which are not always trustworthy. Languages in the past served a largely utilitarian function: they enabled people to communicate. When they ceased to serve that function people abandoned them. Concern to preserve languages for romantic or nationalistic reasons is a relatively modern phenomenon. It would not have occurred to the Picts to retain Pictish speech as a mark of identity or defiance in the face of Gaelic conquerors.

Pictish suffered from one disadvantage: it was not a written language. The puzzle of the ogam inscriptions on Pictish stones suggests that there were serious problems about notating even simple inscriptions in the language. Apart from one version of a king list with curious Pictish spellings of names, there are no Pictish manuscripts. This cannot be explained in terms of loss or destruction; it appears that Pictish writings did not exist on any scale. Like all heroic people, the Picts must have had a learned caste who preserved their oral traditions, origin-legends, king lists, heroic and bardic poetry (the faintest traces have survived); but with the destruction of the Pictish aristocracy, this learned caste disappeared and their lore vanished. Gaelic became the language of kingship and aristocracy, and any Pictish aristocrats who survived and accepted the new dynasty would have become Gaelic speakers within a generation or so. If Pictish survived at lower social levels for a further generation or two, it still had no influence on the speech of the dominant classes.

The Fall of Strathclyde

A generation after the 'destruction of the Picts', we find Kenneth's family becoming involved in the affairs of the Britons of Strathclyde. We have seen how in 870 Olaf and Ivar came from Dublin to Strathclyde and laid siege to Dumbarton Rock, which fell after a siege of four months. In 871 they returned to Dublin with a huge number of prisoners, 'English, Britons and Picts' to be sold into slavery. In 872 the captured king of Dumbarton, Arthgal, was put to death 'by counsel of Constantine son of Kenneth'. Constantine became in effect ruler of Strathclyde. Thereafter for a period Strathclyde kings were clients of the kings of Scots, though it appears that the old British dynasty did continue.[20]

Eochaid son of Rhun (and therefore a grandson of Arthgal) was joint king or sub-king of Scotland 878–89 ruling alongside or under Giric son of Dúngal; he and Giric were expelled in 889, and in the following year, according to a late source, the Strathclyde aristocracy was faced with a stark choice:

> The men of Strathclyde, those who refused to unite with the [Scots], had to depart from their country, and to go into Gwynedd. . . . Thus Gwynedd was freed from the English, through the might of the men of the North.[21]

The Strathclyde aristocrats took with them to North Wales the cult of their patron St Kentigern, for there are dedications to St Kentigern and traditions about him in Gwynedd.

The Vikings had weakened first the Picts and then the Britons and allowed their kingdoms to fall into the hands of Kenneth and his successors. In the 860s Danes destroyed the kingdom of Northumbria and set up their own kingdom, based on York, which had a precarious existence and was seldom able to threaten its northern neighbours. Kenneth's dynasty was left supreme in the north. By the 890s, the only native dynasty left in the south of Britain was that of Wessex under Alfred. The future history of Britain was to be that of the success of these two dynasties, Fortrenn and Wessex, in recovering territory from the Vikings; Wessex expanded northwards until it became the kingdom of England, while the Scots expanded southwards into Northumbria.

Kenneth's dynasty was not without its reversals. Constantine son of Kenneth was defeated and killed by Viking raiders in 877, and succeeded by his brother Áed. After only a year's reign, he in turn was killed by Giric son of Dúngal. Giric ruled jointly with, or in superiority over, Eochaid son of Rhun. Giric is said to have been very powerful, holding sway in parts of the north of England; but he and Eochaid were driven out by Donald son of Constantine in 889. Donald completed the domination of Strathclyde in 890, and may have been responsible for rebuilding the church at Govan near Glasgow and initiating its importance as an artistic centre; the magnificent hunting king on the Govan sarcophagus, the 'shrine of St Constantine', could be his portrait or that of his father Constantine. During the 890s he was faced by Norse invaders from Orkney who seized Caithness and Sutherland and raided as far south as Moray, and even besieged the great coastal fort of Dunottar. Donald had successes against the Norsemen, but he was ambushed and slain by his own men in 900 at Forres in Moray. He was succeeded by Constantine, son of the Áed who had been killed by Giric in 878.

It might appear that the dynasty of Kenneth was petering out in a welter of fratricidal bloodshed of the sort which had weakened the Dál Riata in the seventh and eighth centuries; but the position was to be restored by Constantine son of Áed in the course of a long reign, during which he continued Kenneth's policy of southward expansion.

THE CHURCH AFTER THE VIKING RAIDS

Columban Scotland during and after the Viking Raids

Beginning in the 790s, the Vikings attacked churches, slaughtered monks, and destroyed the political equilibrium of the British Isles. This was felt very keenly on Iona. The island which had been chosen as a remote refuge became an exposed staging post on the raiding route to Ireland. The raids of 794, 795, 798 and 802 were followed by a spectacular massacre in 806, traditionally associated with *Traigh Ban nam Manach* at the north end of Iona, the 'white beach of the monks' whose white sands turned red with the blood of martyrs. As a result of these repeated raids, the monks of Iona acquired an inland site at Kells in County Meath, to which part of the community and some of their most precious possessions, including the famous gospel book still known as the Book of Kells, were eventually transferred. But part of the community remained at Iona with the great shrine of Columba itself. We have seen that this was still an attraction to Viking raiders who descended on the island in 825 and tortured one monk who refused to divulge its whereabouts.

After 825 the history of the relics of Columba is less clear. An 'abbot of Iona' is said to have taken relics of St Columba from Ireland into Scotland in 829, and brought them back to Ireland two years later. So we may presume that after the events of 825 part at least of the relics of St Columba was removed to Ireland. Some time between 831 and 849 it seems to have returned again to Scotland, for in the latter year 'Innrechtach, abbot of Iona, came to Ireland with the relics of St Columba'. But in the same year, 849, a Scottish chronicle records that the Gaelic king Kenneth son of Alpin 'brought the relics of St Columba to a church that he had built', probably at Dunkeld. Kenneth may have been enlarging an existing foundation by Constantine son of Fergus, who died in 820. The most natural interpretation is a division of Columba's relics between the churches of Dunkeld and Kells in 849. The picture is complicated by the fact that the Irish annals record that in 878 'St Columba's shrine, and his relics, were brought to Ireland in flight from the foreigners'. After 878, however, no further movements of Columba's relics between Scotland and Ireland are recorded. By this time Kells had become firmly established as the headquarters of the *familia* of St Columba in Ireland.[22]

Dunkeld may have occupied a similar position in Scotland. It may have been here that the *Brechbennach* or reliquary of Columba (later known as the 'Monymusk reliquary') was preserved. The abbot of Dunkeld is described as *primepscop Fortrenn*, 'chief bishop of [central] Scotland' in 865. According to the continental *Life of Kaddroe* (written *c.* 975), there was a flourishing community ministering at the 'shrine of St Columba' in central Scotland by AD 900.[23]

Surviving artwork appears to bear out this picture. The great crosses of Iona, St Oran's, St John's, and St Martin's appear to belong to an early and formative stage in the development of the Celtic cross. Only the fragmentary 'St Matthew's Cross', which has a scene of the Fall of Man, has close parallels in the art of the Irish

The Cross-slab of
Dunkeld, showing the
front (above left), back
(below left) and right-
hand sides. The first
panel depicts a battle
and Daniel in the Lion's
Den; the second, the
miracle of the loaves
and fishes and the
twelve apostles; and the
third, a saint, possibly
Columba. *(Crown
Copyright: Royal
Commission on the
Ancient and Historical
Monuments of
Scotland)*

midlands of the ninth century. But the Dunkeld cross-slab, with its portrayal of the twelve apostles, the miracle of loaves and fishes, the three young men in the fiery furnace, and Daniel in the lions' den, can be very closely linked with Irish art of the Barrow Valley in Leinster of the ninth and tenth centuries, especially the crosses of Moone and Castledermot. The Dunkeld slab has a battle-scene, presumably depicting war between Gael and Picts, and a large cowled figure on one side – possibly the earliest depiction of St Columba in stone. The reintroduction of the cult of Columba into Pictland at Dunkeld in 849 must have been a significant event. The saint of the Gael, whose monks had been rejected by the Picts in 715, was making a triumphant return, while providing legitimacy for the dynasty of Kenneth son of Alpin.

Christianity in Scotland outwith the Influence of Iona

After the Viking storm, the 'calm' that followed settled on a very different landscape. A new movement of religious reform, the *Céli Dé*, had arisen in Ireland in the late eighth and early ninth centuries. This seems to have been enthusiastically received in Scotland, and there is evidence of *Céli Dé* communities at Iona, Dunkeld, St Andrews and at many other Scottish churches. In essence, these 'servants of God' wanted a return to the simple values of Columba and his contemporaries, away from the development of monasteries into wealthy property-owning corporations presided over by hereditary families of abbots. Communities of *Céli Dé* seem to have lived within monasteries alongside monks, observing their own rule and holding their own services; at St Andrews it is recorded that they had a side-altar in the church which they used for their offices. They were not necessarily celibate, but in some communities priests were required to separate from their wives when they became *Céli Dé*.

We know of other religious centres besides those connected with Columba. In 747 mention is made for the first time of an abbot of *Cennrighmonaid*, St Andrews. Later tradition attributes this foundation to Onuist son of Uurguist, king of Picts (729–61). In 733 Acca bishop of Hexham in Northumbria (a church dedicated to St Andrew the Apostle) was expelled from his diocese, and appears to have spent his exile in Scotland. The dedication to St Andrew at *Cennrighmonaid* may be connected with Acca's exile among the Picts. There were bishops at St Andrews by the early tenth century, and by the eleventh they had overtaken the bishops of Dunkeld as chief bishops of Scotland.

Traditions place the foundation of Abernethy in the Pictish period, and connect the church there with the *familia* of St Brigit of Kildare. There are Class I Pictish stones there, and a Pictish hillfort nearby. There is some evidence of bishops at Abernethy in the eighth century, but by the mid-tenth century the *Life of Kaddroe* mentions only an abbot connected with the 'house of blessed Brigit'. Later still, the kirk of Abernethy, with its tenth-century round tower, was a detached parish of the diocese of Dunblane. It may be that the bishops of Abernethy were ultimately ancestral to the medieval bishops of Dunblane.[24]

Scotland's only other surviving Irish-style round tower is at Brechin, where there were bishops from the twelfth century at latest. A royal grant of liberties to the kirk

The tenth-century Round Tower, Abernethy, Perthshire. *(Historic Scotland)*

of Brechin is recorded sometime between 971 and 995. More common in central Scotland in this period are tall square towers, of which examples can still be seen at Dunblane, Muthill, Dunning, Markinch, St Andrews and Restenneth. Foundations of another have been uncovered at Dunfermline, and the eighteenth-century tower at St Ninians by Stirling was possibly modelled on an early Christian tower.

Other early church sites have different kinds of remains. There are collections of carved stones at Meigle and St Vigeans (by Arbroath) from the Pictish period, and a slightly later collection at Govan in Strathclyde. In the case of some once-important churches, there is little evidence beyond a few scattered stones and later legends to show that they were once places of great spiritual importance. There is no doubt that our picture of Christianity in Scotland both during and after the Viking Age is very incomplete.

SOUTHWARD EXPANSION: THE TENTH AND ELEVENTH CENTURIES

If the main theme in Scottish history during the ninth century is that of unification, that of the following 200 years is of expansion. But the dynasty of Kenneth son of Alpin based in Fortrenn was not the only expansionist force in Britain at the time. The Wessex dynasty of Alfred and his descendants was expanding northward at the expense of the Viking conquests of the ninth century, and eventually these two dynasties were to collide. There was a vigorous, if struggling, Viking kingdom based on York, while other Viking kingdoms or earldoms based on Dublin, Galloway, Man and Orkney contributed from the periphery; there was a powerful Gaelic lordship in Moray, and the British held out in Wales. But it was Wessex and Fortrenn, *Saxonia* and *Scotia*, that were the main contenders for power and territory.

Constantine son of Áed

In Scotland, the first half of the tenth century was dominated by Constantine son of Áed, who succeeded his uncle Donald in 900 and reigned for more than forty years. Even after his abdication in 943 to become a monk at St Andrews he took an active role in politics, inciting his successor Malcolm to invade Northumbria in 949. He faced a serious Viking raid in 903–4, when Dunkeld was plundered but the raiding army was destroyed. In 906 Constantine held a great assembly of clergy and people at the 'hill of faith', presumably the Moot Hill of Scone, where he promised that 'the laws and disciplines of the faith, and the rights of churches and the gospels, should be kept in conformity with the customs of the Scots'. During Constantine's reign we first encounter the term *Rí Alban*, king of *Alba*, Scotland, replacing 'king of Picts' or 'king of Fortrenn'. *Alba* had originally been a name for the whole island of Britain, but from this time it came to be applied only to its northern third.[25]

We have seen that Scottish kings were influential in Strathclyde by the end of the ninth century, even though the ancient British dynasty continued for more than a century. Constantine also pushed south of the Forth and beyond the Pentland Hills. The Norsemen seized Bernicia from its ealdorman *c.* 915 and forced him to seek refuge

A twelfth-century church tower, Dunning, Perthshire. (*Alan Macquarrie*)

with Constantine, who was defeated at Corbridge. Norse domination in Northumbria was short-lived, for the new king of Wessex, Æthelstan, quickly restored his authority in York. A Norse army from Waterford then invaded Scotland in 918. They confronted Constantine with his army on the banks of the East Lothian Tyne, and were defeated with heavy losses. On 12 July 926 Æthelstan met Constantine and his protégé Aldred of Bamburgh near Penrith, and 'With pledges and with oaths they confirmed peace . . . and renounced every kind of idolatry [implying that the heathen Danes were also involved]; and then they departed in peace'.[26]

This peace was short-lived. In 934 Æthelstan attacked the Danes and Cumbrians (under their king Ywain of Strathclyde) and invaded Scotland. English and Irish sources are at variance as to the extent and result of Æthelstan's invasion. In 937 Constantine joined Olaf of Dublin and a great confederation of Cumbrians, Scots and Vikings with the objective of preserving Viking York and curbing the advance of the Wessex kings. The two armies met at an unidentified place called *Brunanburh*, and Æthelstan was victorious; Olaf and Constantine fled with few survivors, and Constantine's own son was among the slain.[27] The victory ensured that Wessex would dominate the north of England, eclipsing York and Northumbria, threatening Strathclyde-Cumbria, and eventually pressing the frontier of England to march with that of the king of Scots.

The death of Æthelstan in 939 brought little relief. In 940 his successor Edmund again defeated Constantine and Olaf, and in 944 expelled the Norsemen from York, annexing it to his kingdom. In 945 he harried Cumbria, and 'commended' it to the king of Scots on condition that he should ally with the English against the Norse of York. By this time Constantine had retired into monasticism at St Andrews, and been succeeded by his nephew Malcolm.

The reign of Constantine was of crucial importance for the formation of the Scottish kingdom. It confirmed the client status of Strathclyde-Cumbria and put paid for the last time to the Viking threat; thereafter no great Viking army dared to invade Scotland. It continued the extension of the Scottish kingdom into Lothian, and even witnessed the dependence of ealdormen at Bamburgh on the king of Scots. Internally, Constantine's reign witnessed a strengthening of Gaelic law and custom in Pictland. When Constantine died in 952 he was buried at St Andrews, the first king of Scots not to be taken to Iona for burial.[28]

Constantine's Successors

The succession to the Scottish kingship in the tenth century has sometimes been viewed as a welter of fratricidal feuding. There were, however, long and successful reigns, notably those of Constantine I (900–43) and Kenneth II (971–95). There were examples of kings who fell as a result of a dispute with a local noble family, and two periods of civil war between rival branches of the dynasty. In both cases order was restored by a 'neutral' contender who reigned successfully.

Malcolm I was killed in 954 in a dispute with the men of Moray at Fetteresso and succeeded by his cousin Indulf or Illulf son of Constantine. During his reign the

English abandoned Edinburgh, and the plain of Lothian was added to the Scottish kingdom. The Viking kingdom of York had been destroyed in 954, despite resistance from its last king, Eric Bloodaxe; although Yorkshire and Bernicia were now annexed to England, the Scots too were able to profit by the changed situation. The Wessex kings now appointed an ealdorman of Northumbria; his task must have been to hold a frontier region of England against Scottish expansion. The role of Northumbria had been established for centuries to come.

Indulf son of Constantine was killed fighting against Norsemen at Cullen in 962. The decade following his death was marred by internal fighting between Dub son of Malcolm and Culén son of Indulf. Culén defeated Dub and the men of Atholl; Dub was driven out and fled north, and was defeated and slain near Forres in 966. 'He was killed in Forres, and hidden away under the bridge of Kinloss. But the sun did not appear as long as he was concealed there; and he was found and buried in Iona.'[29] Culén had enemies in the south, for he alienated Radharc (Rhydderch) king of Strathclyde because of mistreatment of his daughter, and the Britons of Strathclyde slew him in Lothian in 971.

Kenneth Son of Malcolm and His Successors

Culén's death in 971 was followed by the 24-year reign of Kenneth (II) son of Malcolm, who restored order after the civil war of the previous decade. One of his early acts was to make peace with Edgar king of Wessex, whom he met at an impressive ceremony at Chester in 973.

> Edgar landed at the city of Chester; and eight sub-kings met him, as he commanded them, and swore that they would stand by him as his faithful friends, both on land and sea. . . . With these one day he entered a boat, and placing them at the oars, he himself took the rudder's helm, and skilfully steered along the course of the River Dee.[30]

The story of these kings rowing Edgar on the Dee may be a later embellishment, but what is stressed in all sources is the peaceful nature of their agreement with him. Kenneth was accompanied to Chester by Malcolm king of Strathclyde, and his predecessor Dyfnwal, who had resigned in preparation for a pilgrimage to Rome, where he died in 975.

Kenneth II attempted to establish his authority in both south and north. During the feud between Dub and Culén the kingdom of Strathclyde seems to have been able to act independently. Kenneth fought against the Britons of Strathclyde early in his reign, but was repulsed. He then made terms with King Malcolm of Strathclyde, and raided England as far as Stainmore and the Lake District. He married his daughter to Sigurd jarl of Orkney, thus increasing his influence in the north; Sigurd was at war with Finnlaech *mormaer* of Moray. Kenneth was also active in peaceful pursuits: he 'walled the fords on the banks of Forthin' (i.e., built a causeway at Stirling), and made grants to the church of Brechin. Its great round tower, which belongs to this period, could be testimony to his munificence. Kenneth feuded with the *mormaer* of Angus, who brought about his death.[31]

Kenneth's death was followed by a period of renewed disorder and feuding between the sons of Culén and Dub. Constantine son of Culén became king on Kenneth's death, but was ousted and killed after eighteen months by Kenneth (III) son of Dub, who ruled jointly with his own son Giric from 997–1005. In the latter year they were in turn ousted and killed by Malcolm (II) son of Kenneth. His successful reign of nearly thirty years restored order and a policy of southward expansion.

Malcolm Son of Kenneth

It is probably misleading to contrast the eleventh century, dominated as it was by the long reigns of three kings (Malcolm II, 1005–34; Macbeth, 1040–57; Malcolm III, 1058–93), with the tenth; the foundations of their successes had been laid by Constantine II and by Kenneth II in the previous century.

On the death of Æthelred and accession of Cnut in 1016, Malcolm II invaded the territory of St Cuthbert and besieged Durham, but withdrew when ealdorman Uhtred marched from Bamburgh. Two years later Malcolm had his revenge at a great battle at Carham-on-Tweed, where Uhtred's army was destroyed and Lothian was ceded perpetually to the Scots. The significance of the Battle of Carham was far-reaching; eventually the descendants of the ealdormen of Bamburgh would be earls of the kings of Scots controlling Lothian from Dunbar.[32] Shortly after the battle Ywain the Bald, last of the kings of Strathclyde, died. On his death Malcolm gave the southern kingdom to his grandson Duncan.

Malcolm II's successes in Lothian and the south provoked reaction. Cnut, occupied for much of his reign with empire-building in Scandinavia and wide travels, turned his attention to Scotland and in 1031 invaded the kingdom. The result of his invasion is differently reported; English sources record that he 'subdued them with little difficulty' and received the submission of Malcolm and of Macbeth, *mormaer* of Moray; but a contemporary French chronicler records that Malcolm and his people put up stout resistance, so that Cnut was eventually forced to come to terms, make friends with Malcolm, and stand as godfather at his son's baptism. The Norse sagas say that Cnut did make himself master over part of Scotland; but the historian Saxo Grammaticus does not name Scotland among Cnut's many conquests.[33]

Equally serious was a separatist tendency on the part of the *mormaer* of Moray. Their role as protectors of the North from Viking incursions gave them a special importance, and in the eleventh and twelfth centuries they were called 'king of Moray', or even 'king of *Alba*', in the Irish annals. Like the royal house of Fortrenn, the house was periodically dogged by internal succession disputes. One of these ended when Macbeth son of Finnlaech eliminated all his rivals, married his predecessor's widow, and adopted her son Lulach as his heir. For the time being he kept peace with Malcolm II, and is named as one of the 'kings' who submitted to Cnut in the early 1030s.

Malcolm II died in 1034, having procured the recognition of his grandson Duncan, son of Crínán, abbot of Dunkeld, as his successor. How far this constituted an alteration of the system of succession is difficult to say, for Duncan had no obvious rivals and was already of middle years. His brief reign was unsuccessful, marred by two acts of rashness: first, he invaded Northumbria in 1039, but was beaten off before the walls of Durham with heavy losses. Macbeth then raised a rebellion in Moray. Duncan swiftly marched against him, but was defeated and killed near Elgin on 14 August 1040. Duncan's sons, Malcolm and Donald, were young, and there was no other candidate; Malcolm II had efficiently eliminated all rivals. So Macbeth, probably already recognised in the north as king of *Alba*, assumed the kingship of Fortrenn.

Macbeth: 'Son of Life'

When considering the reign of Macbeth (Gaelic *Mac Bethad*, 'son of life'), one must put aside both the fantasies of Shakespeare's sources and the anti-Shakespearean reaction which romanticises Macbeth as a maligned national hero. There is little evidence for either view. Macbeth was certainly an outsider in that he was not a

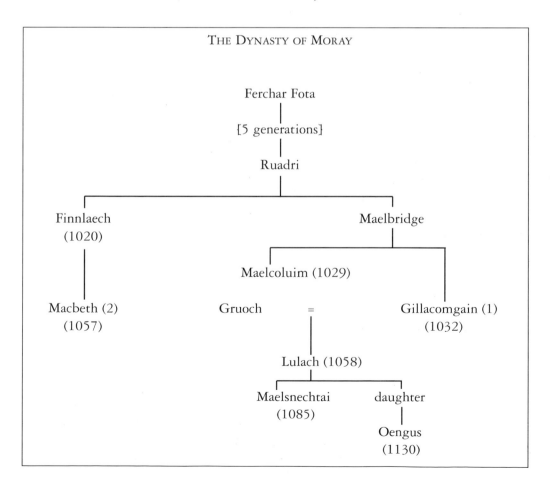

THE DYNASTY OF MORAY

Ferchar Fota

[5 generations]

Ruadri

Finnlaech (1020)

Maelbridge

Maelcoluim (1029)

Macbeth (2) (1057)

Gruoch   =   Gillacomgain (1) (1032)

Lulach (1058)

Maelsnechtai (1085)   daughter

Oengus (1130)

descendant of Kenneth son of Alpin, and his marriage to a lady who was did not legitimise him as king of Fortrenn. But his father and his cousins were recognised as 'kings of *Alba*' in Irish sources. Macbeth was the first member of his house to make his claim recognised south of the Mounth.

There can be no doubt that Macbeth was an effective king of *Alba*. He suppressed a rebellion in Atholl, led by Duncan's father Crínán, in 1045, and fought off a Northumbrian invasion in the following year. He and his wife were generous benefactors to the church of St Andrews, and their names figure among its earliest charters. In 1050 Macbeth went on pilgrimage to Rome, where he 'scattered money like seed'. He returned to find his kingdom intact, with no record of rebellions during his absence. In 1052 he became the first Scottish king to welcome Norman knights into his service; these knights were notably loyal in 1054, when a Northumbrian army drove Macbeth out of southern Scotland, and the Normans were killed to a man. Malcolm son of Duncan, now grown to maturity, led another army into Scotland in 1057, pursued Macbeth into Moray, and defeated and killed him at Lumphanan in Braemar.[34]

Recognition of the rights of the house of Moray to the kingship of all Scotland did not end with the death of Macbeth, for his stepson Lulach was immediately recognised as king, and was killed by Malcolm in Strathbogie in March 1058. Only then was Malcolm's right to the throne of Scone recognised. Thereafter a son and a grandson of Lulach were recognised as 'kings of Moray' in Irish sources, but no later *mormaer* of Moray became king of *Alba*. That position belonged thereafter, as it had done earlier, to descendants of Kenneth son of Alpin.

Malcolm Canmore: the Great Chief

Malcolm III, justly called Canmore, *Ceann mór*, 'great chieftain', is the best documented of the three great Scottish kings of the eleventh century, and the one who pursued his predecessors' policy of southward expansion with greatest determination. At first he enjoyed good relations with the English. In 1059 the archbishop of York, bishop of Durham and Tostig earl of Northumbria conducted him to the English court to confer with Edward the Confessor. Tostig was brother of Harold Godwineson, the most powerful lord in England; he had been imposed on the Northumbrians after the death of Siward, Malcolm's ally in 1054. Malcolm repaid Tostig's kindness (he was called his 'sworn brother') by ravaging his earldom in 1061 and looting Lindisfarne. Tostig resumed his friendship with Malcolm in 1066 after the Northumbrians had expelled him and he had quarrelled with Harold. Leaving Scotland, he sought the friendship of Harold Hardrada, king of Norway, with whom he planned an invasion of England. Malcolm may have been aware of Tostig and Hardrada's plans, but he did not send troops with the great army which Harold Godwineson destroyed at Stamford in Yorkshire on 24 September 1066. Five days later, William duke of Normandy, another foreigner with designs on the English throne, landed his army near Hastings.

A page from Queen Margaret's Gospel Book. MS Lat. Liturg.f.5, f.13v-14r. *(Bodleian Library, University of Oxford)*

William the Conqueror's spectacular success at Hastings presented Malcolm with new opportunities and new problems. High-ranking English refugees, such as Gospatrick of Northumbria, Edgar Ætheling (a descendant of the house of Wessex) and his sisters, fled to his court and afforded him an opportunity for almost unlimited meddling in English affairs; but William and his mail-clad cavalry quickly established themselves as undisputed masters of England who could not be challenged with impunity. When William crossed the Humber in 1068, driving Edgar and his adherents north, Malcolm harboured them, but still came to terms. It was not until 1070 that Malcolm launched a great devastation into Yorkshire and Northumberland, in retaliation for an English attempt to seize Cumbria as far as the Solway; and he strengthened his ties with the English exiles by marrying Margaret, Edgar's sister.

But William was a more formidable enemy than any the Scots had previously encountered. In 1072 he determined to cow Malcolm with a full-scale invasion of Scotland, marching to the Forth and sailing beyond. Malcolm, unable to face the mailed knights in the field, submitted to William at Abernethy and gave hostages.

This did not involve 'doing homage for his kingdom', but it ended Malcolm's attempt to treat with William on equal terms. In the following year, Edgar Ætheling realised that Malcolm could no longer help him, and sailed to Normandy to make his own peace with William, leaving Margaret behind to civilise the Scots.

The reasons for Malcolm's next invasion of Northumbria, in 1079, are unknown. William's response came in the form of a campaign into Scotland by his son Robert 'Curthose'; 'but when he had come to Falkirk he returned without having accomplished anything, and founded a New Castle upon the river Tyne'. Malcolm had given the English exile Gospatrick, descended from the ealdormen of Northumbria, a great lordship in East Lothian based on the coastal fortress of Dunbar, which was to be the foundation of the medieval earldom of Dunbar; the establishment of Newcastle-on-Tyne dashed any hopes Gospatrick and Malcolm may have had of expanding southward. The Tweed frontier was slowly coming into being.

Twelve years later, in 1091, the peace was again broken by Malcolm, who raided deep into England and carried off much spoil; this attack may have been made in favour of Edgar Ætheling, again out of favour in England and Normandy. Shipwreck prevented the new English king, William Rufus, from making reprisals, and he allowed Robert 'Curthose' and Edgar Ætheling to patch up a peace with Malcolm, whereby 'William promised him in land and in everything else all that he had had before' under William the Conqueror.

It was William Rufus who broke this agreement in the following year by annexing Carlisle and Cumbria south of the Solway. Malcolm, seeking recognition of the treaty of 1091, came south under escort to Gloucester; but William refused to see him unless Malcolm would accept the justice of an English court, while Malcolm sought a conference on the borders. Malcolm returned home in haste, gathered an army, and crossed the Tweed for the last time; he was betrayed, ambushed and slain near Alnwick on 13 November 1093.[35]

News of his death provoked various reactions: to the English it came as a surprise that such a wily old campaigner should have been cut down; William Rufus was prompted to shame and promised retribution against the perpetrators; Queen Margaret died of grief at the news.[36] Malcolm maintained the integrity of his kingdom, at least as far as the Tweed–Solway frontier (first arrived at during his reign) in the face of a much more powerful foe than any of his predecessors had had to face, and his occasional submissions made better tactical sense than the heroic last stand of the Old English aristocracy on the Battle Hill of Hastings in 1066. At least on his death Malcolm had a kingdom to pass on to his successors.

This kingdom was much less sophisticated in government and administration than its English counterpart. Malcolm III's administration was capable of nothing comparable with the Domesday Book, but he did have his dues, collected by thane and *toisech*; military service, a local levy led by the *mormaer* of a province, gave him an army of foot which could devastate Northumbria, but could not stand against the Norman cavalry. Malcolm faced only one recorded rebellion, by Maelsnechtai son of

Malcolm III and Margaret, from a fifteenth-century manuscript. *(The Master and Fellows of Corpus Christi College, Cambridge)*

The exterior of Queen Margaret's Chapel, Edinburgh. *(Historic Scotland)*

Lulach, *mormaer* of Moray, which ended with Maelsnechtai's death in 1085; for the most part, he could count on the loyalty of his *mormaer*. Like Macbeth and Malcolm II, records show him making land grants in far parts of his kingdom. Queen Margaret too is credited with grants to churches, including Iona and Laurencekirk.

There is a tendency to regard Malcolm III as the first Angliciser among Scottish kings. Margaret is credited with having 'civilised' Malcolm and his court. But there is little evidence for any great transformation at this time, and it is probable that Margaret has been credited with achievements which belong rather to her sons.

The overwhelming impression of Scotland under Malcolm III is that it was a profoundly Celtic kingdom, with a court life little different from earlier times. What is unusual about Scotland is that it was the only Celtic nation which developed a powerful unitary kingship. It was kingship, and allegiance to kingship by ties of blood, which brought together the 'stately yellow-haired company', the assembled nobility of Malcolm III's court, who first heard the strains of the *Duan Albannach*:

> O all ye learned ones of *Alba*,
> O stately yellow-haired company,
> What was the first invasion, is it known to you,
> That took the land of *Alba*? . . .
>
> Malcolm now is king, Son of Duncan,
> The handsome, of lively aspect;
> His duration no-one knows
> But the Knowing One who knows all.
>
> Two kings and fifty, hear ye,
> To the son of Duncan of princely visage,
> Of the seed of Erc, nobly pure, from the east,
> Held *Alba*, O ye learned ones.[37]

CHAPTER 5

The Twelfth Century

NEW KINGS AND NEW FAMILIES, 1093–1153

By the eleventh century the kingdom of Scotland had become an expansionist force presided over by a dynasty originating in the Gaelic west. Even in the reign of Malcolm Canmore this dynasty and its court were emphatically Celtic. But in the twelfth century a dramatic transformation took place, so that by 1200 Scotland was in many ways a cosmopolitan feudal kingdom. Its kings had a retinue of Anglo-Norman mounted knights, bound to them by feudal ties confirmed by Latin charters; its Church was presided over by bishops with close contacts with the papacy, and contained many monasteries of the reformed orders; and where these ideals came together, Scottish knights joined those of other nations in the great Crusades.

Malcolm III's second wife, Margaret, has been regarded as the initiator of some of these innovations. Her achievements were confined largely to the ecclesiastical field. But also, with more lasting significance, she contributed to change by the education which she gave to her sons. The four eldest of these were given names from the Old English royal dynasty (Edward, Edmund, Æthelred and Edgar); the two youngest were named Alexander, after the reforming pope Alexander II (1061–73), and David, after the Old Testament hero-king. None of these names was traditional among the descendants of Kenneth son of Alpin, so we may see in this a break with the past. The three youngest at least, Edgar, Alexander and David, were educated in England, as was Malcolm's son by his first marriage, Duncan. It was they rather than their mother who transformed the face of Scotland.

Donald Bán and Duncan, 1093–7

When news of Malcolm's death at Alnwick reached Scotland in 1093, the conservative earls and *toisech* chose his brother Donald Bán as king. This was in accordance with ancient Celtic practice, where a king's brother was frequently chosen to succeed. But Anglo-Norman England was getting used to the concept of primogeniture, which excluded brothers and cousins who would have been legitimate claimants according to the Celtic system; and Duncan, Malcolm's eldest son, may have expected to succeed his father. William Rufus, the English king who had kept

Duncan as a hostage, could profit by using him to create confusion and dissension in Scotland after Malcolm's long reign. 'Duncan . . . came to the king and did such fealty as the king would have of him; and with his consent, he went to Scotland, with what help he could get of English and French, and deprived his kinsman Donald of the kingdom, and was received as king. But afterwards some of the Scots gathered together and slew almost all of his followers, and he himself escaped with few. Thereafter they were reconciled, on condition that he should never again introduce English or French into the land.' Duncan's success clearly depended on the support of his foreigners, and without them he was unable to resist Donald Bán's comeback: 'In this year [1094] also the Scots deceived and slew Duncan, their king; and thereafter they took to themselves again as king a second time Donald, his paternal uncle, by whose direction and inspiration he had been betrayed to death.' It seems that Donald had the support of at least one of Malcolm's sons by Margaret. 'Edmund . . . taking part in his uncle Donald's wickedness, was not innocent of his brother's death, bargaining indeed for half the kingdom.' Donald's second reign lasted longer than his first, but it too was curtailed by English intervention in 1097. 'In the same year [1097] soon after Michaelmas [29 September] Edgar Ætheling went with an army into Scotland, with the help of [William Rufus], and in a hard-fought battle won the land, and drove out King Donald, and in fealty to King William set up there his kinsman Edgar.'[1]

Edgar, 1097–1107

This battle, at an unknown location, has with some exaggeration been called 'the Norman Conquest of Scotland'. Duncan and Edgar accepted that they were dependent clients of William Rufus.[2]

Edgar's reign is poorly documented. According to one English writer, he 'was a man sweet and loveable, like in all things to King Edward [the Confessor], his relative, employing no tyranny, no harshness, no greed against his people, but ruling his subjects with the greatest charity and benevolence'. Perhaps the fate of his half-brother Duncan led him to adopt a cautious approach towards the aristocracy.

The complaint against Duncan was that he surrounded himself with English and French, and he was only suffered to rule on condition that he dismiss them. There is no trace of large-scale introduction of foreigners into Scotland under Edgar; one Anglo-Norman knight, Robert son of Godwine, was granted lands in Berwickshire on which he began to build a castle, but no others are known.[3]

The fortunes of Edgar's family were varied. He himself became a king, perhaps with little room for manoeuvre; in 1100 his sister Matilda was taken to wife by Henry I, the new king of England, who thus allied himself by marriage to the family of Edward the Confessor as well as to the royal house of Scotland; two of Edgar's elder brothers were excluded from the succession, Edmund because he had been an ally of Donald Bán and was implicated in Duncan's death, Æthelred because he was a churchman and apparently sought no part in public affairs; his next brother, Alexander, succeeded on his death; and his youngest brother, David, had the most interesting and successful career of all. He played some part in the battle which brought about Donald Bán's downfall in 1097; was present at his sister's wedding to Henry I in 1100; was again present at his brother's deathbed in 1107, when Edgar allegedly promised him a share of the kingdom of some kind; and became a favourite of Henry I, who showered him with gifts. The richest of these came in 1114, when Henry gave him a rich widow in marriage, together with her late husband's great earldom of Huntingdon, to the exclusion of the late earl's sons.

Alexander I, 1107–24

When Edgar died in 1107, it was Alexander who succeeded. His seventeen-year reign is nearly as obscure as that of his elder brother. Notable, however, were his religious innovations, with the foundation of a monastery of monks from Tiron near Chartres at Selkirk (later moved to Kelso), and of a priory of Augustinian canons at Scone. Later generations remembered him as a forceful and rigorous ruler ('Alexander the fierce', because of the way he pursued and hanged thieves) who administered his kingdom *laboriosissime*, with hard work. He cut an impressive figure on a visit to the church of St Andrews (the present St Rule's Kirk) when he arrived on an Arab stallion wearing the finest Turkish armour of the day, which he laid before the altar to be blessed and dedicated.[4] There is no evidence of Anglo-Norman colonisation during his reign.

Alexander's relations with King Henry and with his brother David are complex. King Henry gave him as wife his illegitimate daughter Sybilla; the marriage was probably of greater advantage to Henry than to Alexander. Alexander is found leading a contingent on Henry's Welsh expedition of 1114 – not necessarily the act of a feudal vassal, but perhaps not that of a sovereign equal either.[5]

A twelfth-century writer states that on his deathbed Edgar had bequeathed part of his realm to his youngest brother David. David may have had Edgar's special affection because of his actions during the war of 1097, possibly his involvement in the capture of Donald Bán; perhaps through Edgar's influence, he became a favourite of Henry I. Some time *c.* 1113, Henry compelled the reluctant Alexander to grant David his promised inheritance, and David became prince of Strathclyde (he had previously dwelt at Henry's court as 'brother of the queen'). There is little doubt that Alexander, without legitimate issue, recognised David as his heir.

David used his new position to revive the bishopric of Glasgow and to grant large fiefs to Anglo-Norman knights in return for knight service – the first large-scale introduction of feudalism into Scotland. These knights came from David's newly acquired earldom of Huntingdon. Thereafter for long periods in the twelfth century a great English earldom covering large parts of the East Midlands was held by a member of the Scottish royal family. A large number of families from this region settled in Scotland in the twelfth century, but there are also more subtle connections: e.g. the architectural similarity between the west end of Ely Cathedral and the surviving fragments of Kelso Abbey.

Alexander in his later years seems to have devoted his energies to central and northern Scotland. He made grants to Scone priory and St Andrews cathedral, and his surviving charters are often dated at Stirling, Perth and Scone. He founded a chapel at Stirling Castle (possibly on the site of Holy Rude Kirk), and died there. His one illegitimate son was given the Gaelic name Malcolm (*Mael Coluim*) after his grandfather Malcolm Canmore. Alexander's reign is obscure and contains curious contradictions; but he cannot be regarded as an Angliciser.

David I, 1124–53

The greatest of the sons of Malcolm III was undoubtedly David I. His importance as an innovator and a masterful king is beyond question, and changes were evident in both Church and state. To some extent David was fortunate: the death of Henry I in 1135 and the subsequent 'anarchy' of Stephen's reign allowed him scope for expansion into northern England and opportunities to intervene in English politics; the favour which he found with Henry I brought him the earldom of Huntingdon, and he was able to persuade Alexander to give him his inheritance; and in a limited way his brothers had prepared the way for his reforms. The fact that he had held a lordship in southern Scotland for ten years before his accession gave him experience, and the lordship of Huntingdon gave him a ready supply of colonists for his lordship and kingdom.

But David's successes resulted from his own personality; pious beyond the norms of a pious age, ascetic without severity or remoteness, he never showed such excessive favour to Anglo-Normans as to alienate the traditional magnates, as his half-brother Duncan had done. His court was a curious mixture of natives and incomers. The major offices of state, the new posts of chancellor, chamberlain and constable, were held by highly trusted foreigners; but there is little evidence of a sense of alienation on the part of the traditional magnates.[6]

David's reign was not totally free from internal opposition. Alexander I had left an illegitimate son, Malcolm mac Heth (Gaelic *Mael Coluim mac Áedha*), who made a bid for the throne on his father's death in 1124, but was defeated in two battles that year. His surname, mac Heth, is a mystery, but there appears to have been an earl, called Heth or Áedh, possibly connected by marriage with the family of King Lulach; Lulach's daughter had a son called Angus (*Aonghus*), king or earl of Moray, who does not appear as a witness to any of David's charters. Possibly Lulach's daughter married Heth, who adopted or fostered Alexander's son Malcolm, but also had a son Angus who succeeded as earl of Moray.

In 1130, while David was out of the country, Earl Angus and Malcolm mac Heth raised a great rebellion in Moray and marched south at the head of an army. David's constable, a Northumbrian called Edward fitz Siward, collected an army and opposed them at Stracathro in Angus, where the rebellion was crushed and Angus killed. Malcolm mac Heth escaped, but was captured and imprisoned in 1134. The fact that he was not executed but lived in captivity for more than twenty years before being reconciled and released by Malcolm IV suggests that Malcolm mac Heth was of royal blood, and that David was not of a vindictive nature. David was not naturally suspicious of anyone connected with the royal family: William fitz Duncan, son of David's eldest half-brother, was a favourite at court and was generously treated; David's uncle, Donald Bán, captured possibly by David himself in 1097, was not killed but emasculated and confined, and honourably buried at Iona when he died some years later.[7]

David's mild attitude towards members of his own family could not overcome the hostility of Moray. David's solution was to suppress the title of earl of Moray after 1130 and assume control of the comital lands, some of which he granted to foreign knights; a Fleming called Freskin received Duffus and other lands in Moray for knight service, took the surname *de Moravia*, 'of Moray', and founded the Scottish surname Murray.

The crown's problem with Moray was unusual. In marked contrast was David's relationship with Duncan earl of Fife. Earl Duncan was a frequent witness to David's charters, and frequently present at court; *c.* 1136 the king granted him the earldom of Fife by feudal charter for the service of a specified number of knights.[8] There is no evidence that David attempted to establish similar feudal relationships with other earls.

South of the Forth it was a different story. In Strathclyde-Cumbria, David planted knights with large fiefs in Annandale, Eskdale, Liddesdale, Kyle, Cunninghame and Renfrewshire, and probably elsewhere; in the east, in Lothian and the Borders, he gave out smaller fiefs throughout his reign.

Many, but not all, of the holders of these fiefs came from David's English estates. Typical was Hugh de Morville, a prominent tenant of the earldom of Huntingdon who received extensive estates in Cunninghame and Lauderdale; he became David's constable and is the most frequent witness to David's acts. Relatively unusual was Robert de Bruce, lord of Annandale, who held extensive lands in the north of England in his own right as well as lands in the earldom of Huntingdon.

The development of knight's fiefs was only part of the story. David had other ways of establishing royal control at local level, most notably in the establishment of sheriffdoms. Sheriffs gradually took over from thanes the administration of royal estates and collection of royal dues, and later developed judicial functions as well; in the north of Scotland the term *vicecomes*, 'assistant earl' was curiously appropriate for an official whose jurisdiction was often coterminous with an earldom. The headquarters of a sheriffdom was a royal castle, usually in an area with a concentration of royal estates, as at Roxburgh, Berwick or Haddington. The northern sheriffdoms of Aberdeen, Banff and Inverness became *foci* for towns, but it is unlikely that these towns had any previous existence; the same is probably true of Perth and Forfar. The picture is still very incomplete by the end of David I's reign; there were still no traces of sheriffdoms in Strathclyde-Cumbria or Fife (though a sheriff at Crail appears soon after); in the western seaboard, Galloway, and the far north, there was probably no royal demesne to be administered, and collection of royal dues could be

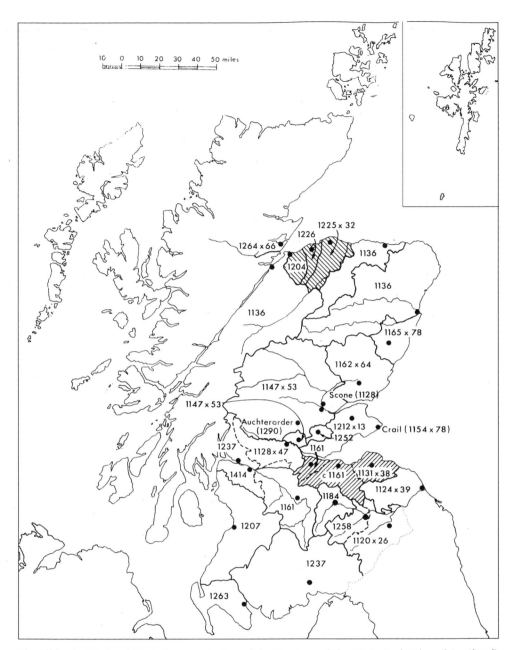

Sheriffdoms. *(Richard Muir; by permission of the Trustees of the Historical Atlas of Scotland)*

left to local lords. The foundation of royal burghs was a development which went hand in hand with that of sheriffdoms.[9]

All these developments, more dense and systematic in the south-east, more haphazard and restricted in the north, absent from Galloway and the far north and west, are indications of the spread of David's royal authority. The crown was still due tribute from the great lords in these areas, such as Fergus of Galloway or Somerled of Argyll, but they had a great deal of local independence.[10]

David's Foreign Policy

Extension of royal authority is evident in the suppression of Moray and the defeat of Malcolm mac Heth; but David also had ambitions for southward expansion, and these occupied the middle years of his reign. David's friend Henry I died in 1135, leaving a succession crisis in England; Henry's only legitimate son had died in 1120. The choice lay between Stephen count of Mortain, son of Henry's sister Adela, who became Henry's favourite nephew and acquired rich fiefs in England and Normandy; and Matilda, Henry's daughter and David's niece, called 'the Empress' because she was the widow of the king of the Romans.

When Henry decided in 1127 that the Empress should succeed him David was the first of his barons to swear loyalty to her. Henry completed his succession plans later in the same year when he arranged the marriage of Matilda to Geoffrey count of Anjou, the most powerful baron in northern France. This match, which would have given Geoffrey the English crown, was unpopular, and a new agreement was suggested which would have recognised Matilda's right, but not Geoffrey's; this was unacceptable to the latter, and he and Henry were at war at the time of Henry's death in 1135. Stephen seized his chance, and swiftly had himself recognised as king.

David seized Carlisle and Newcastle, bringing Stephen to negotiations; this did not lead to a satisfactory solution of David's claims in the north of England, nor did a threatened invasion in the following year. So, in 1138, in a campaign timed to coincide with Geoffrey of Anjou's invasion of Normandy, David gathered a full-scale Scottish army and launched an invasion of the north of England, which had some successes before meeting the English army near Northallerton on 22 August.

English accounts portray the 'Battle of the Standard' as a great English victory; but they exaggerate the brutality of the Scottish army and the scale of the Scots' defeat. The men of Galloway claimed the right to lead the van in battle, which was contested by David's force of some two hundred mounted knights; but the men of Galloway had their way. Before the battle Robert de Bruce, a great landowner on both sides of the border, came to the king and pleaded with him to withdraw. David was not persuaded, and arrayed his men for battle. The description of the Scottish army is an impressive testimony to the support David received from widely scattered parts of the kingdom: Anglo-Norman knights, Northumbrians of Lothian and Teviotdale, Gallovidians, men of Lorn and the Isles, of Moray and Strathearn; 'the army of the Scots cried out the war-cry of their fathers, and the shout rose even to the skies, *Albani, Albani* – but the shouting was drowned in the fierceness and frightful crashing of weapons.' This battle-cry was the Gaelic *Albannaig, Albannaig*, 'men of Scotland'.[11]

David's show of unity may have been impressive, but English sources claim he had the worse of the encounter. The men of Lothian fled when their leader Cospatrick of Dunbar was killed by an arrow, and the Gallovidians, seeing this, were forced to retreat with heavy losses. David and his bodyguard withdrew in good order, their retreat covered by the king's son Earl Henry and his knights; Henry escaped with difficulty to rejoin his father at Carlisle.

It was not, however, a disaster for David; his army remained intact, he maintained his hold on Carlisle, and within a few months the surrender of Wark Castle completed his conquest of Northumbria. In 1139 Stephen granted the title earl of Northumbria to Earl Henry and received him at court, procuring for him the marriage of Ada de Warenne.

King David had achieved all he had hoped to gain from Stephen; but he retained sufficient loyalty to the Empress to join her in 1141, after Stephen had been captured at Lincoln. The Empress's triumph was short-lived; she and David were driven out of Winchester, and David narrowly escaped capture; by the end of the year Stephen was again at liberty, David was back in the north, and the Empress had lost most of her support. For David the most serious blow was when Stephen deprived him of the earldom of Huntingdon-Northampton. But David was untroubled in his control of Cumberland and Northumberland, and these areas escaped the worst ravages of the 'Anarchy', 'when men said openly that Christ and his saints slept'.[12]

David's greatest triumph came in 1149 when Henry, son of the Empress and Geoffrey of Anjou, came to his court at Carlisle to seek knighthood at his hands. Henry returned to Normandy, having sworn to respect David's possession of Cumberland and Northumberland.[13] This perhaps did not amount to a recognition that these lands had become part of the kingdom of Scots, which was David's ambition; but David seems in effect to have treated them as such. Carlisle became his favourite residence; when his son Earl Henry died in 1152 he transferred his earldom of Northumbria to one of his sons, as if it were an earldom of the Scottish crown.

David's Last Years

The death of his son was a blow in David's last year. He had earlier 'designated' Earl Henry as his successor, and had even considered resigning the kingdom into his hands to join the second Crusade (1147).[14] But even in adversity David still showed sure judgement. He caused his eldest grandson, Malcolm, a boy of twelve, to be recognised as his successor, 'and giving him as guardian Earl Duncan [of Fife], with a numerous army, commanded that the boy should be conducted round the provinces of Scotland, and proclaimed to be the heir of the kingdom'. Henry's Northumbrian earldom was given to his second son William.[15]

David died at Carlisle on 24 May 1153. He had ruled over the kingdom for twenty-nine years, which had witnessed enormous changes. Throughout David had always shown great sensitivity in his dealings with the disparate elements in his kingdom, and won their support and loyalty. It was loyalty to kingship, to the monarchy built up by David's predecessors over centuries, as much as to the remarkable personality of David himself, which motivated his subjects. It was David's genius which enabled Scotland to make the transition from an ancient Celtic kingdom to a medieval feudal one with so little disruption.

NEW KINGS AND NEW FAMILIES, 1153–1214

Malcolm IV, 1153–65

The accession of Malcolm IV in 1153 was a phenomenon previously unknown in Scotland: the accession of a minor. Malcolm was twelve years old when he became king. His acceptance in a country where the king had always been chosen from among a group of eligible adult males was a remarkable tribute to the work of his grandfather.

The boy-king might have expected to face serious problems in establishing his right to rule. There were other candidates for the kingship living who were older and more experienced, most notably his grandfather's favoured nephew, William fitz Duncan, and Malcolm mac Heth, an illegitimate son of his great-uncle Alexander I. But William had never been considered a candidate, and David had never regarded him as a threat. Malcolm mac Heth was still in prison following his rebellions in the 1130s.

David's preparations had been thorough. More than five months elapsed before Somerled and Malcolm mac Heth's sons raised the standard of rebellion in the west. Nearer to the centres of royal government, charges of treason were brought against Ness thane of Callander and an unidentified person called Arthur, who were both slain in ordeal by combat. But the most important figures in the country, the earls and the feudatories imported by David, rallied behind the young king. Somerled's rising was short-lived; the lord of Argyll soon found himself embroiled in a long war in the Isles with the Norse king of Man. Malcolm mac Heth's son Donald landed in Galloway and was captured at Whithorn in 1156; son joined father in prison in Roxburgh Castle. The rebellion collapsed, and allowed a reconciliation between the boy-king (now approaching sixteen) and Malcolm mac Heth; the latter was set at liberty and given, or restored to, the earldom of Ross. Thereafter he appears as an occasional witness of King Malcolm's charters, and was never again in rebellion. King Malcolm had weathered the first storm, and was able to act magnanimously towards his former enemy.[16]

But in 1157, as he entered his seventeenth year, he came face to face with a much more powerful force: the Angevin empire of King Henry II of England. Henry had succeeded on the death of Stephen in 1154, by an agreement worked out between the supporters of both parties during Stephen's last years. He was also duke of Normandy and count of Anjou, and husband of Eleanor of Aquitaine, divorced wife of Louis VII of France; Henry was able, ambitious and charming, but had an unpredictable nature capable of outbursts of uncontrolled fury. He was about seven years older than Malcolm when they met in the summer of 1157: 'King Henry took care to announce to the king of Scots . . . that he ought not to be defrauded of so great a part of his kingdom [Northumberland, Cumberland, Westmoreland]. . . . And Malcolm, prudently considering that in this matter the king of England was superior to the merits of the case by the authority of might, . . . restored to him the said territories, and received in return the earldom of Huntingdon.'[17]

Malcolm's motives may have been complex; he was anxious to be knighted by Henry, and realistic enough to wish to avoid armed confrontation. If Malcolm imagined he could give away his brother's earldom without consultation, however, he was mistaken; for William never forgot that he had been earl of Northumberland. Malcolm may also have misjudged Henry II; the two kings met again at Carlisle in 1158, but Henry refused to knight Malcolm, and they parted on unfriendly terms.

Malcolm made a more determined effort to be reconciled in the following year. Henry was proposing an extended campaign against the county of Toulouse, which he claimed as the inheritance of his wife, Eleanor of Aquitaine. Malcolm, now aged eighteen, hastened to join him with a small force which included his brother William, in a quest for knightly adventure and the prized belt of knighthood. On the southward march Malcolm at last fulfilled his ambition when Henry knighted him at Périgueux. He stayed with Henry for about three months at the siege of Toulouse, returning to England in the autumn and reaching Scotland during the winter. Malcolm was back in Perth in the early months of 1160.

The storm of protest which greeted his return that winter was the great crisis of his reign. Earl Ferteth (*Feredach*) of Strathearn and five other earls brought an army to the town and surrounded it while Malcolm was holding court there; they were 'enraged because the king had gone to Toulouse', and wished to get possession of the king's person. The identities of the 'five earls' can be guessed at. Two were almost certainly Fergus lord of Galloway and Somerled lord of Argyll, not strictly earls but of equivalent rank. The loyal earls of Fife and Dunbar were probably not involved; that leaves Angus, Atholl, and Mar as the most likely, with the possibility that Malcolm mac Heth of Ross was also involved.

There is no suggestion that the conspirators sought to depose or harm the king, merely to control and influence him. They were angry specifically that Malcolm had gone abroad in the English king's service in 1159; and they may have been concerned also about the treaty of 1157. The crisis was more serious than the western rebellion in favour of the mac Heth claim in 1153–4. Had the rebellion succeeded, Malcolm would have found his freedom of action severely circumscribed, his grandfather's most trusted counsellors excluded from court, and himself unable to continue the feudal colonisation of the kingdom north of the Tay.

Malcolm escaped capture and slipped out of Perth. Probably he headed south, to Fife, Lothian and Strathclyde where he could count on the loyalty of feudal knights settled by his grandfather and father. Gathering an army, he marched into Galloway and confronted Fergus of Galloway in three battles. Fergus submitted and was forced into retirement, becoming a canon of Holyrood Abbey. Somerled of Argyll, who may have needed Gallovidian support for his campaigns against Man and the Hebrides, came into the kings peace during the later months of 1160, and earned the nickname 'Somerled *site bi the king*'.[18] By Christmas 1160 Malcolm was back in Perth. By 1161 the northern earls appear again as witnesses to royal acts as far south as Tweeddale. That these powerful lords from north of the Forth were making the long journey into the south-east shows the extent of Malcolm's success. The great crisis was over.

Malcolm's success was undoubtedly due to the military superiority he gained by having mounted knights. This brought about his victories in Galloway, the reconciliation with Somerled and with the Celtic earls. There was no trouble on the same scale during the later years of the reign; when Somerled was again in rebellion, apparently in isolation, in 1164, he was defeated and killed at Renfrew by local levies.

In foreign affairs, too, Malcolm showed a more independent spirit. He married his sisters to Conan duke of Brittany (1160) and Florence count of Holland (1162); these marriages can hardly have been pleasing to Henry II, whose northern French empire was close to both lands.[19] When the two kings met in 1163, firm peace and friendship were established between them, secured by Malcolm's giving of hostages, including his youngest brother David. The terms of the peace are unknown, but there was no repeat of the outcry against the 1157 treaty.

Within Scotland, the years 1160 to 1165 probably witnessed the feudal colonis-ation of Clydesdale and the continuation of the colonisation of Moray begun by David I, predominantly by Flemings.

Malcolm IV's later years were dogged by illness. He was seriously ill in 1163, and probably again during the summer of 1165, when he took a vow of pilgrimage to the shrine of St James of Compostela. One writer states that he was chronically ill for several years before his death. He was noted for his piety and chastity (the source of the late medieval nickname 'Malcolm the Maiden'); this befitted a grandson of the austere King David, but there is no suggestion that he would not have married had he lived longer. He died on 9 December 1165, in his twenty-fifth year. His last known act was an unsuccessful attempt to reconcile Henry II with Thomas Becket.[20]

William 'the Lion'

There could have been no dispute about the succession. Malcolm's brother William was a knight in his early twenties, active and strong-willed, whose early succession had been made more likely by Malcolm's illness in his last years. William's active reign of nearly fifty years is by far the longest of any adult Scottish king. Through-out his reign his chief concern was the recovery of the territory granted away by Malcolm in 1157.

He turned his attention to this problem upon his accession, crossing into Normandy in 1166, meeting Henry and finding time to 'attempt certain feats of chivalry'; but he returned to Scotland late in the year without satisfaction. Clearly, an atmosphere of suspicion arose between them, for when one of Henry's knights spoke favourably of the Scottish king, Henry 'roused to his accustomed fury' called him a traitor, threw off his cap and clothes, stripped the covers off the furniture, and sat on the floor chewing straw. William was back in northern France in 1168 to make a secret alliance with King Louis VII of France, at the time at war with Henry, but soon to be reconciled. William too was soon reconciled with Henry, for he and his brother David attended his court at Easter 1170 at Windsor, and Henry knighted David. William and David then accompanied Henry to London for the coronation of

Henry's son, the young King Henry, and did him homage (presumably for the lordships which William held in England). William may have hoped for better satisfaction from young King Henry than from his father, and joined the young king's plot in 1173; his reward for his aid in the rebellion was to be the earldom of Northumberland, and an augmented Huntingdon for David.

With this prize dangling before him, William invaded England in July 1174, while another of Henry's rebellious sons invaded Normandy, and William's brother David raised an army from the Huntingdon estates. But William's campaign was less well organised than David I's campaign of 1138, and castles which David had taken in that year frustrated him. William was out foraging with a troop of knights isolated from the rest of his army and was captured near Alnwick on 13 July 1174. His capture led quickly to the collapse of the Angevin rebellion; David slipped out of Huntingdon castle before it fell to old Henry's troops and fled to Scotland, but soon submitted. William was brought to Henry at Northampton on 26 July 'with his feet shackled below the belly of his horse'.[21] William was taken in chains to Normandy and imprisoned at Falaise, where he accepted humiliating terms. William became Henry's liegeman and did homage for his kingdom; his prelates and barons also acknowledged Henry's superiority. As guarantees Henry garrisoned the castles of Roxburgh, Berwick, Jedburgh, Edinburgh and Stirling, and took hostages. The treaty of Falaise reduced Scotland to the status of a client kingdom.[22]

Internal Unrest: the Mac William Risings

The treaty of Falaise paralysed William's foreign policy for more than a decade; it also left him prey to internal disputes. We know of no uprisings during the first nine years of William's reign; thereafter there was a series. Immediately on the news of William's capture, the 'barbarians' in the king's army turned against the English burgesses dwelling in Scottish towns, and 'the whole kingdom of Scotland was disturbed'. This may be an exaggeration, but there was a rebellion in Galloway. On the retiral of Fergus lord of Galloway in 1160, the rule of Galloway was divided between his sons Uhtred and Gilbert. On William's capture, the brothers expelled all royal officers from Galloway and sent to Henry offering to become his vassals, removing Galloway from the kingdom of Scotland. But they then quarrelled among themselves, and Uhtred was slain. Gilbert then repeated the offer of vassalage to the English king. Henry was not taken in, and upon William's release sent him with an army into Galloway. By the autumn of 1176 Gilbert had been captured, and in October William brought him in chains to Henry's court, to make peace and reparation for the murder of his brother; Gilbert swore fealty to Henry and paid a fine of 1,000 marks of silver, giving his son Duncan as a hostage. But when he returned to Galloway he 'commanded that all foreigners having any holding in Galloway through the king of Scotland should go into exile', and those refusing should be put to death.[23]

Galloway under Gilbert was to be a problem for years to come. But it was not William's only problem, for dissension soon arose in the far north as well. 'William . . .

and David his brother, along with the earls and barons of the land, went into Ross with a great and strong army; and there they strengthened two castles' which guarded the narrows of the Cromarty and Beauly Firths. The threat came from Donald mac William, the son of William fitz Duncan who had been David I's favourite nephew and son of King Duncan II (1094). Donald mac William landed in the north in the summer of 1181 'by a mandate of certain powerful men of the kingdom of Scotland; with a numerous armed host wasting and burning as much of the land as he reached, he put the folk to flight, and slew all whom he could take'. The writer adds that 'Donald had very often claimed the kingdom of Scotland, and had many a time made insidious incursions into that kingdom'.[24]

William fitz Duncan had never pressed his claim to the throne. He had had one legitimate son, William 'the boy of Egremont', who died young. Donald must have been illegitimate, possibly born of a lady of the line of the earls of Moray. A connection may have existed between Donald mac William and the descendants of Malcolm mac Heth, possibly by marriage. In November 1186, Aed or Adam son of Donald (mac William, presumably, but Malcolm mac Heth also had a son Donald) invaded Atholl; his army was attacked by the earl and took refuge in the abbey of Coupar Angus. There the earl violently invaded the sanctuary, captured Aed, beheaded his nephew before the high altar, and burned to death the rest of the band in the abbot's guesthouse.

Donald mac William attempted vengeance in the following year. He appeared in Ross at the head of an army, and King William moved against him. There was dissension in William's army; the king was persuaded to remain at Inverness rather than go with an army of doubtful loyalty into a remote part of his kingdom. In the end it was Roland, son of the murdered Uhtred of Galloway, who rallied those loyal to William and defeated and slew Donald at *Mam Garvia*, now Strathgarve in Easter Ross.

Roland had reason to be grateful to William. His uncle Gilbert, his father's murderer, had continued to oppose King William throughout the late 1170s and early 1180s, attempting to play William off against Henry II. William had been collecting an army against him in 1184 because Gilbert 'had wasted his land and slain his vassals, and yet would not make peace with him' when he was summoned to King Henry's court. Gilbert died in January 1185, still at war with William, but with his son Duncan held as a hostage at the English court. Immediately on his death Uhtred's son Roland collected an army and invaded Galloway and 'slew all the most powerful and richest men in all Galloway, and occupied their lands; and in them he built castles and very many fortresses, establishing his kingdom'. King Henry, hearing this, summoned Roland, but he refused to come; King William persuaded him to come under safe-conduct to Carlisle and stood surety for his good behaviour. Clearly Roland was William's protégé, and this must have influenced his loyalty in the campaign of 1187. Following the pacification of Galloway in 1185–6 and that of Ross in 1187–8, the kingdom enjoyed a period of peace.[25]

The Quitclaim of Canterbury

In the 1180s William's relations with King Henry started to improve. In 1185 he and his brother David were summoned to Henry's court to meet Heraclius, patriarch of Jerusalem, who was travelling in Europe appealing for help against Saladin. The meeting produced few firm promises of help for the kingdom of Jerusalem; but for William's kingdom the result was better. Simon de Senlis, earl of Huntingdon, had died childless in 1184, and Henry now gave the earldom to William, who immediately transferred it to David. In the following year Henry gave his cousin Ermengard de Beaumont in marriage to William, with Edinburgh Castle as her wedding present. Henry retained Berwick and Roxburgh in his own hands.

The fall of Jerusalem in 1187 shook the Christian West, and kings and princes who had ignored Heraclius's warnings in 1185 hastened to take the cross. King Henry and his eldest surviving son, Richard count of Poitou, King Philip II of France and the German emperor Frederick Barbarossa were the most prominent. From Scotland came William's friend Robert de Quincy, lord of Leuchars and Tranent, and Osbert Olifard, lord of Arbuthnott and sheriff of Mearns. Some knights of Alan fitz Walter the Steward appear to have joined the crusade, and there is a tradition that Alan himself did so. Neither William nor David took up the cross, although in the late Middle Ages a tradition existed that David had joined the crusade, which formed the basis of Sir Walter Scott's novel *The Talisman*.[26]

William managed to turn the situation to his advantage. Henry II sent the bishop of Durham to Scotland to demand William's contribution to the 'Saladin tithe', a tax on rents and moveables to finance the crusade. William, with the support of his barons, refused the tithe but offered a substantial lump sum for the restoration of his royal castles; Henry refused. Henry was soon embroiled in a fresh quarrel with his son Richard, which remained unresolved at his death in July 1189. Richard, now king, was anxious to settle matters quickly, and on 5 December 1189 the two kings agreed the Treaty of Canterbury, whereby William paid Richard 10,000 marks in return for all royal castles and the restoration of the status quo as it had existed before the Treaty of Falaise.[27] A few days later Richard crossed into France on the first stage of his journey to recover the Holy Land.

With his kingdom restored to liberty, William could afford to be magnanimous. In 1193 he contributed 2,000 marks to Richard's ransom, securing a letter guaranteeing that the contribution did not establish a precedent. He refused to join John's rebellion in 1193, and Earl David was instrumental in besieging Nottingham in 1194. In 1194 William was present at Richard's second coronation, at which he carried a sword, and offered the king 15,000 marks for the earldom of Northumberland. Richard was willing to accept this on condition that he retained the royal castles, a condition which did not satisfy William. Richard, anxious to return to Normandy where King Philip was attacking his dominions, promised to reconsider the offer when he returned to England; but he never returned, and William never recovered his inheritance.

William's Last Years

The death of Richard and John's accession in 1199 dashed William's prospects. Two internal problems dogged William's later years. One was the succession, and the other disaffection in the north, which persisted even after the death of Donald mac William. The first problem was seemingly solved by the birth of a son, Alexander, in 1198. William also had a number of illegitimate children, including Robert de London who was a favourite at court. But royal bastards, howsoever favoured, could never expect to succeed, and Robert de London, like Earl David, was consistently loyal to young Alexander. William seems to have been fortunate in that those who were closest to him were prepared to put interests of state before personal ambition.

In the far north, William faced disaffection from Harold Madaadsson, earl of Orkney and Caithness. He had been married to a daughter of Duncan earl of Fife, but had put her away in favour of a daughter of Malcolm mac Heth earl of Ross, and thus inherited the old mac Heth claim to the throne. Harold invaded Moray in 1196, and William drove him back, advancing into the far north and sending his troops as far as Thurso. Harold made peace, William demanding his son Thorfinn as hostage and that Harold should take back his first wife. In the meantime Harold found time to defeat and kill a rival for the earldom in battle at Wick. He offered William money to have Caithness restored to him, but refused to take back his wife; in the course of an ensuing struggle the bishop of Caithness was cruelly mutilated. Harold had gone too far this time, and was forced to come to terms with William in 1201 or 1202. He paid 2,000 pounds of silver to the king to have the earldom of Caithness, and the pope imposed a heavy penance for the mutilation of the bishop.[28]

By neutralising the threat from Caithness, William reduced the dangers of the mac Heth and mac William rebels. Guthred, son of Donald mac William, led a rebellion in 1211, which was opposed by the king in person (now in his late sixties); in the following year a force of Brabantine mercenaries was called in under the command of Saher de Quincy and young Alexander, recently knighted by King John. The rebellion did not spread beyond Ross, and was ended when Guthred was captured and hanged. William was also vigorous and decisive in his dealings with Galloway late in his reign: when Duncan son of Gilbert of Galloway married a daughter of Alan the Steward, lord of Renfrew, William immediately took pledges from Alan that he would keep the peace and put the matter to the king's judgement; perhaps William feared an alliance between the Steward and the Gallovidians. In 1200 Roland of Galloway died and was succeeded as lord of Galloway by his son Alan; Duncan son of Gilbert was given a lordship in Carrick which later became an earldom; and a new royal castle, burgh and sheriffdom were established on the River Ayr in Kyle.

The process of planting knights with fiefs, burghs and sheriffdoms, was carried out more systematically under William I than any of his predecessors. Angus and Mearns were important areas of colonisation, with Earl David planting knights from the earldom of Huntingdon in his lordship of Garioch. All the ancient earldoms

Above: Arbroath Abbey, Angus: from south. *Below:* Looking west. William the Lion's monument. *(Both courtesy of Historic Scotland)*

remained in native hands, but there was an element of royal interference in Lennox, Mar and Buchan as well as in the south-west; in Moray the comital house was not restored, and William intensified King David's feudalisation; a new burgh, castle and sheriffdom were founded at Invernairn *c*. 1187. The foundation of Nairn closely parallels William's building of the castle and burgh of Dumfries *c*. 1185 on the death of the last native lord of Nithsdale.

For all William's vigour and the achievements of his reign, his last years were an anti-climax. His attempts to negotiate with King John over the northern counties went badly. Treaties between them in 1209 and 1212 have not survived, but appear to have involved William giving hostages and paying a large sum in return for vague promises; all the concessions were on William's side.[29]

Perhaps William's grasp was slipping as he approached his seventieth year. Insensitive towards his Gaelic subjects and at times rash in his foreign policy, William was at the same time on good terms with his feudal vassals; he overcame the crisis of 1174 and maximised his advantage throughout Richard's reign. There is the hint that from the time of the 'king's aid' raised to pay for the Treaty of Canterbury in 1189, William had the machinery to raise large sums of money, which none of his predecessors had been able to do; but this did not provoke the fury that John faced.

With all these apparent contradictions, William remains above all else the Norman feudaliser, welding his kingdom together more closely and extending the bounds of his authority. An English writer commented: 'The more recent kings of Scots profess themselves to be rather Frenchmen, both in race and in manners, language and culture; and after reducing the Scots to utter servitude, they admit only Frenchmen to their friendship and service'.[30] Although this statement exaggerates somewhat, it was with good reason that William's Gaelic subjects called him *Uilleam Garbh*, 'William the harsh'. His popular nickname William 'the Lion' is relatively modern, based either on the fact that medieval chroniclers call him a 'lion of justice', or on the adoption of the lion as the heraldic beast on his shield. William himself chose to be remembered through his great monastery of Arbroath, founded in 1178: a fitting memorial to a proud, stern and ambitious king.

CHAPTER 6

Reform of the Church

BISHOPS AND PARISHES

It has been seen that the Scottish Church in the sixth and seventh centuries had a high and deserved reputation for piety and scholarship. This it lost during the years of the Viking onslaught, when Iona was repeatedly pillaged and its community reduced. Churches also tended increasingly to become concerned with their worldly possessions. Adomnán's *Life of Columba* reads as an affectionate account of the life and works of a great and holy man; some Celtic saints' lives read like collections of title deeds, describing their heroes travelling the country and being given lands, churches and rights, which were carefully recorded for posterity.[1] By the eleventh century some of the great religious foundations, such as Dunkeld and Brechin, had come to be presided over by lay abbots who administered the abbey lands as a hereditary possession.

As well as monasteries there were bishoprics: the ancient churches of St Andrews, Dunkeld and Brechin had bishops, and there was a bishopric in Strathearn which eventually settled at Dunblane; further north, bishoprics are found later at Aberdeen and in the provinces of Moray, Ross and Caithness. In the south-west, Glasgow was the episcopal centre of the kingdom of Strathclyde, and there were bishops of Galloway at Whithorn. Many of these bishoprics were very obscure, and there appear to have been long episcopal vacancies. David, as prince of Cumbria, held an inquest into the possessions of the Church of Glasgow, and had to summon the ancient wise men of Strathclyde to reconstruct the bounds of the diocese and its episcopal lands and churches, because the bishopric itself had been vacant for so many years.[2] King David, when he set himself the task of remodelling and revitalising the Scottish Church, had much to do.

The Bishopric of Glasgow

The bishoprics had complex relations with kings, popes and English archbishops. The archbishops of York claimed that they had always exercised metropolitan rights over Scotland as part of the northern province. Durham was the only diocese in the province of York, so in order to be able to consecrate without recourse to bishops from the province of Canterbury, York maintained in his household two bishops with the titles of Orkney and the Isles (which they never visited); from the 1120s Galloway was added, when its bishop acknowledged the authority of York, and in the 1130s a diocese of Carlisle was created out of the southern part of the bishopric of Glasgow.[3] The rest of the Scottish bishops vigorously resisted English claims to superiority.

The tone of the struggle was set in the 1120s by a dispute over Glasgow. There were shadowy holders of the title 'bishop of Glasgow' in the eleventh century, but they may have been York titulars rather than resident bishops. When David became lord of Strathclyde c. 1113 he appointed John, a Tironensian monk, as bishop and carried out an inquest into the possessions of the see. David was concerned that Bishop John should be subject to no authority outside the kingdom of Scotland; but Thurstan archbishop of York demanded John's immediate submission. John, at David's insistence, appealed to the pope and travelled to Rome. When he got there, in 1122, Pope Calixtus II refused to uphold his case, and John, rather than return to face either David's wrath or submission to York, made a further journey to Jerusalem, where he occasionally took the patriarch's place at services in the Church of the Holy Sepulchre. But the pope would not let him rest, and ordered him to return at once to his diocese and make his submission to York. John did return to Scotland, but withheld his profession of obedience; the new pope (Honorius II) was still instructing him to do so in December 1125, having sent a cardinal legate to Scotland to resolve the dispute. David met the legate at Roxburgh and refused him entry to Scotland; and in 1126 he went further by sending Bishop John to the pope to ask for a *pallium* for the bishop of St Andrews and his creation as an archbishop.

Shortly before his death in 1124, King Alexander I had appointed Robert, prior of Scone, as bishop of St Andrews following a long vacancy. In 1128 Thurstan consecrated Robert without profession of obedience, and effectively admitted the independence of the Scottish Church.

But he would not give over his vendetta against Bishop John of Glasgow. In 1131–4 he was working on the new pope, Innocent II, to secure John's submission; one move was the erection of the new bishopric of Carlisle in an area which John claimed as part of his diocese and David as part of his kingdom. John was bombarded with bulls demanding his submission. By 1138 John had withdrawn from his see to live as a monk at Tiron.

King David and his bishops threatened to withdraw from the allegiance of Pope Innocent and transfer themselves to that of the antipope Anacletus II, but they were dissuaded by a new papal legate. Despite his 'defeat' at the Battle of the Standard, where the English troops had been commanded by Thurstan, David came out of it all rather well. He was forced to accept the bishopric of Carlisle, but probably intended to treat it as a Scottish bishopric after he obtained Cumbria; and he did not get the archiepiscopal *pallium* for St Andrews. But he did get the northern counties, he did preserve the independence of the Church in his kingdom, and John was able to return to his church at Glasgow without having to profess obedience to Thurstan.[4] When Bishop John died in 1147, his diocese remained free, and David was able to appoint another Tironensian monk, Herbert abbot of Kelso, as his successor. The archbishop of York could expect no more obedience from him than he had had from Bishop John.

During this long dispute, the archbishop of York did score one notable success. In about 1126, Fergus lord of Galloway appointed a new bishop to the see of Whithorn, who offered his submission and obedience to York.[5] The lords of Galloway may have been anxious that their bishops should not get sucked into a close-knit ecclesiastical system under the control of the Scottish kings. The diocese of Whithorn continued to offer its obedience to the archbishops of York from the twelfth to the fifteenth centuries, despite efforts to bring it into line with the other Scottish bishoprics.

No later bishops of Glasgow were consecrated by the archbishop of York. When Herbert was appointed (1147) the archbishopric was vacant, so he went to Pope Eugenius III; in 1164 his successor Ingram was consecrated by Alexander III 'although the messengers of Roger, archbishop of York, very greatly opposed it';[6] in 1175 Jocelin was consecrated by a papal legate. By the time of Jocelin's death in 1199, the battle was won. Popes would only support archbishops when it suited them.

The Bishopric of St Andrews

After the death of Bishop Robert of St Andrews in 1159, Pope Alexander III was reluctant to agree to Malcolm IV's proposal that St Andrews should have an archbishopric with metropolitan status. Malcolm's choice as the new bishop was Arnald abbot of Kelso. He held the legatine office, by virtue of which he consecrated a new bishop of Ross in 1161, and died in 1162. Malcolm then chose his chaplain Richard, for whom he clearly hoped for the legatine position and the archbishopric; when Roger archbishop of York appeared at Norham trying to enter Scotland as legate on pretext of the vacancy at St Andrews, Malcolm opposed him, 'and he returned thence in confusion'. Richard was consecrated at St Andrews by the bishops of Scotland in the presence of the king on 28 March 1165; a late chronicle says this was done 'be the papys lettrys speciall'.[7]

With the consecrations of Ingram to Glasgow and Richard to St Andrews in 1164–5, the question of supremacy over the Scottish Church fell into abeyance for a number of years. William's capture by Henry II in 1174 allowed that king to revive the claim of English superiority in church matters as it was being newly asserted in secular affairs; but Henry's heavy-handed methods proved counterproductive.

'A Special Daughter': Scotland and the Papacy

Henry II is best remembered by church historians for his infringements on ecclesiastical liberties which led to the murder of Archbishop Thomas Becket in Canterbury Cathedral in 1170. Pope Alexander III was unlikely to allow Henry a free hand in Scotland. Already in 1175 Alexander had written to Jocelin, bishop of Glasgow, taking his church under the special protection of St Peter, and calling the

Scottish Church 'our special daughter without intermediary'. But clauses in the Treaty of Falaise claimed rights for the Church of England over Scotland. Scottish bishops were summoned to York in 1175 and did homage to the archbishop, acknowledging his overlordship and right to consecrate. After William's release, they showed a much more combative attitude. When in 1176 Henry demanded that the Scottish bishops should profess obedience to York, 'they replied to him that their predecessors never made any subjection to the church of England, and neither ought they. . . . Then a great dispute arose between the archbishops of York and Canterbury about the receiving of that subjection. . . . And the bishops of Scotland . . . sent secretly to Pope Alexander, requesting that he would receive them in his own hand, and protect them from the subjection which the English church demanded of them.' Alexander replied to the Scottish bishops that they should 'attempt not to obey by metropolitan right any but the Roman pontiff by pretext of these oaths'.[8]

In church matters at least, the overbearing demands of the Treaty of Falaise had backfired for Henry II. The Scottish bishops exploited the fact that he had extracted these concessions due to William's capture, and played upon the disputes between king and pope and between York and Canterbury.

William and his bishops were united in resisting the demands of Henry II. When these demands were no longer a threat, William began to exercise his own authority, and became embroiled in a dispute over the bishopric of St Andrews. When Bishop Richard of St Andrews died in 1178, the chapter elected a well-educated career churchman, John Scott; but William ignored the election and presented one of his household servants, Hugh, and had him consecrated irregularly. John Scott appealed to Alexander III, who sent a legate to Scotland in 1180. John was consecrated by Scottish bishops with English protection, but William's hostility forced him to withdraw. He appealed to Henry II, who arranged a compromise whereby John was to accept another bishopric, the office of chancellor, and 40 marks from the revenues of St Andrews, and William was to end his hostility to the bishops who had consecrated John. This was unacceptable to the pope, who commanded John Scott to accept no bishopric other than the one to which he had been elected, made the archbishop of York his legate, and ordered him to excommunicate William and interdict the kingdom (in effect, to close all the churches and forbid all sacraments) if William continued to resist. William refused to comply, and the sentence was duly carried out in the autumn of 1181. A lengthy interdict, forbidding masses, baptisms, weddings, funerals and other sacraments, would have led to a crisis. William quickly sent Bishop Jocelin of Glasgow and others to the papacy; their task was made easier by the death of Alexander III and the archbishop of York, and the election of Lucius III as pope. Jocelin secured the lifting of the interdict and absolution of the king in March 1182, and Lucius, as a mark of special favour, awarded William the golden rose.[9] This was a token granted to a favoured secular ruler, often the prefect of the city of Rome, on mid-Lent Sunday; but Lucius had quarrelled with the prefect and citizens, so the contrite William was the recipient.

Dunkeld Cathedral. *(Alan Macquarrie)*

John and Hugh were summoned to appear before legates in Scotland in the summer of 1182. John, fearing for his safety, refused to come, and William persuaded the pope to allow Hugh to hold St Andrews. The pope secured the resignation of both pretenders early in 1183, conferred St Andrews on Hugh, and granted John Dunkeld with the other concessions offered by William. William appeared to have won. Hugh held St Andrews undisturbed from 1182 until 1186, when the new pope Urban III reopened the case. Thereafter John seems to have prevailed at the papal *curia*, and secured the deprivation and excommunication of Hugh early in 1188; John made peace with William, gave up St Andrews and was given Dunkeld. Hugh went to Rome, was absolved by Pope Clement III, and died in the city on 4 August 1188. William's troubles were over: St Andrews was given to his servant and chancellor Roger; Hugh of Roxburgh became chancellor in his place; John held Dunkeld.[10]

The dispute indicates William's determination to have his way, his bullying of opponents, and the strange mixture of stubbornness and skill which characterised many of his actions. Pope Alexander III could rightly claim that he had 'laboured with solicitude for the peace and liberty' of the Scottish Church; William, who had

Above: East End and St Rule's Tower, St Andrews Cathedral. *(Historic Scotland)*
Below: Elgin Cathedral from the south-east. *(Historic Scotland)*

to north-east and finally into the west. David I planted many churches on royal demesne, and he was imitated by his successors and knights. The practice began at an early date of giving a parish church to a religious house, a cathedral or monastery, to administer the revenues and appoint a clergyman; this was known as 'appropriation', and became an abuse in the later Middle Ages, though in the twelfth and thirteenth centuries it probably seemed the best way of ensuring sound administration. Thus David I gave many parishes in Clydesdale to Glasgow Cathedral; the Steward gave most of the parishes of Strathgryfe to his foundation, Paisley Abbey; William I gave many parishes in Angus and Mearns to Arbroath Abbey; and his brother Earl David gave the parish churches of his lands of Garioch to his foundation of Lindores. By the time of the first surviving survey of the Scottish Church for papal taxation in 1274, almost the whole country was divided into parishes, and already many of them were appropriated.[12] The process became more intense in the later Middle Ages, until by 1560 some 80 per cent of Scottish parishes were appropriated.[13]

THE NEW MONASTICISM

'At that time very many men, shut up in cells apart, in various places in the districts of the Scots, were living in the flesh, but not according to the flesh; for they led the life of angels upon earth. Queen [Margaret] endeavoured to love Christ in them, and to visit them often with her presence and conversation, and to commend herself to their prayers.' Thus Thurgot, St Margaret's biographer, describes the state of monasticism in Scotland c. 1070.[14] He does not name any of these anchorites or the places where they dwelt, except to imply that they were all north of the Forth ('in the districts of the Scots'). Since Thurgot had in his youth attempted unsuccessfully to revive the ancient monastery of Melrose, he was in a position to speak authoritatively of the lack of monasticism in south-east Scotland. Twelfth-century records do contain some fleeting references to these holy men: *Céli Dé* or Culdees at Lochleven, St Andrews, Abernethy, Muthill, Brechin and Monymusk, *clerici* at Deer in Buchan, *fratres* at Inchaffray, monks at Iona, hermits at various places.[15] So even in the eleventh century there were remnants of Celtic monasticism. But there were also signs of decay; at Brechin and Dunkeld, and probably elsewhere, the office of abbot and control of the monastic revenues had become the possession of a family of laymen. Some monasteries became colleges of secular clergy with wives and families.

Monastic Reform under Queen Margaret, Edgar and Alexander

How far it was St Margaret's influence which transformed Scottish monasticism in the twelfth century is arguable, but no one can doubt the importance of her sons in the process.

Whether Queen Margaret was responsible directly or indirectly, it is clear that a transformation took place; the number of monasteries increased (as did the number of monks), the new reformed Benedictine congregations were introduced into Scotland,

West door looking east, St Andrews Cathedral. *(Historic Scotland)*

Opposite: Dunblane Cathedral. *(Historic Scotland)*

and vast amounts of royal and non-royal land were given to religious houses, so that they became great and wealthy property-owning corporations. Although some Celtic communities of *Céli Dé* or *clerici* survived into the thirteenth century, none survived beyond it; most were converted into Augustinian or Benedictine houses. Celtic monasteries seem to have followed their founder's rules. The Benedictine Rule enjoined the threefold virtues of poverty, chastity and obedience, the seven daily offices with their emphasis on the psalter, more frequent mass and less fasting than Celtic rules. It did not become popular until it spread widely in Gaul and England in the eighth century; it was taut but not over-demanding, and it was adaptable. Successive relaxations led to attempts at collective reform by families of monasteries. The earliest of these 'reformed Benedictine' congregations was that headed by the Abbey of Cluny in Burgundy, founded in 909. At Cluny there was emphasis on contemplation and the service of the choir and altar with magnificent ceremony, and a reduction of emphasis on manual labour. Some later reformed Benedictine congregations, most notably the Cistercians, stressed simplicity and austerity in the church and manual labour. The other popular rule of the period was the so-called Augustinian Rule, a rather vaguer set of precepts for the religious life practised by canons rather than monks, which made it suitable for the conversion of houses of *Céli Dé*. All new monasteries in Scotland followed rules based on either the Benedictine or the Augustinian Rule. Reformed congregations sought to maintain a close relationship between the mother house and the daughter houses of its congregation by regular visitations and summonses to attend chapters-general. Those monasteries which were not members of reformed congregations were autonomous, maintaining their own discipline without supervision.

The reformed monasticism which was sweeping the West in the tenth, eleventh and twelfth centuries would find great favour with Queen Margaret and her sons. The story began soon after Margaret's marriage to Malcolm III in *c.* 1070, when she entered into correspondence with Lanfranc archbishop of Canterbury. She complained of certain abuses permitted by the Scots, and requested that the archbishop send her monks from Canterbury to found a monastery at Dunfermline. Lanfranc replied:

> I send to your glorious husband and yourself our dear brother Goldewine, as you request, and two other brothers, because he cannot perform alone the service of God and your desire. And I ask insistently, that what you have commenced for God and your own souls, you should bring to completion quickly and efficiently; and if you can and wish to continue the work by means of others, we request earnestly that you send these our brothers back to us, because they are necessary for the offices of our church. But let your will be done; we desire to obey you in all things.[16]

Her will was in effect the foundation of the Benedictine priory of Dunfermline, colonised by three monks from Canterbury. Within half a century it had become very wealthy. There is also evidence of a continuing relationship between Dunfermline and Canterbury well into the twelfth century. The church, whose nave survives as one of the great Romanesque monuments of Scotland, was dedicated in 1150 at a great ceremony attended by King David and a host of magnates clerical and lay. In 1245 the abbot received the honour of wearing the episcopal mitre and ring from the pope as a mark of special favour. Also in the mid-thirteenth century the choir and east end were rebuilt as a sumptuous shrine for the tomb of St Margaret, in emulation of Henry III, who rebuilt Westminster Abbey as a shrine for Edward the Confessor.

We have a record of Edgar's generosity to Dunfermline, but his reign was too short for him to found any other monasteries. His brother Alexander did more of this work. Alexander's achievement was the foundation of the Augustinian priory of Scone, near the royal palace and enthronement seat. It was colonised by canons from Nostell in Yorkshire. Inchcolm, Loch Tay and St Andrews were projected Augustinian foundations of this time, but none of them came into being during Alexander's lifetime, and only Inchcolm and St Andrews did so during David I's reign.[17]

The Foundations of David I

King David I was the founder of monasteries *par excellence*, 'a sair sanct for the croun', as his descendant James VI called him. Even before he became king he was already a generous benefactor of monasteries and churches. His earliest foundation was a house of Tironensian monks at Selkirk *c.* 1113. The abbey of Tiron had been founded by St Bernard of Tiron in 1109 as a very austere community reacting against the grandeur of Cluny, and had early won the patronage of Henry I and of Earl David. Selkirk was the first monastery of its order in the British Isles, and the earliest congregation of reformed Benedictines founded in Britain. In 1128 the monastery was moved from the royal town of Selkirk to Kelso near the royal centre of Roxburgh. The abbots of Kelso had great pretensions. The abbey church, built in the second half of the twelfth century, must have been magnificent. The west end has similar arrangement and proportions to Ely Cathedral, which stood close to the lordship of Huntingdon: a great west tower, short western transepts and porch, and a tall, narrow nave.

King David, having taken the step of introducing reformed Benedictines into his principality in 1113, was by no means finished. His next major foundation, though, was of Augustinians, at Holyrood beside Edinburgh *c.* 1128. David's monastic foundation beside Stirling, Cambuskenneth Abbey (founded in 1140), was a house of monks from Arrouaise in Picardy, the only monastery of the Arrouaisian order in Scotland.

David completed his brother Alexander's project of founding an Augustinian house at Inchcolm in the Firth of Forth, and converted houses of *Céli Dé* at Lochleven and St Andrews into houses of canons regular. At St Andrews (founded 1144), site of the premier bishopric of the kingdom with the most magnificent cathedral, the Augustinian Rule was used for the chapter. The great cathedral, begun by Bishop Arnald in 1160, was by far the biggest and grandest church in Scotland.

More complete, and perhaps giving a better idea of what a great Augustinian abbey church should look like, is David's great border abbey of Jedburgh. It was founded in 1138 and colonised by canons from the monastery of St Quentin at Beauvais.

Kelso Abbey: west tower and transept. (*Historic Scotland*)

Jedburgh is one of the most complete Romanesque buildings in Scotland, belonging mostly to the second half of the twelfth century.

Other new religious orders entered Scotland under David I. Hugh de Paiens, first grand master of the Knights Templars, visited Scotland in 1128, met King David, and was given Balantrodoch (now Temple), Midlothian, for the founding of a Scottish commandery of Templars. The rival military order of Hospitallers also came to Scotland during King David's reign and was given Torphichen, West Lothian, for its preceptory.

The monks of Cluny had only one royal foundation at this time: David brought monks from Reading to the Isle of May *c*. 1140. They soon acquired a mainland base at Pittenweem in Fife, but the choice of so wild a spot for the least austere of the Benedictine congregations is curious. Scotland's greatest Cluniac abbey, at Paisley, was founded by the king's Steward, Alan fitz Walter lord of Renfrew.

David's other foundation for unreformed Benedictines was Coldingham Priory. This was a daughter house of the great Benedictine monastery of Durham; the lands of Coldingham were given to Durham by King Edgar *c*. 1105, but there is no evidence of a religious community there until *c*. 1140, when a prior of Coldingham is mentioned. Coldingham maintained a close relationship with Durham until the Wars of Independence and beyond; there were still English monks from Durham there in the fifteenth century, though not without intermission.

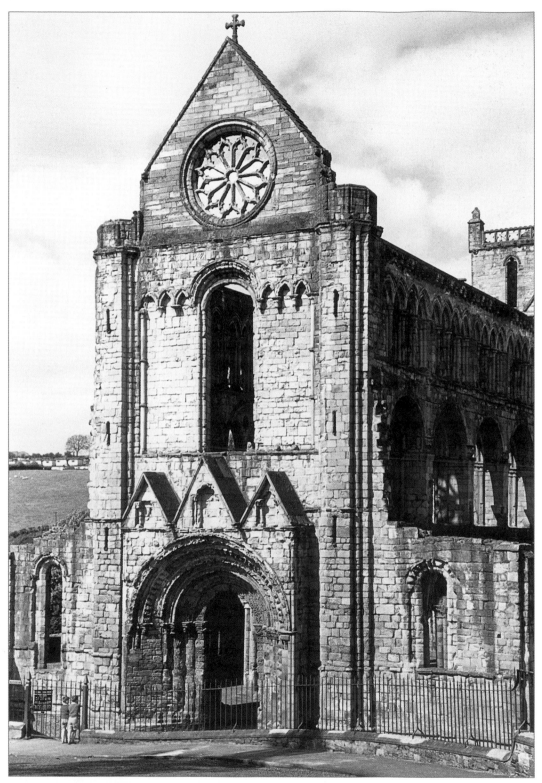

Jedburgh Abbey. *(Historic Scotland)*

But the religious order which is most closely associated with King David I is the Cistercians. The monastery of Cîteaux in Burgundy was established in 1098 by Robert of Molesme. It was inevitable that this great austere and intellectual order, with its stress on simplicity and manual labour, should have made a profound impact on the king. His first Cistercian foundation was at Melrose on the Tweed. This was about three miles upriver from Old Melrose, where St Cuthbert had been a monk in the seventh century. The abbey buildings are among the finest monastic remains in Scotland. Melrose produced monks of the highest integrity and ability, and many of the abbots became bishops. One of the greatest achievements of Melrose was its fine *Chronicle*, the best Scottish monastic chronicle, kept in a series of fine contemporary hands continuously for over a century. Another Cistercian stress was on labour, and here the monks of Melrose were again successful; they ran profitable sheep-farms on the Southern Uplands, and shipped vast amounts of wool to Flanders each year from the port of Berwick.

Sheep-farming was also practised by Melrose's first daughter-house at Newbattle in Midlothian, founded in 1140. This too was a royal foundation, in which King David was joined by his son Earl Henry. No motive for the foundation is known, but the king may have felt it was desirable to have a Cistercian house nearer to the important centres at Edinburgh and Haddington.

David's other Cistercian foundation was at Kinloss in Moray in 1150. Despite its remoteness, Kinloss was generously endowed. Its foundation should probably be associated with the plantation of Moray in the years following the death of the last native earl, Angus, in 1130, when we find knights building castles, and a sheriff and royal burgh at Inverness.

David's successors were not lacking in piety, but none of them equalled him in generosity to the religious orders. Malcolm IV founded the great Cistercian house of Coupar Angus (*c.* 1161), following a project of his grandfather's; William I founded the Tironensian house of Arbroath (1178) and dedicated it to St Thomas Becket, the churchman murdered by his enemy Henry II; his brother Earl David founded another Tironensian monastery, at Lindores in Fife *c.* 1191; William's son King Alexander II founded a Valliscaulian house at Pluscarden in Moray *c.* 1230.

Non-royal Foundations

The royal house was not alone in founding monasteries in the twelfth and thirteenth centuries. Scotland's greatest Cluniac house was Paisley, founded by the Stewart lords of Renfrew *c.* 1163. David's trusted counsellor Hugh de Moreville, lord of Cunninghame and Lauderdale, founded two monasteries: a Tironensian house at Kilwinning, and a Premonstratensian house in a beautiful setting at Dryburgh on the Tweed. This order was established by St Norbert at Prémontré near Laon in 1120. Dryburgh was their first and most important house in Scotland; they had others at Soulseat in Galloway, founded by Fergus of Galloway *c.* 1161; at Whithorn, where Premonstratensian canons formed the cathedral chapter from *c.* 1175; and at Fearn in

Above: Melrose Abbey. *(Historic Scotland) Below:* Dryburgh Abbey. *(Historic Scotland)*

Easter Ross, whither Fearchar earl of Ross brought canons from Whithorn in the 1220s. There was also an obscure Premonstratensian house at Tongland in Kirkcudbright from 1218, probably founded by Alan of Galloway, son of Fergus's grandson Roland. Roland had founded a Cistercian house at Glenluce c. 1191, following Fergus's own example of the foundation of Dundrennan, with Cistercian monks from Rievaulx, in 1142. The surviving crossing and transepts at Dundrennan are typically Cistercian in their fine proportions and austere restraint.

The religious orders penetrated into other parts of the kingdom into the thirteenth century. Ranald son of Somerled brought Cistercians to Saddell in Kintyre from Melifont in Ireland c. 1200, and transformed Iona itself into an independent Benedictine house c. 1203. The very austere and small order of Valliscaulians, named from Val des Choux near Langres in eastern France, had no monasteries outside France except for three small Scottish priories, at Pluscarden in Moray (founded by Alexander II), Beauly in Easter Ross, and Ardchattan in Argyll (founded by Duncan Macdougall of Lorn); all were founded c. 1230. The Celtic monastery of Inchaffray was converted into an Augustinian abbey by Gilbert, earl of Strathearn in 1200. Duncan son of Gilbert, lord of Carrick, brought Cluniacs from Paisley to Crossraguel in south Ayrshire c. 1214. There was a hospital of 'canons of Bethlehem' at St Germains in Tranent, possibly founded by Robert de Quincy c. 1170. There were many other small religious houses about which very little is known. Trinitarians and Gilbertines, and orders of mendicant friars, Franciscans and Dominicans, entered Scotland in the second quarter of the thirteenth century.

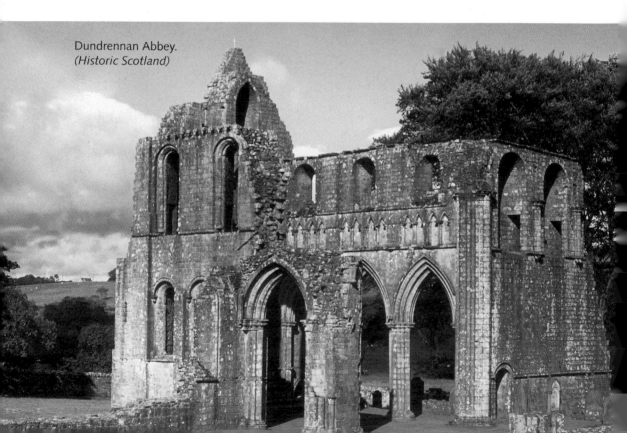

Dundrennan Abbey.
(Historic Scotland)

An example of a Cistercian foundation late in the thirteenth century is Dervorgilla (*Derbforgaill*) of Galloway's foundation of Sweetheart Abbey with monks from Dundrennan in 1273, where she was buried before the high altar holding her Balliol husband's embalmed heart in a silver casket. The ruins of Sweetheart, in its buildings typical of the best thirteenth-century Cistercian work, are a fitting crown to the religious houses of Galloway and to the work of Dervorgilla's ancestors.

Sweetheart Abbey. *(Historic Scotland)*

Medieval Monasticism

What were the motives behind this great outburst of generosity to religious institutions in the twelfth and early thirteenth centuries? What was the *raison d'être* of the monasteries, and the social contribution of the monks? Of course, kings and nobles were imbued with the conventional piety of the time; they believed that generosity of this sort would aid their passage into the heavenly kingdom. Their grants to religious houses were usually made 'in alms' or 'free and quit of all secular exaction', for the benefit of the souls of the grantors, their ancestors and successors. Often their grants specified certain pious works to be performed by the monks, the saying of certain masses for the souls of the grantor and his family, feeding and clothing certain numbers of poor folk, maintaining hospitality, and so on. Cluny and other great monasteries viewed their existence as being primarily for the purpose of the *opus Dei*, celebrating masses and offices, and all other tasks were secondary. The early twelfth-century reformed houses, like the Cistercians, stressed austerity, manual labour and the good lives of the monks; in their chronicles and sheep-farms we might see more of utilitarian value, and these considerations must have weighed with contemporaries as well. Monasteries provided other benefits: monks ran schools, so they were centres of learning; the monks were an educated literate elite at a time when even kings could not write their own names.

There were few nunneries compared with houses of men. Pious women were considered laudable, but the social position of women restricted their range of activities. Medieval Scotland had only about a dozen nunneries, and only the Cistercian nunnery at Haddington was really wealthy; it was founded by Countess Ada, wife of Earl Henry and mother of Kings Malcolm and William, the most important female personality in twelfth-century Scotland. Some nunneries were founded in the interest of a female member of a powerful family: for example, at Iona nunnery, founded by Ranald son of Somerled *c.* 1203, the first prioress was Ranald's sister Beathoc.

The monasteries were to retain their value and usefulness for centuries; it was not until the rise of lay literacy and learning in the sixteenth century, and the questioning of the old values of monastic prayer, the *opus Dei* and contemplative life, that the monasteries were swept away by the rising tide of the Reformation. For four hundred years they had provided essential services to the kingdom, and had mostly done it well.

CHAPTER 7

Economy and Society in Medieval Scotland

FEUDALISM: A NEW WAY OF LIFE?

Of all the social innovations associated with David I and twelfth-century Scotland, the best known is feudalism. Feudalism is a form of land tenure whereby the grantee holds his land of his lord in return for the performance of military service. The grant and its conditions are guaranteed by a written deed, in Latin, called a charter.

Feudalism had its origins in northern France during the late Carolingian period. It was stimulated by the need for defence during the period of Viking attacks and the development of the Carolingian monarchy. Cavalry warfare was a new development of this period, unknown in Britain; it demanded a level of training, equipment and discipline unknown since the days of the Roman legions. With the mounted knight went the castle, a natural site or man-made earthen mound fortified against attack. Although later sanctified by chivalry and Christianity, early knighthood had a brutal and ruthless ethos. By the early eleventh century, this 'feudalism' had spread across northern France from Brittany to Flanders and included Viking Normandy. Effectively exploited by the dukes of Normandy, feudalism provided them with a powerful cavalry force which could challenge and defeat the infantry levies of the most efficiently governed kingdom in Europe – Anglo-Saxon England. The result of William's victory was the occupation of England by an alien and unpopular foreign army, the need for military strength to counter the threat of rebellion, and the parcelling of the country into knight's fees to maintain a standing army. Between 1066 and 1100 England became as intensely feudalised as any kingdom in Europe.

Feudalism is not the only form of exploitation of land and its occupants for military purposes; the army Harold Godwineson led to victory at Stanford Bridge and destruction at Hastings was based on land exploitation (hidage), but was not a cavalry force, and was not a 'feudal army'. The Anglo-Saxon *fyrd* or common army, a levy led by warrior-aristocrats under their chosen king, went back to Germanic models of the heroic age. Celtic society was similar in many ways, so we should expect to find broadly similar forms of non-feudal military exploitation in Celtic countries.

Pre-feudal Scotland

Senchus fer nAlban is a survey and assessment of seventh-century Argyll for military purposes. At a later period and in a different part of the country, the Gaelic notes in the Book of Deer show exactions due to king, *mormaer* and *toisech*, all of whom had military as well as fiscal functions.[1] *Mormaer* are also called *duces*, *comites* and *satrapes*, and probably developed out of the *exactatores* (exploiters, tax-gatherers) who surrounded Pictish kings in battle. All of this shows that military service was an imposition on the land, even if it does not imply the contractual nature of the bond guaranteed by charter. Pre-feudal society was both rural and hierarchical, presided over by a military aristocracy and exploited for their purposes – war and such other pursuits as hunting, feasting, and generosity to churches and poets. So in one sense at least feudalism was not new; it allowed the aristocracy to continue the activities of centuries. Twelfth-century charters contain many references to types of military service which must be pre-feudal, and include summons to 'common army', 'Scottish service', and 'forinsec service'. It is uncertain what regional variations existed within the term 'common army'. In the north and Fife, where 'Scottish service' is mentioned, the army was led by the *mormaer* and obligation was assessed by the local unit of arable, the *davoch*, perhaps as much as 200 acres or more. South of the Forth there were officers with an equivalent function. Perhaps under the leadership of Cospatrick of Dunbar and his like, they were administrators of the royal demesne, collecting the kings rents and dues, and summoning and leading his common army. In this area the unit of assessment was the carucate, a unit familiar also in English Northumbria. In Lennox, part of ancient Strathclyde, there are traces of different arrangements for the 'common army' or pre-feudal host, based on a unit of land called the *arachor*. One of these has given its name to the village of Arrochar at the head of Loch Long.

The Scottish kings had plenty of provision for military service in the eleventh century. But Malcolm III's experiences showed clearly that the Scottish common army of footsoldiers led by earls and thanes could not withstand William's Norman cavalry with their superior weapons, tactics and discipline. And the sons of Malcolm, with their close association with the English court, felt the need to have a court of knightly retainers on the continental model.

The Introduction of Feudalism

Sir Archibald Lawrie's great collection of *Early Scottish Charters*, containing 270 texts prior to 1153, includes only two documents which mention knight service. There are a number of explanations for this. The vast bulk of the surviving documents are ecclesiastical charters, and churches did not contribute knights, though they were due for common army service. One of Lawrie's charters, a grant of Annandale to Robert Brus, does not mention knight service, though subsequent confirmations make it clear that knight service was involved. Charters were the title deeds of the grantee, drawn up for their benefit, and were more concerned to enumerate the benefits conferred on them than their obligations. Thus they often have extensive lists of the bounds of their lands and the privileges which went with them, ending with the laconic phrase 'for the service of one knight', without stating what knight service involved – as if that were well understood and did not need to be explained. We know of knights who served the king but whose charters have not survived. The proportion of survival of ecclesiastical charters to that of secular ones is very much greater, because churches did not undergo the vicissitudes of hereditary landed families.

The first Norman knights to take service in Scotland were the small band exiled from England in 1052, who under their leader Osbern Pentecost came to Scotland and served Macbeth. They were all killed in battle in 1054, and there was no repeat of this innovation.[2] Although Queen Margaret is said to have surrounded herself with foreigners and civilised the manners of Malcolm III's court, her attendants seem to have been women and churchmen, and there is no evidence for feudal knighthood during Malcolm III's reign. But Malcolm's sons were much more open to influences from the south, as hostages of English kings or attendants at their court. Malcolm's son by his first marriage, Duncan, was accepted as king by the pre-feudal magnates who had earlier chosen his uncle Donald Bán, when 'he hastened to the kingdom with a host of English and Normans and drove him out'; they expelled the foreigners, and 'after this they allowed him to reign; but on this condition, that he should never again introduce into Scotland English or Normans, or allow them to give him military service'.[3] So there is the suggestion that in 1094 Duncan began the process of introducing knights and knight service into Scotland, but was opposed by the earls and other leaders. King Edgar (1097–1107) was, like Duncan, heavily dependent on foreign help in obtaining and holding his kingdom, but there is little evidence of new knights being introduced and given fiefs. A rare example is Robert son of Godwine, an English knight to whom the king gave lands in Lothian on which he began to build a castle, and who later accompanied Edgar Atheling to the Holy Land. But Robert was not part of a general trend; the Scots who joined the first crusade (1095–9) were mostly noted for their lack of knightly arms and their simple faith.[4] The beginnings of real evidence for feudalism in Scotland come from the reign of Edgar's brother Alexander I (1107–24). Alexander's brother David became lord of Cumbria c. 1114, and over the next ten years proceeded to parcel it out into large fiefs for Anglo-Norman knights. This reflects determination on David's part to feudalise his new lordship as quickly as possible, and to do it with colonists from his great English lordship of Huntingdon-Northampton.

When David I became king in 1124, he continued the process of settling Anglo-Normans for knight service, but now this was extended into Lothian as well; the fiefs involved were smaller, and the knight service demanded was less. But it was not only Anglo-Normans who received grants on this basis. David granted Calder in West Lothian to Earl Duncan of Fife by charter, in return for knight service. Another charter of King David to Earl Duncan stated that the king granted him the earldom of Fife itself in return for a specified knight service. This is a 'striking testimony to the lengths to which David was prepared to go in the introduction of feudalism into

Scotland. Yet it should not be regarded as typical.' In Fife we do begin to find the introduction of Anglo-Normans during David's reign, evidently with the cooperation of the earls.[5]

With the forfeiture of the earldom of Moray in 1130, David had the opportunity to make infeftments on comital lands in that area. Freskin, granted lands in Duffus and Spynie, was a Fleming, and there are later indications of a degree of Flemish settlement in Moray. His descendants took the surname *de Moravia*, 'of Moray' (now Murray), which indicates an important position in the northern province.

The obvious gaps in the feudalisation of David I's reign were Clydesdale and the land north of the Forth. The plantation of these areas belonged to the reigns of David I's grandsons, Malcolm IV and William I.

In between, as what has been described as a bridge between the earlier and later phases of Anglo-Norman colonisation of Scotland, we should set the marriage of Earl Henry to Ada de Warenne, daughter of Earl William de Warenne. Earl Henry may have been given Haddington by his father – certainly Countess Ada resided there during her later life – and some tenants of the Warenne estates in Upper Normandy were given fiefs in East Lothian.

Feudalism under the Grandsons of David I

During Malcolm IVs reign (1153–65) the colonisation of Clydesdale was carried out. Baldwin the Fleming, lord of Biggar and sheriff of Lanark, is first recorded in 1162. David Olifard received land at Bothwell, the origin of the Scottish family of Oliphant, and also of the great lordship of Bothwell with its castle. Malcolm IV also gave lands to a Fleming called Tancard, who has given his name to Thankerton near Bothwell and Thankerton near Lanark. Other Clydesdale towns and villages bear names of Flemings: Wiston (Wice), Lamington (Lambin), Symington (Simon Lockhard). A charter of Malcolm IV to the church of Glasgow in 1165 hints that he had been systematically depriving the church of lands from which it had been accustomed to draw certain royal rights; in compensation, Malcolm gave the church Glasgow Green.

The colonisation of the lands between Tay and Spey was a phenomenon of the reign of William I (1165–1214). The main features of his colonisation of the north-east were in ecclesiastical terms the foundation of his great abbey of Arbroath, and in secular terms the creation of the great lordship of Garioch in Aberdeenshire for his brother David, which he held for a service of ten knights;[6] grants on this scale had become uncommon. Perhaps more typical was the almost contemporary (c. 1178) grant of Errol in the Carse of Gowrie to William de Hay for the service of two knights, or the grant of lands in Fife near Abernethy to Henry Revel for one knight's service. William planted a number of knights in Angus, Mearns and Gowrie throughout his reign. In some cases he granted a thane's rights with the lands. The number of sheriffdoms in the north-east was increased, and their tenure became more continuous. William had to suppress major rebellions in Galloway and Ross; but

Top: Bothwell Castle. *(Historic Scotland)*
Below: Caerlaverock Castle, Dumfriesshire. *(Historic Scotland)*

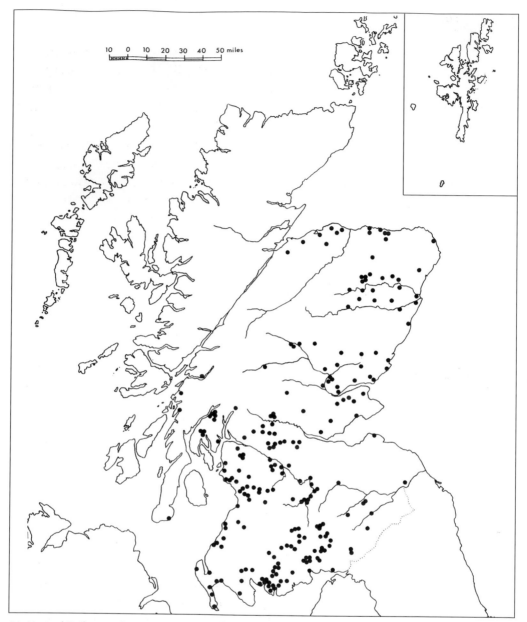

Motte and Bailey castles. *(Geoffrey Stell; by permission of the Trustees of the Historical Atlas of Scotland)*

these areas do not figure in his charters as great areas of plantation of knights. Mottes, a sure sign of the knight's fief, are thickly distributed in south-west Scotland as far as the Cree, but are thin in Wigtownshire. Similarly, they spread evenly from the Forth to the Ness, but not beyond. Mottes are mostly a twelfth-century phenomenon; in the thirteenth century castles tended to be built of stone. So the map of mottes is in effect the map of feudal Scotland by the end of William I's reign.

The Significance of Feudalism

The military context is the most obvious *raison d'être* of feudalism; it is clear that the Scottish kings built up a military machine of some cohesion and effectiveness. On the other hand, the contrast between the effectiveness of the feudal army in suppressing internal rebellion and its inadequacies in a pitched battle against the English is a recurring theme.

But feudalism had other significances as well. It was a force for social cohesion; knights were bound together by their chivalric code – courage and loyalty, respect for the persons of women and churchmen and for church property, conventional piety, love of hunting, jousting and adventure, and a taste for chivalric lore and poetry enshrined in the newly popular Arthurian romance. The only Scottish romance which survives from this period is the *Roman de Fergus*, a skilful interweaving of chivalrous romantic themes with Scottish topography and persons composed for a Galloway prince in the early thirteenth century.[7] An interest in the crusades and the fortunes of the Holy Land is evident among Scottish knighthood, especially from the time of the fall of Jerusalem (1187) onwards.[8]

Was the feudalisation of Scotland a great social revolution? It certainly meant that kings could not be overthrown by internal opponents, as tenth- and eleventh-century kings had been; feudal vassals knew their place in a way which the great hereditary *mormaer* sometimes did not, and the crown was more secure in its relation with its nobility than before. The social ethos of knighthood also made great changes, so that a prince of Galloway could be regaled with a French Arthurian romance rather than a Gaelic praise-song. But many traditional features of society remained: the earldoms themselves, the common army, the ancient loyalty to the kings of Scots and their kingdom. It was perhaps these, more than feudalism, which were to see Scotland through the darkest days of the Wars of Independence.

BURGHS: TOWNSMEN AND TRADERS

The Roman empire was a collection of urban centres, each with specialist artisans and traders. In the fifth century this trade declined and many towns, particularly in the northern parts of the Empire, fell into decay. London had been a flourishing Roman port as late as *c.* 400, but within twenty-five years a money economy had disappeared in Britain, and the great buildings of the city were falling into disuse. At York, a great Roman basilica was still standing centuries later, and was systematically demolished to make way for Anglo-Saxon buildings. North of Hadrian's Wall there were no urban centres. Trading posts on major routes, and the tribal *oppida* of local kings, hardly constitute an equivalent to Roman cities. Scotland had never been part of the Roman empire, so there were no cities to fall into decay; and, with the upswing of north–south trade in the tenth and eleventh centuries, there were no towns to be revived.

There was, of course, trade in Dark Age Scotland. The Church needed certain imports, wine and precious materials, for ritual purposes. Adomnán tells a story of how Columba went to a port to await the arrival of ships from the continent which brought news from Italy. But there was no equivalent of the Anglo-Saxon town, often built over a Roman city, which carried on in a limited way the trade of the Empire.

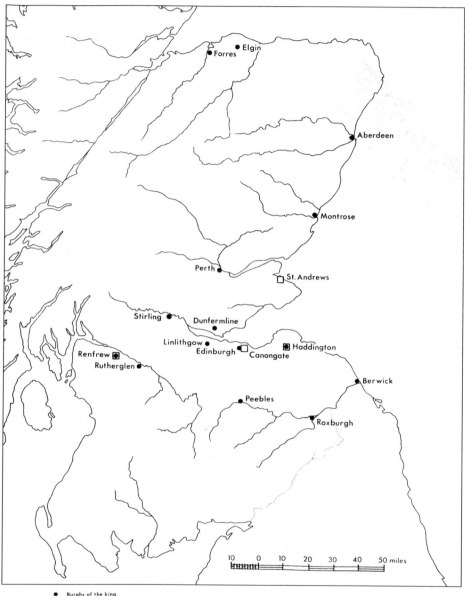

Burghs by 1153. *(A.A.M. Duncan; by permission of the Trustees of the Historical Atlas of Scotland)*

We should expect to find important trading centres in eastern Scotland at the junctions of land, river and sea routes, close to royal centres. Edinburgh stood below the royal castle guarding the gap between the Pentland Hills and the Firth of Forth, astride a major land route and served by the natural harbour at Leith. At Stirling, the castle controlled the lowest fords on the Forth at the highest point to which seagoing ships could ascend. St Andrews has a fine natural harbour at a place which was a major religious centre from the eighth century. On the Tay, Perth stood at the highest point to which seagoing ships could navigate, at a crossing of the Tay, and at the seaward end of a great complex of land and river routes. Further north, Montrose stood at a natural harbour where the South Esk narrows between Montrose basin and the sea. Aberdeen also stood at a natural harbour near the mouth of the Dee and controlled land and river routes down from Mar, but was also near the mouth of the Don with its religious centre of St Machar. Banff, Forres and Invernairn, at the points where the Deveron, Findhorn and Nairn flow into the Moray Firth, were natural trading sites. The most important of all these northern trading sites is Inverness, at the northern outlet of the Great Glen. Here timbers from the Caledonian Forest were floated down Loch Ness to Inverness and fashioned into ships for export, and other rural produce of the brae of Moray came to be sold and shipped south. As at Perth, there was no natural castle site at Inverness, so the castle was placed on an artificially raised mound near the river.[9]

Burgh is a Germanic word meaning a fortress. The town seems to have been normally a place where trade developed naturally because of the advantages of the site and where a king or lord chose to erect a place of protection, a *burgh*. Commerce came first, defence later. Some burghs, however, had few natural advantages for commercial development. Here the presence of a royal hall or castle must have been the dominant factor. The royal hall was an important centre in any area, a place to which the king's rents in kind were brought, livestock, cheeses, grain, etc. At these places there must have been surpluses to be disposed of when the king and court were not in residence; and when the king was present with a large court, there must have been the need to acquire extra produce. A market and commercial centre were ideal for such a place, and became so important as to be almost indispensable at major royal centres. This is why the name *burgh* came to be applied to towns; the king's castle and the king's market went together.

A town also provided accommodation when the court was meeting. In the autumn of 1209 a large court was assembled at Perth to discuss ways of raising the sum which William I had promised King John by the treaty of that year. A sudden flood on the Tay carried off the royal castle, a motte-and-bailey structure between the town and the North Inch. The great magnates saved themselves by climbing into the uppermost rooms of the houses in which they were staying, from which they were rescued by a fleet of small boats. The chamberlain, an officer of the king's household, had the responsibility for arranging accommodation for the magnates and courtiers attending the king as he travelled; this must have been much easier where there were many burgesses' houses in the locality. So all big courts, summoned to discuss taxation, war, or great events, must have met in or near towns, which were fostered by the king for such purposes.

Some towns must have existed before the twelfth century, but from the reign of David I we read about burghs. *Burgh* is, above all else, a legal status. It implies a set of rights and privileges conferred by the king on a place either where commerce already exists or where he wishes it to develop. A charter granted by William I to Perth in *c.* 1209 speaks of dealing with matters as was done in the time of David I, so burghal privileges were well established by the first half of the twelfth century.

A burgh had a regional area over which it had privileges and in which it had a right to tolls on merchandise and fines for merchandise sold illegally outwith the burgh. Within its bounds the burgh had a right to tolls and customs on all merchandise, and could exact a fine or confiscation for items on which toll had been withheld; nothing was to be sold within the bounds which had not first been exposed for sale at the burgh market. The grant of burghal status conferred protection and privilege, ensuring that trade would thrive in areas designated by the king.

William's charter to Perth speaks of burgesses, or some of them, as men of status; but not all burgesses were so free. Some transactions implied that some burgesses were not 'free', but clients who could be given to another master, as some categories of unfree men could be passed from one master to another. By contrast, we read of a burgess 'free and quit of all burgess service except watch', and with the right that 'if he wishes to leave the town he may do so, and may sell his house and toft in the burgage'. William's charter to Perth gives the burgesses the right to have their merchant guild, 'except for the fullers and weavers'. Clearly, some professions were beginning to rise in status and others were becoming depressed. Merchants, who controlled capital, were rising in status, and some craftsmen who required wealth for their trade, such as goldsmiths and dyers, were rising with them.

Already early in the thirteenth century guilds were becoming exclusive societies which would come increasingly to dominate urban politics, forming an oligarchy which would govern the town to the exclusion of non-capitalist artisans. The documents say very little about burgh organisation in its earliest phase. *Prepositi* and *ballivi* are mentioned, but we have not yet got to the stage of having a single provost who presides over a group of bailies in the town council. But by the time the *Leges burgorum* were drawn up in the late twelfth century, burgess status had become clearly defined and self-regulating conditions for admission to burgesship established.

Burghs sought to be self-governing communities free from interference from the king's sheriff and custumar. Originally, burghs and sheriffdoms with their royal castles were closely associated, and the king's sheriff played an important part in the administration of the burgh, collecting rents and gathering tolls and customs, often through the intermediary of a custumar. Increasingly from 1200 the burgesses farmed the burgh themselves and elected their own provosts; burgh seals appear, which must indicate some measure of urban self-government. In some cases, natural events helped the burgesses to escape from control by the sheriff, as at Perth where the destruction of the castle in the floods of 1209 obliged the sheriff to set up his storehouses outside the town; the castle was never rebuilt. In other cases, political events must have helped: when Roxburgh, Berwick, Edinburgh and Stirling castles were occupied by English garrisons from 1175, royal authority in these burghs must have been curtailed and the burgesses became more independent. William I's acts show that he was anxious to maintain his authority in towns; but twenty years later he had bowed to the inevitable and accepted burgh self-government. The maps show that the increase in numbers and spread of burghs in the twelfth and thirteenth centuries correspond closely to the spread of royal authority throughout the kingdom.

Burghs were planted by the king, colonised by Englishmen from Newcastle, Norwich or King's Lynn, or by Flemings. Flemish settlement seems to have been particularly significant in the Moray Firth burghs. There are parallels with the planting of Flemish knights as feudal colonists in Moray after 1130.

By far the biggest burghs were Berwick and Perth, which had 80 and 70 burgesses respectively subscribing Edward I's homage rolls in 1291. That does not indicate the total population, but may approximate closely to the number of prosperous burgess families, which would have had women, children and servants; in addition there were probably more, or at least as many, poorer artisan families who would at one time have had, but later lost, burgess status. There were also the houses of royal officers, sheriffs, custumars and chamberlain's men; the great magnates and religious institutions, bishops and monasteries, would have had their town houses in Berwick, Edinburgh or Perth. The biggest burghs must have been towns of several thousand people. Archaeology and documents suggest that Perth was very crowded in the thirteenth century, and the same is probably true of Berwick and Edinburgh.

The earliest burghs were enclosed with a ditch and palisade, more to prevent thieving and straying of livestock than for defence; at Perth, however, the defences must have been stout enough to prevent the rebellious earls from seizing the king in 1160, or at least to hold them up long enough for Malcolm IV to slip out of the town. By 1312, probably earlier, Perth had stone walls. This was unusual; Berwick, the town most vulnerable to English attacks and the greatest urban prize in Scotland, had only a ditch and palisade when Edward I seized it in 1296. Towns had gates and watch-towers (often represented on their seals) to control commerce as much as to repel invaders, and burgesses had an obligation to perform watch and to enclose their tenements. At Inverness, in hostile countryside during the mac Heth and mac William risings, 'provision was made for enclosure by a good ditch and stout palisade', and after 1296 the burgesses of Berwick paid a tax for the upkeep of the walls.

Within the burgh, the main feature was the market-place, usually a widening of the High Street or a cross street near its junction with the High Street, marked by a mercat cross. A few burghs had a double main street. There were few other necessary features, but they included the castle and the town church. There was not the proliferation of urban churches in Scotland on the English scale; most burghs had a

The burgh cross, Stirling *(Historic Scotland)*

single parish church, some had a few additional chapels built by guilds and burgesses, and in the most extreme case of St Giles, Edinburgh, guilds and burgesses haphazardly tacked on new chapels and aisles to the existing church.

Most burghs had a castle; most Scottish towns have a 'Castle Street' even where no vestiges of the castle remain today. Perth was unusual, for when the castle was swept away in 1209 it was not replaced. At Perth the strength of the walls may have compensated for the loss of the castle. Ditch and palisade (or walls), market-place with mercat cross, one or two main streets, church and castle, and of course the houses of the burgesses and other inhabitants – these were the main physical components of the burgh in Scotland as elsewhere; these features, and indeed many burghs, changed very little between the twelfth century and the eighteenth.

Most burghs were centres of local trade; cattle and other livestock and grain and dairy produce were brought into burghs from the countryside on market day and exchanged for crafted materials, shoes, clothes, dishes and pots, joinery, bread and ale (though most households would make the last two themselves, and only buy when extra was required). But there were also interregional imports and exports. The east coast burghs, especially Berwick, imported corn from England on a large scale, while Ayr in the west imported corn from Ireland; Scotland's climate was better for bere (barley) and oats than for corn. The monasteries of the southern uplands and Lothian sent carts to Berwick to fetch corn, and by inference the religious houses north of the Forth must have sent to Perth. Some other foodstuffs were imported, most notably pepper and cumin for seasoning meat. The most common drink was ale; water could, and often did, carry diseases, so alcohol was safer. We have very little information from this period about taverns, but the Perth privileges of *c.* 1209 state that no *vill* in the sheriffdom of Perth may have a tavern unless its lord was a knight who resided there, in which case it may have one tavern only; taverns, and therefore extra-residential ale making, were a privilege of the burgh. The luxury drink was wine, brought in first from Normandy and Maine, later increasingly from Bordeaux and

Gascony. The king's household was the principal user, with great lords and religious households following, but every parish church required wine for ritual purposes. Much of the wine came through English inter-mediaries, but much also came direct, handled by Scottish merchants, especially after Henry III's war in Gascony in 1242.

Another import was fine cloth, mostly from Flanders but also to some extent from Italy; this supplemented the poorer quality cloths produced in Scotland. In the later thirteenth century fulling mills, which waulked cloth by water power, were being built in Scotland; this enabled Scottish weavers to produce better quality cloth, but it is not clear that the burghs were able to take advantage of this development.

Scotland's main export by the thirteenth century was wool, either

St Giles' Kirk, Edinburgh, before the nineteenth-century restoration.

in sacks or on hides. This was exported in great quantities from the great sheep-farms of the Border abbeys and other monasteries to Flanders, where Bruges, Ghent and Douai were industrial centres for the cloth trade. Flemish merchants had a house, the 'Red Hall', at Berwick by 1296, and German merchants had a 'White Hall' close by, for exporting Scottish wool. Berwick was by far the most important burgh in this trade, with only Perth (the main outlet for the wool of Coupar Angus) coming close. The pre-eminent position of Berwick is shown by its status as a mint town, with a mint producing silver pennies from David I's time, but with discontinuities during the twelfth and thirteenth centuries. Roxburgh, Edinburgh and Perth also had mints, but for most of this period Berwick was the main mint. Scottish coinage was not advanced, the number of surviving coins in hoards is far outstripped by English coins, and English and continental coinage was just as acceptable as the relatively scarce native coinage.

Burgh, a country gentleman who had risen through royal service and been well rewarded by John, becoming earl of Kent and justiciar of England, married Alexander's sister Margaret. Hubert was effective regent of England for the young Henry for most of the 1220s through his control of the justiciarship and the support of the archbishop of Canterbury, Stephen Langton. His marriage to the king of Scots' sister was a useful cloak over his relatively modest origins, but his *de facto* power, justiciarship, and earldom of Kent may have made Alexander feel that the marriage was without disparity. Relations between the two kingdoms remained good so long as Hubert de Burgh's power lasted.[4]

Peace with England allowed Alexander to turn his attention to the remoter parts of his kingdom. Not for the first time, violence flared between the bishop of Caithness and the earl of Orkney, resulting in the bishop being burned alive in his palace at Halkirk. Alexander pursued the earl and brought him to submission. The incident strengthened the king's hand in Caithness; but he still faced trouble in other regions. In 1221 and 1222 Alexander was in the west and north against one Donald mac Neill, perhaps the eponym of the MacNeils of Gigha and Barra; in the latter year he was at Glasgow and founded the burgh of Dumbarton and possibly built the castle of Tarbert on Loch Fyne.

Among those who joined the king's army in the west in 1222 were the men of Galloway, but Galloway tended increasingly to go its own way again in the early thirteenth century. The lord of Galloway was Roland's son Alan of Galloway (d. 1234), who campaigned in Man and Ireland independently of the king of Scots, and was seldom at Alexander's court. His career was that of an independent sea-lord in the Western Isles, Man and Ireland ruling from Galloway; Norse sources state that 'He was the greatest warrior of that time; he had a great army and many ships. He plundered about the Hebrides for a long time'. His father had had good relations with King William, and this may have influenced Alexander in allowing Alan free rein, even making him constable in 1214. Nonetheless, Alexander must have been relieved when he died in 1234, leaving only an illegitimate son and three daughters.

There seems to have been no shortage of candidates to take on the mac William inheritance, despite the violent fate which had met its protagonists in 1186, 1187, 1212 and 1215. In about 1230, Alexander took steps for the suppression of a northern lord called Gillescop, sending an army under William Comyn earl of Buchan into Moray; soon after William's son Walter Comyn is found as lord of Badenoch, possibly through Gillescop's deprivation.[5] About the same time Farquhar Mactaggart was made earl of Ross.

The mac William risings always began in the north, in Moray and Ross; the race of mac William was persistent in its claims, suggesting a genuine belief on their part in the rightness of their cause, and they were always opposed by the crown with unremitting violence. Taken together, we may suppose that the mac Williams inherited a claim to the throne from the house of Moray which Earl Angus had died prosecuting in 1130, and which he in turn inherited from the kingship of Macbeth and Lulach in the eleventh century. The claim can hardly have been inherited from William fitz Duncan alone.

The chief beneficiary of the elimination of the mac Williams was the family of Comyn. This Anglo-Norman family first came to Scotland during the reign of David I, when a cleric called William Comyn was the king's chancellor *c.* 1136–41. His nephew, Richard Comyn, was given the marriage of a Northumbrian heiress, Hextilda, daughter of Uhtred son of Waltheof, at the time when Earl Henry held the earldom of Northumbria; he founded the fortunes of the family in Scotland. He later acquired lands in Angus and Mearns during the feudal colonisation of that area, and was justiciar under William I, and possibly keeper of the royal forests. His son William was lord of Lenzie and Kirkintilloch (lands of feudal colonisation under William I), and sheriff of Forfar before he married into the comital family of Buchan and was one of the very first members of a non-native family to acquire an earldom. This William's second son Walter Comyn appears as lord of Badenoch from 1230, and later acquired the earldom of Menteith by marriage and probably the lordship of Lochaber by royal gift. Another son, Alexander, succeeded to the earldom of Buchan and was justiciar and constable under Alexander III; another, Richard, inherited the lordship of Lenzie, while a brother, David Comyn, had acquired the lands of East Kilbride by marriage to the de Valognes heiress. By the middle of Alexander II's reign, this family had become the most powerful and wealthy in Scotland after the royal house, controlling the earldoms of Buchan and Menteith and the great northern lordships of Badenoch and Lochaber, and lands in Strathclyde and Tynedale.

Thus under Alexander II ancient earldoms and lordships were no longer the preserves of native families. Perhaps the most striking imposition of feudal law as opposed to native practice came when Alan of Galloway died in 1234, leaving an illegitimate son (Thomas) and three daughters. Under feudal law, the inheritance was divided between the three daughters and their husbands, Roger de Quincy, William de Fortibus and John Balliol. Of these, only Roger de Quincy had a strong connection with Scotland. William de Fortibus, earl Albemarle, had no connection with Scotland, while John de Balliol was lord of Barnard Castle and of Bailleul in Picardy, and his family's earlier connection with Scotland was slight. Nonetheless, King Alexander insisted that the ancient lordship of Galloway should be divided between these three co-heiresses and husbands, to the exclusion of Alan's natural son Thomas or the sons of his brother. The men of Galloway petitioned the king to preserve the lordship intact, and, when he insisted on feudal principle, revolted in 1235. Thomas of Galloway invaded Galloway with an army of Irish mercenaries which came close to surrounding the king, but was defeated by the arrival of Farquhar Mactaggart of Ross with reinforcements. The Irish force fled north, to be destroyed by the burgesses of Glasgow; Thomas of Galloway was captured and imprisoned in the Balliol stronghold of Barnard Castle, where he lived to a great age (he was still alive in 1296). Alexander thus imposed an unpopular settlement on Galloway. Resentment still simmered there ten years later: in 1246, when the countess Albemarle died childless, her share of Alan of Galloway's inheritance passed to Roger de Quincy; when he came to Galloway to claim it, the men of Galloway tried to capture him, but he escaped with difficulty to King Alexander, who again punished the Gallovidian rebels.[6]

Alexander II and Henry III

The 1230s, which saw Alexander defeating rebels in Galloway and Moray, also saw him dealing less successfully with Henry III. Relations between the two kings had been good while the power of Hubert de Burgh lasted, but declined as Henry became increasingly independent of the justiciar in the late 1220s. Henry at one point (1231) proposed to marry another of Alexander's sisters himself, but was dissuaded by Hubert's enemies; and when Hubert divorced his wife in 1232 there was friction between Henry and Alexander. In 1235 Henry demanded the renewal of the Treaty of Falaise and the agreements between William and King John, and got the pope to intervene on his behalf. Alexander countered with a demand for the earldom of Northumberland. The peace which was worked out in 1237 involved Alexander quitclaiming his right to the northern counties and the sums paid by William to John for services unfulfilled in return for £200 worth of lands in Northumberland and Cumberland, without the building of castles. The Treaty of York, ratified by both kings at a great assembly under the eye of the cardinal legate Otto on 25 September 1237, marked a major turning point in Anglo-Scottish relations.[7]

Alexander, who had come so close to making real gains by his intervention in the civil war in 1216–17 and ended up empty-handed, was at last prepared to cede all claim to further territory in northern England. This left him free to pursue expansionist policies in the west, which occupied the rest of his and his son's reigns. The Treaty of York did not include an unequivocal statement of the sovereignty and equality of both kingdoms. This was tacitly admitted in the wording of the treaty and in the fact that both kings swore its observance vicariously (it was regarded as a derogation of kingly dignity to swear an oath in person). But it left the way open for English kings to resurrect the Treaty of Falaise and claim to homage for the kingdom of Scotland in future. For the time being, however, it seemed a statesmanlike compromise.

There may have been teething troubles for the new treaty: in 1242 it is recounted that goodwill was 'restored' between the two kings, implying that it had been disrupted. The restoration of goodwill was cemented by the betrothal of Alexander's baby son Alexander to Henry's infant daughter Margaret. The immediate cause of friction was a baronial feud within Scotland, a vendetta by the Comyns against the Bisset family on pretext of the murder by them of Patrick of Atholl, nephew of Alan of Galloway and heir to the earldom of Atholl. Matters came to a crisis again in 1244, resulting in warlike preparations on both sides, but in the end Alexander and Henry were reconciled and a marriage alliance was arranged.[8] With peace restored, Alexander was able to turn his attention to other parts of his kingdom.

The West Highlands and Western Isles

The situation in the Western Isles was one of in-fighting between segments of the Manx royal dynasty, with the kings of Norway exercising what moderating control they could. Such a situation was ideal for Scottish royal intervention, but Alexander

Traprain Law, a hill-fort of the Votadini. *(Historic Scotland)*

Dunadd, a hill-fort of the Scots. *(Historic Scotland)*

Dumbarton Rock, a hill-fort of the Britons of Strathclyde. *(Historic Scotland)*

Left: The Battle of Dunnichen, 685(?). This Pictish stone at Aberlemno, Angus, shows the defeat and death of an invader. The dead king (Ecgfrith?) lies at bottom right, being eaten by a raven. *(Historic Scotland)*

Opposite page: Hilton of Cadboll, Easter Ross, showing a mounted female Pictish aristocrat. *(Historic Scotland)*

An archway from the palace of Kenneth son of Alpin (d. *c.* 858), Forteviot, Perthshire. *(National Museums of Scotland)*

Sueno's Stone, Forres, Moray, possibly commemorating the death of Dub son of Malcolm, 966(?). Near the foot is a bridge and under it decapitated corpses and severed heads. *(Historic Scotland)*

A Pictish king portrayed as David, possibly a memorial to Onuist son of Uurguist (d. 761), St Andrews. *(Historic Scotland)*

The Govan Sarcophagus, portraying a king hunting, possibly a memorial to Constantine son of Kenneth (d. 877) or his son Donald (d. 900). *(Historic Scotland)*

Beehive cells on Eileach an Naoimh, Argyll, probably the monastery of Ailech founded by St Brendan. (*Historic Scotland*)

Malcolm IV's charter to Kelso Abbey, 1159. The Initial M shows David I and Malcolm IV seated side by side in majesty, as they had done in 1153. (*National Museums of Scotland*)

Jacob von gots genaten küng von Schottland

James II in a contemporary portrait. He is shown as a fashionably-dressed young man with a red birthmark covering the left side of his face. (Stuttgart, Landesbibliothek)

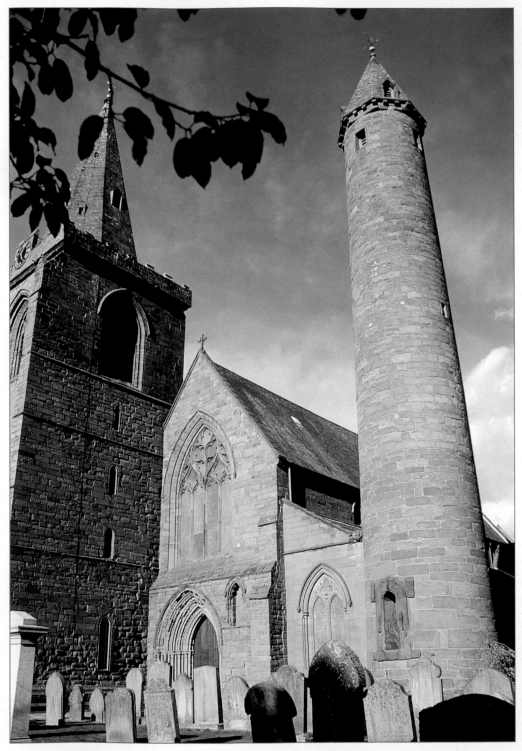

Brechin Cathedral, Angus. The tenth-century Round Tower is on the right, possibly built by Kenneth II, (d. 995). *(Historic Scotland)*

The interior of Queen Margaret's Chapel, Edinburgh. *(Historic Scotland)*

The interior of Dunfermline Abbey. The nave is possibly from David I's reign. *(Historic Scotland)*

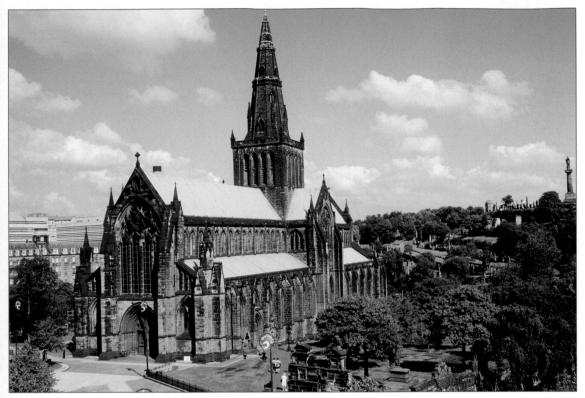

Glasgow Cathedral. Scotland's most complete medieval cathedral. *(Historic Scotland)*

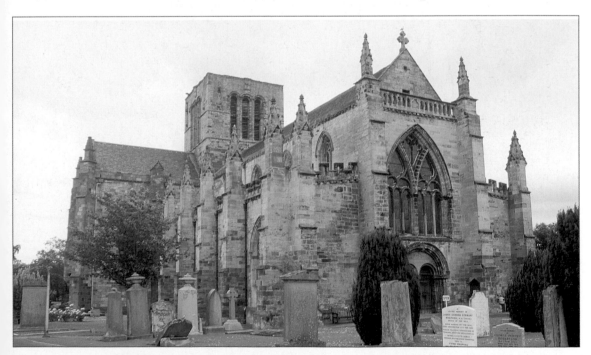

St Mary's Kirk, Haddington, was rebuilt after Edward III's 'Burnt Candlemas' of 1356. *(Historic Scotland)*

St Monans Kirk, Fife, built by David II (d. 1371). *(Historic Scotland)*

In 1297 Stirling Bridge was a timber structure, a little upstream from the medieval bridge. The Wallace Monument stands where the Scottish army lay in wait. *(Historic Scotland)*

Duffus Castle, Moray, consists of a motte and bailey with later stone castle. *(Historic Scotland)*

Threave Castle, a Douglas stronghold. *(Historic Scotland)*

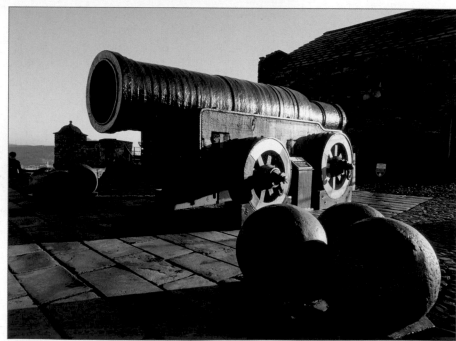

One of James II's guns, Mons Meg, Edinburgh Castle. *(Historic Scotland)*

could do little while faced with a baronial crisis and the suspicions of Henry III. After 1237 Alexander must have hoped to turn his expansionist energies to the west, but was delayed for a number of years, most notably by the crisis of 1242–4. In 1244 Alexander sent a powerful embassy led by two bishops to the court of King Haakon IV of Norway, demanding the cession of the Isles to Scotland on the grounds that Magnus Barelegs had acquired them unfairly during the reign of Malcolm III. Haakon replied that the transaction had been legitimate. The envoys said that the king of Scots was prepared to offer 'refined silver' for the Isles, but Haakon replied that he did not think he had such need of silver that he was prepared to sell the lands of his kingdom. Hearing this the envoys departed.[9]

There is no doubt that Alexander was the aggressor in his new attitude towards the Isles; they had not formed a notional part of the Scottish kingdom since the eleventh century. Godfrey son of Fergus had been *toisech Innse Gall*, 'lord of the Hebrides', in the mid-ninth century, but his descendants had been increasingly restricted to a coastal area in Morvern and Ardnamurchan. From this base his descendant Somerled and his sons had launched a great reconquest of the Isles in the mid-twelfth century. This family was frequently at war with the Norse kings of Man, and not always on good terms with the Scottish crown; Somerled was in revolt against Malcolm IV for part of his reign, but his son Dugald (ancestor of the Macdougalls of Lorn) had a better relationship with William I. Their lordship effectively split the kingdom of Man into north and south, which were often ruled by different members of the Manx dynasty. In the 1240s, the whole kingdom was ruled by Harold, who was knighted by Henry III and honourably entertained by Haakon IV at Bergen. When he was drowned in Shetland in 1248, the kingdom was divided between Reginald in Man and John (*Eoin*) son of Dugald, a descendant of Somerled, in the northern Hebrides; the former was soon slain in Man in the interest of a rival claimant, Harold son of Godfrey, but John was able to make himself master of the Hebrides with Haakon's support. At the same time Dugald mac Ruaidri, a great-grandson of Somerled, held a lordship in the southern Isles.[10]

In 1249 Alexander aggressively summoned John to do him homage, and gathered an army against him. John demanded pledges of safe-conduct from the king, but Alexander countered by demanding the surrender of Cairnaburgh Castle in the Treshnish Isles and three other island castles. When John refused, Alexander summoned an army and fleet to gather in Oban Bay early in July 1249. While he lay at Kerrera waiting to sail, he was taken ill with fever and died. Norse sagas claim that as he lay dying he saw a vision of St Olaf, St Magnus and St Columba rebuking him for his aggressive purpose against the Norse Isles.

In spite of the king's death, the expedition succeeded in driving out John, establishing a royal bailie in Argyll, and imposing a royal candidate as bishop of Argyll. In 1249 there are also signs of the eclipse of Comyn power: Walter Bisset was restored to royal favour; Alan, grandson of Malcolm of Lundy, hereditary door-ward of the king (hence his surname, Durward), became increasingly prominent at court and in the royal council; Earl Patrick of Dunbar, the most powerful lord in southern

Scotland and an ally of the Comyns, died on crusade in 1248; and Walter Comyn and his family seem to have been seldom at court in 1248–9. If continuity of the royal administration was to be maintained, it could only be through Alan Durward.

Alexander II was about fifty-two when he died, and at the height of his power. At home, he had pacified Galloway and Ross, terminated the mac William feud, and established the power of the Comyns in the north. To prevent their total dominance he had at the end of his reign restored Walter Bisset to favour and promoted Alan Durward, and maintained a broadly based court of prelates, earls and barons. He had failed to gain very much by the English civil war of 1215–17, but had gained material concessions in return for the quitclaim of the northern counties in 1237; thereafter, despite the distractions of 1242–4, his foreign policy had been directed towards expansion into the Isles, a policy which was to be successfully continued by his son. He well merited the description given to him in a Norse saga: 'he was a great chieftain and full of ambition'.[11]

THE REIGN OF ALEXANDER III, 1249–86

> Quhen Alexander our kynge was dede,
> That Scotlande lede in lauche and le,
> Away was sons of alle and brede,
> Off wyne and wax, of gamyn and gle.
> Our golde was changit into lede.
> Crist, borne in virgynyte,
> Succoure Scotlande and ramede,
> That is stade in perplexite.[12]

These words were written by an anonymous Scots poet in the 1290s, when the problems caused by the death of Alexander III at Kinghorn in 1286 produced a state of acute political crisis. Men might well at that time look back to the reign of King Alexander as something of a 'golden age'. Thereafter came days of political uncertainty, and war with the misery and hardship which it brought.

The Minority of Alexander III

Alexander II's death came unexpectedly, so there was no time for the smoothly organised transition which had occurred in 1214. The king's heir was his son Alexander, a boy of eight, whose person was controlled by the queen mother, Mary de Coucy, and by Alan Durward. He was immediately taken to Scone and inaugurated in the traditional way.[13] Alan Durward proposed to knight the young king himself, which would have given him the right of guardianship, but was opposed by Walter Comyn. While Durward maintained his position in Scotland, the Comyns curried favour with Henry III. Comyn does not appear as a patriotic figure in 1249–51. Intervention by Henry III in 1251 led to Durward's removal from power and the formation of a new government dominated by the Comyns. This took place during the celebrations of Alexander III's marriage to Henry's daughter Margaret at York in December 1251; when Alexander returned to Scotland early in 1252, he was accompanied by his new bride (a child of his own age), the Comyn faction, and two guardians appointed by Henry III, Sir Robert de Ros lord of Wark and John de Balliol lord of Barnard Castle and of a share of the Galloway lordship. Durward was accused of having sought the legitimating of his wife, a natural daughter of Alexander II, which would have given his offspring a place in the royal succession. Having resisted Henry's demands while the Comyns curried favour with him in 1249–51, Alan Durward then exchanged roles with them during the period 1251–5. He served Henry in the Gascon campaign of 1254 and even accompanied his son Lord Edward to Burgos for his marriage to a Castillian princess; thus 'he not only recovered the king's friendship, but also accused in many ways those who had accused him before the same king [in 1251] with their accomplices'. Henry was told that his daughter was a virtual prisoner in Edinburgh Castle, denied association with the young king her husband, and mistreated by Robert de Ros. He came north, removed the royal couple from the custody of the Comyns, and established a new governing council similar in composition to that of 1249–51, dominated by Durward and his partisans, but more broadly based. This government in turn lasted only two years, and there are signs of moves towards a reconciliation with the Comyns in 1257.

The funeral of King Alexander III, from a fifteenth-century manuscript. (*The Master and Fellows of Corpus Christi College, Cambridge*)

These were frustrated by one of the few acts of political violence during the minority, the seizure of the king and queen's persons by Walter Comyn at Kinross on 28/9 October 1257. The great seal was taken from the chancellor, the bishop of Dunkeld, and Alan Durward fled. But Walter Comyn's triumph was short-lived. Early in 1258 Alexander escaped from his control and began to act independently. He summoned a parliament at Stirling in April 'to amend the transgressions done' to Henry III, himself and the queen; from there he went south to Roxburgh to negotiate with Durward and his associates, waiting at the border. They could not be enticed into the kingdom to a meeting at which Alexander hoped to reconcile them and the Comyns to himself; but towards the end of the year a compromise was agreed, and a new governing council was formulated to include members of both groups and some neutrals.[14]

Alexander was fortunate in being able to take control of the government himself at a time when England was sliding into civil war between the king and Simon de Montfort; and his position must have been eased when at the end of November Walter Comyn was killed by a fall from his horse. Thereafter Alexander (now nearing eighteen) had no rival for power, and the English king had neither the excuse nor the power to intervene.

The years 1249 to 1258 read like a series of political crises, with successive *coups d'état* and rivalry between Comyn and Durward factions. Walter Comyn and Alan Durward may have been self-seekers masquerading as defenders of the royal dignity; but they were no more self-seeking than Henry III. The difference between Comyn and Durward on one hand and Henry III on the other is that they at least had clear objectives; Henry was incompetent and vacillating, creating political instability but not replacing it with order, seeking his own political advantage in Scotland but never achieving it; not even the tired old issue of Scottish homage was used to his advantage.

This decade witnessed a royal minority and a series of political crises with almost no violence; only Walter Comyn's seizure of the king and queen in 1257 involved the use of force, but even then (as far as we know) there was no bloodshed. This contrasts with the crisis of Malcolm IV's youth, the great rebellion of 1160; Scotland had matured politically in the hundred years in between, and this political maturity was to be again in evidence in 1286–90, when Alexander's death left a new crisis. Then it was again English intervention, in the shape of the much more purposeful Edward I, which was to destabilise the political equilibrium. The majority of the prelates, earls and barons would not let the particular ambitions of Walter Comyn or Alan Durward get out of hand, but worked for compromise and reconciliation.

Alan Durward rose spectacularly from obscurity in the last years of Alexander II's reign, from being a country laird and hereditary household officer to being the king's chief adviser, son-in-law, and a claimant to two earldoms (Atholl and Mar, neither of which he successfully acquired). After Alexander's death his control of the young king's person enabled him to cling to power, and he received widespread support from those who feared the power of the Comyns; during Alexander III's personal reign Durward was used by the crown but never trusted to the same extent, and never allowed to fulfil his dynastic ambitions. It made little difference, for on his death in 1275 he left only daughters.

Alexander III's Personal Reign

By 1260, Alexander was his own master and determined to continue his father's policies of friendship towards England and aggression in the Hebrides. He and the queen visited London in 1260, and Queen Margaret, well advanced in her first pregnancy, was allowed to stay in England for her confinement. Some Scottish nobles objected that the king's firstborn should be born outwith the kingdom, but Alexander ignored their criticisms; the queen gave birth to a baby daughter at Windsor in February 1261.

The peaceful state of Scotland in the early 1260s contrasted with the English civil war between the Plantagenets and Simon de Montfort; some Scots joined the royalist side, notably Robert de Bruce, John Balliol and John Comyn, who were all captured along with King Henry and Lord Edward at the Battle of Lewes in 1264. But in Scotland Alexander was able to plot the acquisition of the Western Isles without fear of English aggression. In 1262–3 the Mactaggart earl of Ross and Kenneth, ancestor of the Mathesons and MacKenzies of Wester Ross, raided in Skye. King Haakon in Bergen was told that Alexander intended to subdue the Hebrides to himself. Certainly the kings of Man and the island chiefs could not resist the king of Scots alone. Haakon realised that only his personal presence in the Hebrides would keep them Norse, and to that end made preparations for a great naval expedition in 1263.

Haakon's fleet was not ready to sail before July, which meant that the campaign would continue well into the autumn. They reached Orkney in early August, rounded Cape Wrath and came to Skye, where they restored Norse rule and made threatening noises against the men of Ross. Sailing through Kyleakin (*Caol Hacann*, 'Haakon's narrows') they rounded Ardnamurchan and came down the Sound of Mull to Oban Bay. Here, near the spot where Alexander II had died, Haakon gathered a fleet of between one and two hundred ships for the final stage of the journey to the southern Isles. He sailed on to Gigha and Kintyre, received the submission of Angus Macdonald of Islay, and sent ships ahead to seize the islands of the Firth of Clyde; following them, Haakon rounded Kintyre and landed on Arran.

It was at this point that things began to go wrong. Haakon sent word to Alexander demanding the cession of Arran, Bute and the Cumbraes; Alexander refused and bided his time, knowing that the invaders' supplies were running low and that a deterioration in the weather could be expected soon. In a bold move to acquire supplies, Haakon sent ships up Loch Long, across the porterage at Tarbet, and on to Loch Lomond to plunder the rich pastures of Lennox. The equinoctial gales struck at the end of September, driving ashore Haakon's ships anchored in the Sound of Cumbrae; some ships were wrecked on the beach at Largs.

On 1 October there was skirmishing between Norse sailors and local levies, and on the next day King Haakon himself came ashore. A company of about fifty Scottish knights from Renfrewshire and Cunninghame rode up, and Haakon's commanders forced him to return to his ship. The battle raged up and down the beach at Largs, with the Scots ending up in command of the battlefield, but the Norse withdrawing to their ships in good order. On 5 October, as the autumn gales subsided, Haakon's depleted fleet raised anchor and began the long journey home. He imposed taxes and tribute on the Hebridean islands as he went, but the fleet suffered further losses due to bad weather, arriving back in Orkney at the end of October. Soon after his arrival Haakon fell ill and died in the bishop's palace at Kirkwall on 16 December.[15]

The expedition had not been an unmitigated disaster for the Norwegians. The fight at Largs had gone against them, and the weather had preyed upon their ships without threatening to destroy the fleet. More serious was the difficulty of ever repeating such an expedition, with the sullen antipathy of the southern island chiefs and the king of Scots now unquestioned master of the western seaboard from Kintyre to Ross. Alexander now pressed home his advantage. He prepared an invasion of Man, whose king submitted and became his feudal vassal in 1264, and when the king died in the following year Man was annexed as a bailiary of the Scottish crown; the Manx Chronicle records that 'in this year [1265] kings ceased to reign in Man'. In 1264 Alan Durward and the earl of Buchan launched a punitive expedition against Ross and Caithness for their submission to Haakon, and in 1265 they invaded Skye and took hostages. Islay and the southern Hebrides were also attacked in 1264–5, with Angus Macdonald of Islay and John Macdougall of Argyll submitting to Alexander.[16] It was perhaps the swift punitive campaigns of 1264–5 as much as the Battle of Largs which led to the cession of the Western Isles to Scotland.

Certainly when the new king of Norway, Magnus Haakonsson, sought to enter into negotiations with Alexander over the Isles in 1264, Alexander was in no hurry. He had bided his time during Haakon's great expedition, and after its failure he was not going to be rushed. It was not until July 1266 that the final terms of the treaty of Perth were agreed, whereby the Western Isles were ceded to Scotland for 4,000 marks plus an annual tribute of 100 marks.[17] The acquisition of the Western Isles was the great triumph of thirteenth-century Scotland.

Alexander III's Last Years

England, in a state of exhaustion after the civil war, then with Lord Edward absent on crusade until 1274 (his father Henry III had died two years earlier), had little time to devote to relations with Scotland, and allowed the conquest of Man and the Isles to go unchallenged. One slight ruffling of the placid surface of Anglo-Scottish relations came in 1278, when Edward I tested the waters by suggesting that he was owed homage for the Scottish kingdom.[18] The question came to nothing, and could only have been serious had there been any doubt about the succession.

But in the 1270s and '80s death robbed Alexander of an assured succession. Queen Margaret died in 1275. In 1281, her daughter, Margaret, was married to King Eric of Norway, but within two years she was dead, leaving only a baby daughter, Margaret 'the Maid of Norway'. The greatest tragedy was the death of young Alexander, the king's only son, a promising young man of twenty, in 1284.

King Alexander was now forty-four, and still had hope of fathering more children; to this end he married Yolanda de Dreux in 1285. On the night of 18/19 March

Bishop's Palace, Kirkwall. (Historic Scotland)

1286, the king proposed to spend the night with his young bride at Kinghorn, and so left his council meeting at Edinburgh to cross at the Queen's Ferry. Both the ferryman and the provost of Inverkeithing rebuked him for travelling on such a night, but he was given guides to bring him safely to his wife's chamber. He became separated from his guides, who searched in vain along the cliffs. In the morning the king's body was found on the seashore near Kinghorn; he had been killed by a fall from his horse.[19]

Alexander III's reign was a period of unparalleled stability in medieval Scotland; the chronicles have little to report of violence and upheaval. The development of trade and burghs, and the material evidence of Scotland's fine late thirteenth-century Gothic architecture, suggest a degree of prosperity; the conquest of Man and the cession of the Isles were positive achievements in foreign affairs. There are hints that Alexander was more sensitive to the feelings of his Gaelic subjects than some of his predecessors: the men of the Isles were to keep their own laws, and their rulers seem to have accepted Scottish lordship on this basis. The record of Alexander's conversation with the ferryman at Queensferry and the provost of Inverkeithing on the night of his death suggests that he was approachable and affable, at ease with his subjects. His letter to Edward I on the death of his son in 1284 is dignified and moving.[20] There is reason to believe that Alexander was well liked by his subjects in a way that few kings were, and presided over a period of peace. Scots, looking back to his death from the turbulence which followed, were surely right to consider that 'Our gold was changit into lede'.

CHAPTER 9

Scotland's Great War

THE 'GREAT CAUSE' AND THE REIGN OF KING JOHN

Throughout the twelfth and thirteenth centuries Scotland's relations with England developed so that peace and friendships were the norm, and it was possible for great magnates to hold lands on both sides of the border. Despite occasional English reminders of the terms of the Treaty of Falaise, there was no reason to believe on Alexander III's death in 1286 that the same relationship could not continue.

The Succession Crisis

The first signs of impending crisis came in 1284, when Alexander's heir-apparent, Lord Alexander, died. This elicited a sympathetic response from Edward I of England, to which the Scottish king's reply has survived. Its reference to Alexander's granddaughter, the 'Maid of Norway', might be taken as a reminder to Edward that the king did have a legitimate heir.[1] Alexander was anxious to remind his own baronage of this fact; in February 1284, a week after his son's death, he had summoned the nobles to Scone to agree to accept the child Margaret as his heir. Only Robert Bruce of Annandale had any reason to feel aggrieved at this, for he was later to claim that Alexander II had when childless recognised him as heir as nearest descendant of Earl David of Huntingdon.[2] There is no doubt that the Bruces were always convinced of the rightness of their claim; their actions during the period after 1286 can only be understood in this context.

The sudden death of Alexander III on the night of 18/19 March 1286 deepened the crisis, but did not plunge the kingdom into immediate chaos.[3] A parliament met at Scone in early April, a fortnight after the king's death. Old Robert Bruce of Annandale asserted his family's claim, but was opposed by John Balliol, who could also claim descent from Earl David through a female. Neither claim could be put to immediate test, because Alexander III's queen claimed to be pregnant, and there existed the possibility of a posthumous heir. Parliament imposed a carefully vague oath of peace-keeping on all parties, and appointed six guardians – two bishops, two earls and two barons – to carry on the administration in the name of the community of the realm; this group included sympathisers with both the Bruce and Balliol parties.[4]

By the autumn of 1286 it had become clear that the queen's pregnancy had come to nothing, so the oaths of 1284 to acknowledge the 'Maid of Norway' as heir-designate came back into prominence. But the Bruce faction had prepared against this eventuality by agreeing the Turnberry Bond on 20 September, promising common cause for the rights of the English king and the heir to the Scottish throne.[5] In the winter of 1286/7, when most Scottish nobles were remembering their oath to the Maid of Norway, Robert Bruce of Annandale and his son the earl of Carrick were raising the standard of rebellion in the south-west, seizing the royal castles of Dumfries and Wigtown and attacking the Balliol estates in Galloway. The guardians quickly brought the situation under control, but tension remained, and it was clear that the guardianship could not continue indefinitely without a king.[6] In 1289 two guardians – the earls of Fife and Buchan – died and were not replaced, so there was a danger of the guardianship disintegrating.

It had probably all along been Alexander's intention to marry off his granddaughter to an English prince, and as the crisis deepened in 1289 the remaining guardians looked to this as a possible solution to their problems and a way out of the Bruce-Balliol rivalry. Three kingdoms were involved in the Scottish succession crisis: Scotland itself, England and Norway. The heir to the kingdom was the daughter of the king of Norway. Edward I was strong and ambitious, and had raised the old question of feudal superiority as recently as 1278. It was unlikely that he could be approached without the question being raised again; but if the Maid's husband and ruler of Scotland were to be a son or other relative of his, he might be persuaded not to assert himself.

Envoys of the three kingdoms met at Salisbury in October 1289. The Scottish representatives were the bishops of St Andrews and Glasgow, John Comyn of Badenoch and Robert Bruce senior; they were empowered by the guardians to negotiate only on a basis that would preserve 'the liberty and honour of the realm of Scotland'. Whether the Treaty of Salisbury (November 1289) did so is another matter. The Scottish parliament met in March 1290 to ratify the treaty and to appoint a fresh embassy to negotiate a marriage treaty with Edward, who was writing to the pope to secure a dispensation for the marriage of his son Edward of Caernarfon to the Maid. The Treaty of Birgham (July 1290) was more explicit in its defence of the integrity and liberty of the Scottish kingdom.[7]

Since Edward had seized Man in May 1290, and was trying to secure the payment of taxes from the Scottish Church, such safeguards seemed prudent. One chronicler remembered the fate of the Welsh, whom Edward had defeated in the 1270s and '80s. But this fear was replaced by a graver one when the Maid died in Orkney on her journey to Scotland at the end of September 1290. All the careful plans for the succession lay in ruins.

Tensions increased during the last months of 1290. It was clear that there was continued rivalry between Bruce and Balliol claims, and uncertainty as to what could be done to decide between them. The competitors themselves looked to Edward for support, and neutral parties looked to him to keep the peace and act as an honest arbitrator between them. The realities of power dictated that all parties should curry favour with the English king.

The 'Great Cause'

The 'Appeal of the Seven Earls' of late 1290/early 1291 is of interest in that it claimed that the 'seven earls', presumably the whole body of Scottish earls, and the 'community of the realm', had the right to elect a king and place him upon the throne; but more significantly, it is a protest by Bruce and his adherents that certain of the guardians favoured Balliol's claim and wished to make him king, and an appeal from the guardianship to King Edward to intervene on Bruce's behalf.[8] There is no evidence that the guardians themselves formally invited Edward to intervene in the succession crisis. But on the basis of the letters he received from Bruce and Balliol supporters, Edward I appeared at Norham early in May 1291 demanding acknowledgement of his overlordship and his right to 'negotiate certain business' in the kingdom.

There was a more sinister side to Edward's dealings. During the early months of 1291 he had circulated a request among the religious houses of England asking for evidence from their chronicles which would show the historical superiority of England over Scotland. He enlisted might as well as historical right on his side; ships were prepared to blockade Scotland, and the shire levies of the northern counties were summoned to muster at Norham in June. Aware of the dangers, the Scottish nobles who met Edward at Norham in May delayed before giving an evasive reply. But Edward demanded that all the claimants should acknowledge his claim to overlordship before he would hear and determine their claims to the kingship. They had little choice if they hoped for a hearing, and on 5 June 1291 nine claimants acknowledged Edward's superiority and right to try the case. His next step was to secure the acquiescence of the guardians and the constables of Scottish royal castles. Since the chief competitors had already acknowledged Edward's overlordship, there was no point in any further resistance on their part.[9]

The guardians resigned on 11 June and were 'reappointed' by Edward as king of England and 'superior lord of Scotland', and two days later they did him homage as 'superior and direct lord' of the kingdom of Scotland. In this act they were joined by an impressive list of prelates and barons, and Edward made a progress as far as Perth collecting further fealties and making provision for fealties to be made at Berwick and Perth during July. By 2 August Edward was back at Berwick for the opening of the great court which would adjudicate on the claims of the competitors for the kingdom of Scotland.

Edward's actions had been skilful; he had taken control of Scotland without striking a blow, and had had his right to do so accepted by all interested parties. Scotland would now be unequivocally a vassal kingdom, and the safeguards which he had accepted in the Treaty of Birgham no longer mattered. The court which met at Berwick in August 1291 consisted of 104 auditors and 13 claimants. Forty auditors each were nominated by Bruce and Balliol as the two most interested parties, and twenty-four by Edward himself. The claimants included the legitimate descendants of Earl David's three daughters, illegitimate descendants of William I and Alexander II, and others with more remote claims: King Eric of Norway suggested that he had an ascending right through his daughter the Maid; John Comyn of Badenoch claimed descent through a daughter of Donald Bán (king 1093 and 1094–7); Florence count of Holland claimed that Earl David had resigned his right to succeed and that King William had then recognised his sister Ada and her descendants as heirs, and said there were documents in the Scottish archives to prove this. Florence was granted a ten-month prorogation to produce the documents; but by the time the court reassembled in June 1292 he had been unsuccessful, and his claim was dismissed.

The ten-month delay, during which Edward acted unopposed as lord of Scotland, worked in his favour. His position and rule were becoming accepted, and he offered generous inducements to prelates and barons to cooperate. In November the court reached its decision. Balliol's claim, based on his descent from Earl David's eldest daughter, was preferred to Bruce's, based on nearness by generation through the second daughter; the claim of John Hastings, that the kingdom was a partible inheritance and should be divided among the three daughters' descendants, was rejected on the grounds that a kingdom was indivisible. King Eric's claim by ascent was also rejected.

On 17 November 1292, judgment was pronounced in favour of John Balliol, a secondary Bruce claim based on partibility being also rejected. Two days later, on 19 November, the seal of the guardians was broken up and its pieces deposited in the English treasury, as a symbol that the guardianship was at an end. King John was escorted to Scone and enthroned on St Andrew's Day, and had a new great seal made, showing him enthroned and crowned. Then he went south again to spend Christmas with Edward at Newcastle, and on 26 December did homage and swore fealty for his new kingdom.

Throughout the process Edward had behaved with apparent legality and fairness. It cannot be claimed that Edward favoured Balliol because he believed that he would be more complaisant than Bruce – Bruce's actions since 1286 had shown that he was prepared to be subservient to Edward if it served his interest.

Where Edward's fairness can be questioned is in his whole attitude towards the kingdom of Scotland and its relationship with England. What he was doing was more than reviving the Treaty of Falaise; he was putting a concept of superior lordship into practice. Henry II had exercised superiority over William I because of the latter's capture and submission to *force majeure*, not because of any notional legal superiority. What Edward I was doing was different; and he was soon to find that the Scottish aristocracy had second thoughts about the surrender of their liberties without a fight.

The Reign of King John, 1292–6

Even without the benefit of hindsight, it is clear that the new king was not going to have an easy reign. At his adjudication, Edward had issued a stern admonition to the new king to act justly and in accordance with his lord's wishes, lest he be forced to intervene in Scottish affairs. Since the Treaty of Birgham had effectively lapsed with the Maid's death (though the Scots were soon reminding Edward of its terms), there existed no guarantees for Scottish integrity. The new king had been relatively inexperienced in public affairs before the death of three elder brothers projected him unexpectedly to the headship of his family in 1279. He faced the problem of reviving a royal household and administration after a lapse in royal government of seven years. Perhaps most seriously of all, his right was not universally recognised throughout Scotland, for the Bruces and their adherents did not give up the conviction of the rightness of their claim. They could spread disaffection within Scotland and pass poisoned reports of King John's conduct to Edward at Westminster. The problems which Balliol would face would have taxed a stronger personality than his.

King John, however, at first attempted to rule like a king. He held parliaments, revived the royal household, and commissioned a new great seal. But his reign had hardly begun when his difficulties began to mount. Within a week of his enthronement a burgess of Berwick appealed to Edward at Newcastle against an adverse judgment which he had received from the Court of the Guardians; when Edward upheld part of the appeal, Balliol protested. His resistance was short-lived; on 2 January he issued a written declaration releasing Edward from the terms of the Treaty of Birgham or any other concessions which he had made during the interregnum. Other appeals from John's court to Edward's followed, the most protracted being from 'Macduff', a member of the comital family of Fife which was friendly towards the Bruces. Rather than face the alternatives of open defiance or a humiliating admission of his clienthood, John sought to evade a confrontation by seeking a series of adjournments in the case; but Macduff and his lawsuit would not go away.[10]

Another, more serious, problem arose in 1294 when Edward was preparing for war against France, and induced King John to promise Scottish aid. North Wales was again in revolt at the prospect of its levies being drafted into the English king's wars, and the Scots began to consider a similar move. In July 1295 John's great council sent envoys to negotiate a secret treaty with the French and appointed a council of twelve – four bishops, four earls and four barons – to implement the new policy; the community of the realm had gradually realised that John could not be trusted to defend their aristocratic liberties, and effectively relieved him of office.

On 23 February 1296, the treaty with France, precursor of the 'auld alliance' which was to last for 250 years, was ratified at Dunfermline.[11] The 'patriotic' community, led by the Comyns, rallied round King John and the new council of guardians; and the increasing importance of 'middle folk' in the kingdom is suggested by the fact that the common seals of six burghs were appended to the treaty as well as the great seal and those of the great prelates and barons. Notably absent were the Bruces and their adherents. The old competitor had died the previous year, well into his eighties, but his son and grandson continued the Bruce cause, and quickly distanced themselves from the growing rebellion. King John was now under the direction of a broadly based group of aristocrats and clerics, who had a further grievance in the collection of taxes for the benefit of the Plantagenet king. Although he had little stomach for the encounter, and was to some extent responsible for the difficulties in which he found himself, King John gave in and on 5 April sent Edward a formal 'defiance' with a list of his grievances.[12]

In fact, Edward had long before made his preparations for a confrontation with the Scots, before he knew of the French treaty; Balliol's failure to answer in the Macduff case gave Edward a pretext to invade Scotland early in 1296. He crossed the Tweed on 26 March and found Berwick held against him; when the town fell on 30 March there followed an indiscriminate massacre of men, women and children. On 27 April Edward faced the Scottish feudal army and levies at Dunbar, and completely defeated them. Balliol escaped and fled north into Angus, but offered his submission on 2 July at Kincardine. Eight days later, in a humiliating ceremony at Brechin, Balliol was brought before Edward and ceremonially stripped of his royal regalia and left only in his bare surcoat, or 'toom tabard', the name which has stuck with him through seven centuries. John was taken to London and confined in the house of Anthony Bek, bishop of Durham. Later he was allowed to retire to his estates in Picardy, and ended his days (in 1313) at Bailleul, the castle from which his family was named.

By the middle of 1296 Balliol had managed to alienate almost everybody. The aristocratic community who in 1292 had accepted him had found that he was incapable of protecting their liberties against Edward's infringements; they had pushed him into unwilling defiance and then deserted him when the war went badly. The Bruce faction had always been hostile, and may have engineered trouble between Edward and John. Edward had put Balliol in an impossible position by setting him up as a vassal king and then not leaving him to be master in his own house; this was perhaps the first serious miscalculation in the English king's Scottish policy.[13]

The Scottish Rising, 1296–1306

If his maltreatment of his own client king was Edward's first false move, he soon compounded it with others. The massacre of Berwick was not calculated to win him friends. Edward appointed English sheriffs and officials and placed English garrisons in Scottish royal castles; he ordered English churchmen to be appointed to Scottish benefices, first in Galloway, then throughout the kingdom, and earned the hatred of the Scottish clergy. He alienated the Bruces, the only aristocratic faction on whose support he had hitherto been able to count, by refusing to hear their case after the Battle of Dunbar. The summer months of 1296 were spent preparing the 'Ragman Rolls', a great list of all Scottish tenants who came into the king's peace;[14] this did nothing to reconcile him with the defeated Scots. The kingship itself was to lapse, and to be replaced by direct rule – a move which violated feudal law, since if Scotland were an escheated fief its constitution should be preserved unaltered. Scottish feudal contingents and levies were to fight in Edward's wars; many of the captives of Dunbar were dispatched thither, and others secured their release by promising to send contingents. If Edward had set out systematically to antagonise every section of the Scottish population in 1296, he could not have done so more effectively.

Almost immediately, the edifice which Edward had assembled began to crumble. His control over Scotland in 1291–6 had been based on a skilful manipulation of divisions and suspicions; he had now done much to unite the kingdom against him. Renewed resistance was led by lesser men. William Wallace was probably the son of the laird of Elderslie who had not signed the Ragman Rolls, and was consequently outlawed by the English justiciar. He escaped capture by the English garrison of Lanark with the help of his mistress, who was killed in the process; in revenge, Wallace killed the sheriff of Lanark and fled into the forests of the Southern Uplands, setting himself up as head of a band of outlaws in May 1297.[15]

Wallace was not alone. In Moray there was a rebellion led by Sir Andrew Murray which by July 1297 had driven the English garrisons from the castles of Inverness, Urquhart, Nairn and Banff, and had overrun the countryside as far east as the Spey. He joined forces with Wallace's men some time in August, by which time the castles of Angus and Mearns had fallen, and Perth and Dundee were threatened. In July an aristocratic force under the youngest Robert Bruce and the Steward rose in arms at Irvine, then quarrelled with Wallace because he was carrying on the revolt in the name of King John, and finally capitulated on generous terms. It was left to Wallace and Murray, proclaiming themselves 'leaders of the army of Scotland', to wage a struggle that was popular as well as nationalistic. The closest parallel anywhere in Europe was the 'Sicilian Vespers' revolt against Angevin rule in Sicily in 1282.

The great Scottish revolt of 1297 was the most remarkable episode in the whole drama. In the short term, the revolt had successes. By the end of August, the English army had been expelled from all Scotland north of the Tay, and Wallace's forces terrorised much of the southern countryside, confining the English garrisons to their castles. The English regime was in the hands of John de Warenne, earl of Surrey, and Hugh de Cressingham, the treasurer. They sent alarming reports to Edward, who ignored them and crossed into Flanders with an army, including his Scottish noble captives, in late August. Warenne and Cressingham assembled an army which must have included at least three hundred heavy cavalry, the shire levies of the northern counties, and a large number of Welsh archers; they determined to move rapidly against the Scottish rebels. What they lacked were ships to cross the Firth of Forth, and Wallace's intelligence knew this. When Warenne and Cressingham advanced to Stirling Bridge, the lowest crossing of the Forth, the Scots were waiting for them on the north bank. Cressingham may have been swayed by financial considerations when he decided to attempt the crossing of the bridge and causeway; he urged, 'Why should the king's treasure be wasted in prolonging the war?'

The attempt turned out to be suicidal. The cavalry could only cross two abreast, the archers three abreast; unable to deploy cavalry on the swampy carse around the causeway, they were attacked on both flanks and cut down. Cressingham, one of the first to attempt the crossing, was killed, and his body reportedly hacked to pieces. The Welsh archers, who might have been able to give the cavalry covering fire, were of doubtful loyalty and fled. The cavalry suffered terrible losses, with Warenne barely escaping with his life to flee ignominiously to Berwick. The Scottish triumph was complete, and resulted in the surrender of Stirling Castle; within a few weeks the English held only Edinburgh, Dunbar, Roxburgh and Berwick, and before the end of the year the Scots were raiding over the border into Northumberland. So confident were Wallace and Murray that they issued letters of protection to English religious houses which came into their peace. They wrote on 11 October 1297 to the mayors and communities of Lübeck and Hamburg, informing them that the kingdom of Scotland had been delivered by God's grace and victory in battle from the power of the English, and in consequence the ports of Scotland were once more open for trade with German merchants.[16]

All this was happening while Edward was in Flanders. In March 1298 he returned to England, and immediately began preparations for a new campaign. By July he was at Edinburgh with a powerful army; on 22 July he came face to face with Wallace's forces near Falkirk. The Scots had few cavalry, but grouped their spear-bearing infantrymen into tight 'hedgehog' formations or schiltroms; between these they placed their archers, with the mounted knights in the rear. The Battle of Falkirk was a victory for the English mounted knights and Welsh archers, who wore down the schiltroms by repeated cavalry charges and discharges of arrows; most of the Scottish mounted knights fled. Wallace escaped and extricated the survivors as best he could; but the English casualties had been light, and Wallace's power was shattered. He resigned the guardianship, and seems to have gone abroad to recruit support for the Scottish cause at the courts of Europe.

Wallace's resignation left the way open for aristocratic elements to reassert themselves, and by the end of the year the youngest Robert Bruce, earl of Carrick, and John Comyn of Badenoch were acting as joint guardians. Although the two men quarrelled in 1299 and Bruce resigned the guardianship in 1300, it was clear that resistance would continue, and other guardians served through the following years. Edward faced lasting troubles.

His troubles were not helped by a changing attitude on the part of the papacy. Normally favourable to the Plantagenets against the Scots, in 1299 the Scots found themselves for once basking in papal protection. Pope Boniface VIII opposed the pretensions of powerful secular monarchs; and the information supplied to him by William Lamberton and David Murray, the new bishops of St Andrews and Moray, gave him an opportunity to intervene in Scottish affairs. The bull which he issued on 27 June 1299 might have sounded reasonable to Scottish ears (despite the pope's extravagant claim that Scotland was a papal fief), but it aroused Edward I to a transport of fury. The intervention of the papacy introduced a new element of international diplomacy.

Indeed, the years following his victory at Falkirk were difficult ones for Edward, and brought no comparable success. He campaigned in Galloway in the summer of 1300, capturing Caerlaverock and dispersing a small Scottish force on the River Cree; in the following year he advanced up Tweeddale and over into Clydesdale, capturing Bothwell Castle before withdrawing to Linlithgow to overwinter (1301/2). In 1303 Edward launched a great invasion of Scotland, with a massive show of force as far

Wallace and Murray's letter to Lübeck, 1297. *(Archiv der Hansestadt Lübeck)*

north as Kinloss; he wintered at Dunfermline in 1303/4 without having brought the army of the guardians to battle. In 1304, Edward found that persuasion counted for more, and the Comyns, finally despairing of a Balliol restoration, accepted easy terms. Stirling Castle held out until July 1304, battered into surrender by Edward's siege-engines; its defenders claimed to be fighting not for King John but 'for the Lion'. They were imprisoned but not executed.

The only Scottish martyr was Sir William Wallace. He continued the fight, now a shadowy fugitive, long after the submission of the guardians in early 1304; defeated on the Earn in September, he remained at liberty until betrayed by Sir John Stewart of Menteith in August 1305. He was brought from Glasgow to Westminster, summarily tried for treason (to a king whom he had never acknowledged) and denied any defence. Then he was dragged for four miles at the tail of a horse to Smithfield, where he was put to death by being strangled, disembowelled, beheaded and dismembered. The form of execution was specially devised by Edward for the occasion.

The death of Sir William Wallace should, for Edward, have been the end of the struggle. In September 1305 a parliament held at Westminster with many Scottish representatives issued an 'Ordinance for the order of the land of Scotland', which revived some of the old household offices and allowed Scots to hold sheriffdoms and custodianships of royal castles. Scotland was still to be a 'land' without a king, directly administered but with some degree of 'devolution'. Edward must have felt that his life's work was complete: the Comyns had come into his peace in 1304, extinguishing the last hopes for a Balliol restoration; Sir William Wallace was dead; Stirling Castle, which had held out for so long 'for the Lion', was in his hands.[17]

If a lingering doubt remained in Edward's mind, it concerned Robert Bruce earl of Carrick. Bruce had come into the king's peace in 1297, 1300 and 1302, and since then had given no grounds for complaint. Bruce's father died in 1304, leaving him heir to the Bruce claim. Edward did not know of the 'Cambuskenneth bond' of mutual support which he had reached with Bishop Lamberton in the summer of 1304, but some nagging doubts may have remained. In 1305, Bruce was commanded 'to place Kildrummy Castle in the keeping of a man for whom he is prepared to answer'.[18]

That Bruce himself had not forgotten his family claim is made clear by his actions in 1305–6, when he had a series of secret conferences with John Comyn of Badenoch. The two men had never got on well; when they had served as guardians in 1299 they had quarrelled and come to blows. On 10 February 1306 they held a meeting in the Greyfriars kirk at Dumfries, but in the course of the discussions old rivalries resurfaced, and in a fit of temper Bruce drew his dagger and stabbed Comyn; his companions joined in the fray and made sure Comyn was dead.[19] The new conspiracy, ill-prepared as it was, could not be concealed; after years flitting about in the wings, Robert Bruce was projected to the centre stage.

KING ROBERT I, 1306–29

Bruce's Bid for the Throne

After the murder of the 'Red Comyn' Bruce's conspiratorial aims could no longer be kept secret from Edward I or the Comyns and their allies. The bold and, as it turned out, correct decision was to come out of concealment. Gathering such support as he could, Bruce advanced to Scone, where on 25 March (the Feast of the Annunciation) he had himself crowned with a gold circlet and set on a substitute enthronement stone. The English chamberlain, when he heard the news of Comyn's murder and Bruce's intention to make himself king, demanded his surrender; Bruce reportedly replied 'that he would take castles, towns and people as fast as he could, until King [Edward] had notified him of his will concerning his demand, and if he would not grant it to him, he would defend himself with the longest stick that he had'.[20]

His enthronement was necessarily poorly attended. Bruce's friend and adviser, Robert Wishart bishop of Glasgow, was absent in the west, awaiting Irish mercenaries; Bishop Lamberton of St Andrews did not have time to attend, though he joined Bruce a few days later and said mass for him; the senior churchmen were the abbots of Scone and Inchaffrey. There were few notable laymen present. The earl of Fife was a minor, so the enthronement was carried out by Isabella countess of Buchan, sister of the late Earl Duncan; the earls of Atholl and Menteith also attended, and possibly Lennox. Bruce's wife, Elizabeth de Burgh, daughter of the earl of Ulster, was present and was made queen; she rebuked her husband for making them play at kings and queens like children, and when she later fell into Edward I's hands he ordered lenient treatment for her because of this remark.

Bruce's enthronement was followed by a rapid tour of the country recruiting soldiers. Fortunately, the English had been as ill-prepared as Bruce had been himself, so he had two months to prepare for confrontation. When it came, at Methven near Perth on 19 June, Bruce was defeated with heavy losses by forces gathered by Aymar de Valence, earl of Pembroke. Bruce fled west, suffering further losses in skirmishes at Loch Tay and at Dalry near Tyndrum; entering Lennox, he had his men ferried across Loch Lomond in a small boat. He then slipped away to Kintyre and abroad. His whereabouts during the winter of 1306/7 are unknown.[21]

Meanwhile, his adherents who remained behind were being harried mercilessly by Edward. A reign of terror occupied the autumn of 1306, with Bruce's brother Neil, the earl of Atholl, and others being executed with varying degrees of cruelty. The new queen, the countess of Buchan, and the royal ladies were dragged from the sanctuary of St Duthac at Tain to be displayed in cages at Berwick Castle. The bishops of Glasgow and St Andrews were placed in dungeons, their lives being spared only because of their holy orders. Edward, uttering bitter denunciations against his enemies, roused himself to march north, but illness halted his progress at Lanercost Priory near Carlisle, where he spent the winter of 1306/7.

While he lay there in the early months of 1307, he learned that Bruce had slipped back into Scotland at the beginning of February, to his own earldom of Carrick, and had seized Turnberry Castle. Two of his brothers landed at Loch Ryan in Galloway with Irish reinforcements, but were soon taken prisoner by Dungal Macdowell of Galloway, sent to Edward at Carlisle, and hanged and beheaded. King Robert himself was more fortunate. By May he had gathered a sufficient army to defeat Aymar de Valence at Loudoun Hill in Ayrshire. One of King Edward's supporters sent news from Forfar that Bruce's support was growing all the time. After Loudoun, Robert Bruce was a force for the English to reckon with, and a rallying point for Scottish support.

Edward, roused to one final outburst, tried to rise from his sickbed to be avenged on the traitor. He rode on horseback towards the Solway, but was so infirm that in four or five days he only managed to cover about six miles. Making his son swear never to abandon the struggle until the Scots were utterly defeated, he died at Burgh-on-Sands on 7 July 1307. He had already chosen the epitaph to be carved upon his tomb in Westminster Abbey: 'This is Edward I, hammer of the Scots; obey the oath'. He had had great triumphs, and could have been a great king; but the greatest ambition of his life, the unification of Britain into a single English empire, had ended in failure.

Fortunately for Bruce and his adherents, Edward's son Edward of Caernarfon had little desire to 'obey the oath'. He took his father's body to Richmond, where he entrusted it to the archbishop of York, then turned north again to advance as far as Cumnock in Ayrshire; but Bruce was long gone. Edward II turned his great army about and headed back to England for his coronation and for years of conflict with the English baronage, which were to give the Scots a breathing space.

Enemies at Home, 1307–9

Bruce's murder of the 'Red Comyn' had embroiled him in a blood feud with the whole Comyn dynasty and their adherents, including the Balliols and Macdougalls. The Comyns were a family whose interest in Scotland stretched back to the twelfth century. The great concentration of their power was north of the Tay, with the highland lordships of Badenoch and Lochaber, the earldom of Buchan, and rich estates in Angus and Mearns. By marriage they were allied to the Macdougalls of Lorn, the senior descendants of Somerled, lords of a great island and mainland lordship on the western seaboard. The 'Red Comyn's' mother was a sister of John Balliol. Bruce's family lands of Annandale and Carrick encircled Balliol's Galloway, and the Bruce family share in Garioch was close to the Comyn lands in Buchan; these proximities, together with the need to neutralise the Macdougall power in the west, dictated the course of the civil war of 1307–9.

In the autumn of 1307 Bruce was in Galloway, forcing some of its leading men to flee to Edward II seeking help; then he turned swiftly north to fight a winter campaign in Moray, Mar and Buchan. This consisted of months of indecisive sieges and skirmishing through the winter, until Bruce decisively defeated the Comyns at Inverurie (23 May 1308) and ordered the 'herschip of Buchan', a pillaging of Comyn lands which ended their power in the north. Meanwhile Sir James Douglas and the king's brother Edward Bruce continued operations in Galloway, recapturing and burning Sir James's castle of Douglas and defeating Dungal Macdowell. In August 1308 King Robert was in Argyll, making war on the Macdougalls and gaining the submission of Alexander of Argyll and his son John of Lorn; but their loyalty was not lasting, and a year later he was back in the west, this time decisively breaking Macdougall power in the Battle of the Pass of Brander in the autumn of 1309.

By March 1309, King Robert felt strong enough to hold his first parliament. A major act was the issuing of a declaration in the name of all the clergy of Scotland and sealed by the bishops affirming King Robert's right to the throne and their loyalty to him. The parliament also received probably the first foreign embassy to Bruce's court, an invitation from Philip IV to Bruce and Edward II to drop their quarrel and join with him in a new crusade.[22]

These documents show how completely Bruce had won over the Scots in the space of four years; those who were irreconcilable had been neutralised in battle. Some enemies, like William earl of Ross, surrendered to Bruce, promised him loyal support, and thereafter were unfailing in their loyalty. Most of the clergy supported Bruce, despite his murder of Comyn and consequent excommunication, because they saw him as the best guarantor of their liberties. As for the 'middling folk' and townsmen, there is evidence that they began to perceive that they had a stake in an independent kingdom, freed from English sheriffs, castellans and garrisons. Bruce's aristocratic enemies in the north-east had to punish their tenants and husbandmen for going over to Bruce against their lords' wishes; and some men of relatively humble origins played a part in the recovery of castles from the English.

Dunollie Castle, a stronghold of the Macdougalls of Lorn. *(Alan Macquarrie)*

Already on the 23rd the signs were auspicious. As Bruce reviewed his division near the Bannock Burn (probably near the present Bannockburn village), a knight from the English advance division, Sir Henry de Bohun, advanced alone and challenged him to single combat. His soldiers watched in horror as the king stood alone before the English knight's charge, but their apprehension was turned to joy when King Robert side-stepped the charge and struck de Bohun down with his battle-axe. The Scots infantrymen charged, and the English withdrew. Meanwhile another part of the English army was trying to make a swift dash to Stirling along the marshy banks of the Forth, to outflank the main Scots army stationed near St Ninian's Kirk. Sir Thomas Randolph, newly knighted and created earl of Moray, led his infantry schiltrom down into the carse of Stirling and drove the English back. Had the English cavalry had archery support, they would certainly have created real difficulties for Randolph's spearmen; but the move was too quick for the archers to be deployed to fire into the schiltrom. By nightfall the English found themselves forced to bivouac in the low-lying carse of the Forth between loops of the Forth and the Bannock Burn. Once Bruce and his captains knew that the English were hemmed in, they decided to attack in the morning.

The night of 23/24 June was short, offering at most three or four hours of semi-darkness before daybreak. As soon as it was light, three of the four Scottish infantry battalions, led by Edward Bruce, Thomas Randolph and Sir James Douglas, advanced into the carse of the Forth. In a cavalry charge against Edward Bruce's leading schiltrom, the earl of Gloucester was killed and his men repulsed. Only when they managed to deploy their archers into an effective position did the English have a chance of disrupting the tight infantry formations; but this was done so slowly that the Scots had time to counter the move, dispersing the archers by a charge of their own cavalry under Sir Robert Keith. Then King Robert, who had been holding back his own rearguard division near Bannockburn village, threw them into the battle. The English knights, unable to spread out along the narrow front, found themselves driven back towards the Forth and the Bannock Burn. From there there was no escape, and defeat soon turned into disaster. The English rearguard tried to flee across the Bannock Burn, but were ridden down by the mounted knights fleeing in panic. Thousands of men were drowned or trampled underfoot, until it was said that the burn was bridged with corpses of men and horses; and as the survivors struggled across they were attacked by King Robert's camp followers, who had been waiting to the west. King Edward was led from the field away from the Bannock Burn towards Stirling; but when he reached the castle Mowbray declared his intention to surrender since the siege had not been lifted. Edward fled south-west and then east, avoiding the fiercest fighting as he sped to Linlithgow. Sir James Douglas pursued, but he did not have sufficient force to prevent the king reaching the safety of Dunbar and a ship to the south.

Of those who had escorted Edward from the battlefield, Sir Giles d'Argentine declared that he could not flee and returned to a suicidal charge into the Scottish schiltroms near the Bannock Burn; Aymar de Valence marshalled a band of Welsh archers and infantrymen together and led them (probably on foot, since his horse had been killed) across 100 miles of hostile terrain to the safety of Carlisle.

King Robert's triumph was complete. Thousands of English mounted knights and infantrymen had been killed, and as many captured. The spoils and booty were immense, as were the ransoms of the noble captives. The greatest prize of the day was Stirling Castle, the objective of the whole engagement; but Bruce's victory was greater than that. A really decisive battle was a rare event in medieval warfare; Bannockburn made Robert Bruce undisputed master in his own kingdom, won over the last wavering Scots (such as Alexander de Seton, whose defection had influenced Bruce in fighting the battle, and Sir Philip Mowbray, custodian of Stirling Castle), and left Berwick as the only Scottish castle in English hands. The war was not over, but there was little doubt left who was going to be the victor.

If Bannockburn had a serious failure, it was the failure to capture Edward II. His ransom alone would have financed the war effort for years, and could have brought about a peace treaty within months. But King Robert's army was so small, and the scale of his victory so unexpected, that not everything was possible at once. The sources hint that Douglas's pursuit of the king was half-hearted, because he did not have the numbers to tackle King Edward's escort of knights.

In the months following Bannockburn, many Scots hastened to come into King Robert's peace. On 6 November 1314 a parliament was held at Cambuskenneth Abbey, where 'it was agreed and made statute . . . that all who have died in the field against the faith and peace of the lord king, or who on the same day have not come into his faith and peace . . . are to be disinherited forever of lands and tenements and all other status within the kingdom of Scotland, and they are to be held in future as foes of the king and kingdom, debarred forever from all claim of heritable right. . .'. In fact Robert was willing to receive back any of the 'disinherited' who chose to make peace with him at later times.

Some of his enemies could not be reconciled, however, and the lands of Balliol, Comyn, Macdougall and their adherents were parcelled out among Bruce's most loyal supporters, such as James Douglas and Thomas Randolph; the records are full of regrants of forfeited lands of Bruce's enemies in favour of his friends. The disinherited were to prove a problem to Robert's successor, but for the time being any such problem must have seemed very remote.

The Irish Campaign, 1315–18

The war was continued with an even more ambitious scheme. In the summer of 1315 the king's brother Edward Bruce crossed into Ireland with an army, with the intention of winning the land from the English and being made high king of Ireland. Robert Bruce was the earl of Ulster's son-in-law, and his patrimony of Carrick was Gaelic-speaking; but the war in Ireland was also designed to divert English resources and prevent recruitment of Irish mercenaries to fight in Scotland. In May 1316 Edward Bruce was crowned high king near Dundalk, and in September the English garrison of Carrickfergus surrendered. For another three years Edward Bruce campaigned widely throughout Ireland, ravaging the Pale without fragmenting it. Early in 1318 Bruce's Irish supporters, led by Donald O'Neill of Ulster, sent the 'Irish Remonstrance' to the pope, claiming that O'Neill had a hereditary right to the high kingship, which he was willing to renounce in favour of Edward Bruce, 'a pious, prudent and modest man of ancient Irish descent, powerful enough to redeem the Irish from the house of bondage'. Edward's brother was the king of 'lesser Scotia' (Scotland), 'whose kings have all derived their original blood from greater Scotia' (Ireland), 'keeping our language and way of life to a certain extent'. This document is of interest as an early promotion of pan-Celtic consciousness, an appeal to racial and linguistic links between Scotland and Ireland. In fact, there was little enthusiasm for Edward Bruce's invasion in Ireland; all his marching and counter-marching only led him to defeat and death near Dundalk in October 1318. One Irish annalist called his death 'the best deed that was ever done for the Irish since the driving out of the Fomorians'. King Robert may have been glad to find an alternative outlet for the ambitions of his aspiring brother; but the appeal to pan-Celtic loyalty was not a success. The Scots withdrew from Ireland, abandoning even Carrickfergus Castle.

King Robert's Later Campaigns

Earlier in 1318, however, King Robert had had a happier moment with the storming of Berwick, the last English garrison in Scotland; in this he was aided by the betrayal of the town by John Spalding, an English burgess who had quarrelled with the commander of the garrison. This prize was so valuable that Bruce did not destroy Berwick, but strengthened and garrisoned it with his own troops, a move which facilitated the many raids into northern England which occupied the following years, and which proved a valuable source of revenue to the Scots. The fall of Berwick again roused Edward II, and he marched north to besiege the town with 8,000 men in September 1319. Douglas and Randolph, rather than tackle such a big English force, raided deep into England, destroying a motley assembly of soldiers and clergy under the archbishop of York (the 'chapter of Myton') on the Swale. When news of this disaster reached the English lords before Berwick, they 'discorded' and the siege was lifted. The raid had failed in its objective of capturing the queen, who had prudently withdrawn, but it succeeded in driving Edward back home.

If Edward II was losing the war on the battlefield, he was having more success in the war of words. The pope, John XXII (1316–34) was a Gascon, and Gascony was still an English possession. Bruce's legal position was weak; he was still excommunicated for the murder of Comyn, and his title to his throne was little recognised outside Scotland and France. In an effort to secure papal recognition for Bruce's kingship, the barons of Scotland sent an eloquent appeal (the 'Declaration of Arbroath') to the pope on 6 April 1320. This is usually associated with the name of Bernard abbot of Arbroath, the king's chancellor. It asserted King Robert's right to his throne in succession to 113 kings of royal stock who had reigned, under the protection of Andrew the Apostle, free from subjection. Should King Robert abandon the struggle, however, the barons would turn against him and make another their king; 'For so long as a hundred of us remain alive, we will never submit to the domination of the English. For we fight not for glory, nor wealth, nor honour, but for freedom alone, which no good man gives up except with his life.'[23]

Within months of this impressive show of baronial unity, King Robert faced an obscure crisis, the 'Soulis Conspiracy', which allegedly sought to assassinate him and place Sir William Soulis on the throne. Soulis was a son of one of the unsuccessful competitors of 1291, whose claim derived from an illegitimate daughter of Alexander II; an uncle, Sir John Soulis, had been guardian in 1301–2, nominated by Balliol and supported by the Comyns; Sir William Soulis's mother was a Comyn, a daughter of the earl of Buchan. The whole episode appears to be a Comyn conspiracy. Soulis and his Comyn aunt, the countess of Strathearn, confessed and were sentenced to perpetual imprisonment; another conspirator, Sir Roger Mowbray, had died before being brought to trial, so his corpse was brought into court and sentenced to be drawn, hanged and beheaded. The king magnanimously pardoned the corpse, but four conspirators who were unlucky enough to be still alive suffered the full punishment. Such severity was uncharacteristic of King Robert, and the chronicles record shock at his action. The conspiracy was an obscure affair, and little can be said about it with certainty.

The 1320s saw continued stubbornness on the part of Edward II, who refused to acknowledge Bruce as king of Scots, further Scottish raids which devastated the north of England but had little effect at Westminster, and some local attempts at *rapprochement*. In 1323 the earl of Carlisle, Sir Andrew Harclay, sought to alleviate the suffering of his own earldom by agreeing a private treaty with the Scots. This is of interest in that it foreshadows a truce agreed later in the same year. But for his pains Harclay was arrested by Edward II, summarily tried for treason, and sentenced to be drawn, hanged, disembowelled and beheaded.

More successful were Scottish negotiations with the pope, carried out by Thomas Randolph in the late months of 1323. A thirteen-year truce was agreed between England and Scotland at Bishopsthorpe in 1323, but Edward still refused to recognise Bruce's kingship and Scotland's independence (now inextricably intertwined), and so a final peace could not be negotiated. When an English rebellion in the winter of 1326/7 deposed Edward and replaced his rule with that of Mortimer and Queen Isabella, Robert put pressure on the new government by a campaign in Weardale in 1327. The English army, accompanied by the fourteen-year-old Edward III, marched up and down in search of Sir James Douglas's disappearing army, then tried to coax them down from a high position on to an open front for battle, receiving the reply that Douglas 'had come to England to burn and slay', and it was up to them to try to stop him. When he did descend from his strong position it was in a night attack on the English camp, during which he rode among the tents shouting, 'Douglas, Douglas! Ye shall all die, thieves of England!', and cut the guy-ropes of the king's tent before vanishing into the night. Two days later, when the English woke to face battle, the Scots had struck camp in the night and were already far away heading for the border. It is hardly surprising that King Edward was 'sore afraiede' and 'ful hertly wepte with his yonge eyne'. At the same time as the Weardale campaign, King Robert himself descended on Ulster and extracted a truce from the English there. Returning to Scotland, he followed up Douglas's Weardale campaign by appearing before the walls of Norham and erecting mighty siege engines, making public his intention to annex Northumberland and even issuing charters granting out lands there.

With discontent growing in England, Mortimer and Isabella let it be known that they were at last ready to negotiate a final peace. In October 1327, King Robert set out his demands. Negotiations lasted through the winter, and resulted in the Treaty of Edinburgh ratified on 17 March 1328 at Holyrood, where King Robert lay ill. The peace was to be sealed by a marriage between King Robert's son David and King Edward's sister Joan.

Although King Robert recovered sufficiently to make another visit to Ulster later in 1328, he was now mortally ill, and had retired to a country mansion which he had had built at Cardross. He now had a son to succeed him, so earlier doubts about the succession were removed. On his deathbed King Robert bequeathed his heart for burial at the Holy Sepulchre. It is indicative of the Scots' confidence that peace would hold that Sir James Douglas departed on crusade with the king's heart within a few months of his death. King Robert died on 7 June 1329, bitterly mourned by the people he had led so well.

THE REIGN OF DAVID II, 1329–71

When Robert Bruce died on 7 June 1329, none of the subjects who mourned him doubted that the peace which he had won would be long-lasting and effective. King Robert's most able captain, Sir James Douglas, immediately made preparations to fulfil the king's dying request and take his heart on crusade.[24] Meanwhile, the guardianship was to be vested in Thomas Randolph earl of Moray, the late king's nephew, on behalf of the five-year-old David II. Randolph carried out his guardianship with a rigorous enforcement of justice; he hanged many felons as far afield as Wester Ross, and refused to have any dealings with the 'disinherited', those who had failed to come into King Robert's peace before the end of his reign. The high point of his administration came on 24 November 1331, when the boy king was crowned and anointed by the bishop of St Andrews at Scone. He was the first Scottish king to receive the full ceremonial form of coronation and anointing; the occasion must have been a source of immense pride to Randolph and those who had fought with him over the years. But Randolph was now an old man. He died at Musselburgh on 20 July 1332.

Renewal of War with England, 1332–41

Many important participants in the first War of Independence died around the same time: King Robert, Sir James Douglas, Walter the Steward, the bishops of St

Andrews and Moray, Bernard the chancellor, and Thomas Randolph, all died within a few years (1329–32). The men who followed them soon found themselves faced with difficulties and powerful enemies; for the problem of the 'disinherited' remained unresolved, and could provide a focal point for discontent and an excuse for English intervention. Already Edward III had interceded on behalf of Henry Beaumont and Thomas Wake, two of the disinherited, without success. In 1331, Beaumont began a scheme to recover his inheritance in which he involved Edward Balliol, the son and heir of King John. Edward Balliol's father had died in 1313, and since then Edward had been living on the family's estates at Bailleul in Picardy, without apparently showing any interest in the kingdom which his father had once ruled. Now Beaumont, claiming the earldom of Buchan through his Comyn wife, brought Edward Balliol to England, to meet Edward III and to perform a secret homage for his prospective kingdom of Scotland.[25]

This was, of course, a breach of the Treaty of Edinburgh of 1328. But Edward III was later to claim that the treaty was not binding on him because it was made by Mortimer and his mother during his minority. Edward had overthrown and executed Mortimer in October 1330, sent his mother into seclusion, and was determined to undo their work. The conspiracy of Henry Beaumont and Edward Balliol, matured during the winter of 1331/2, gave him an opportunity. Although the young king did not share his grandfather's legalistic turn of mind, he was not yet prepared for an open breach with the Scots, but supported Balliol and Beaumont quietly until he saw what success they had.

On the last day of July 1332, only ten days after Randolph's death, the army of the disinherited sailed for Scotland. They numbered about fifteen hundred and were led by Edward Balliol, Henry Beaumont and some other English aristocrats with claims to titles or lands in Scotland. They landed unopposed at Kinghorn and marched towards Perth, presumably with the intention of crowning Balliol at Scone. The Scots hastily assembled a force to meet them at the crossing of the Earn, near Dupplin Moor; they greatly outnumbered Balliol's army, and were led by Donald of Mar, a veteran of Douglas's Weardale campaign of 1327. As a result of confusion and dissent among the Scottish captains, Edward Balliol and the disinherited won a complete and unexpected victory against superior odds (11 August 1332). The guardian and many other leading Scots were killed. As a result, Balliol was left master of the region, and was able to force many nobles and churchmen into attending his 'coronation' at Scone on 24 September. He proceeded to distribute titles to the disinherited, but was still far from being recognised as king of Scots; so he moved to Roxburgh where he could call upon English support. A move by the new guardian Sir Andrew Murray (son of the victor at Stirling Bridge in 1297) to capture him backfired, and it was Sir Andrew who was captured. More successful was an attack on Annan by Sir Archibald Douglas, brother of Sir James; Balliol was surprised and nearly taken, and fled towards Carlisle on an unbridled horse, 'one leg booted and the other naked'.

Edward Balliol had been 'king of Scots' for less than two months when he was forced to flee to the protection of Edward III. Even before his flight to England,

Balliol had agreed the terms by which the English king was to aid him: Balliol and his heirs would do homage and fealty for the kingdom, and Edward and his heirs would maintain him in power; for services already done Balliol granted to Edward £2,000 worth of land in southern Scotland, to include Berwick and its shire, to be annexed in perpetuity to the kingdom of England. Edward now made public his intentions and mounted a full-scale invasion of Scotland which laid siege to Berwick in March 1333. The guardian, Sir Archibald Douglas, marching to the relief of the town, which was the only fortress not to have been demolished by King Robert I, found himself forced to offer battle on disadvantageous ground at Halidon Hill on 19 July 1333. The English archers proved the effectiveness which they were to show in the great battles of the Hundred Years' War, and the Scots were defeated with heavy losses, including the guardian and five earls. Berwick immediately surrendered and was possessed by Edward as the first part of Balliol's promised payment. The impression of the invincibility of Scottish arms built up since Bannockburn was shattered, and that heavy defeat was avenged.

Edward III did not follow up his victory, but left it to Balliol to make himself master of Scotland, believing that Scottish opposition and the Bruce cause had been crushed. Balliol was able to summon a parliament in 1334, but, apart from a number of churchmen who were bullied into being present and the disinherited who turned up in full strength, it was sparsely attended. Balliol's position was weakened when he made public his agreement with Edward III and asked parliament to ratify it: the cession of the whole of the Border and Lothian counties in perpetuity to be annexed to England, and homage and fealty for the remainder of the kingdom to be held as a vassal state. This announcement (February 1334) led to a general uprising in southern Scotland, directed by John Randolph earl of Moray and Robert the Steward, soon joined by Sir Andrew Murray on his release from captivity. Meanwhile King David and his queen were sent from Dumbarton Castle to the safety of France, where King Philip VI promised support for the war. Quarrels soon broke out among the disinherited (some of them claiming the same lands) and between them and Balliol; some of them went over to the Scottish side. By the autumn Balliol had once again fled from his kingdom and taken refuge with Edward III; and the lands recently annexed by England, with the exception of Berwick, were back in Scottish hands.

Edward III's campaign in Scotland in 1335 was one of the biggest military offensives of the war; with well over twenty thousand men involved it was greater than the Bannockburn campaign of 1314 and comparable with some offensives of the Hundred Years' War. Edward III and Edward Balliol marched to Perth without encountering opposition, and stayed there in the hope of bringing Sir Andrew Murray to battle; but he had learned the lessons of Dupplin and Halidon, and reverted to Robert Bruce's tactics of avoiding battle. By the autumn, Edward III had withdrawn without an engagement, leaving Sir Andrew Murray and Sir William Douglas of Liddesdale free to attack, defeat and kill David de Strathbogie, the 'earl of Mar', in Culblean Forest on the Dee. Edward mounted another expensive campaign in Scotland in the summer of 1336, which was no more decisive. Robert I had destroyed so many castles and fortresses that there were very few points which could be garrisoned, so Edward could not hold Scotland by garrisons; he either had to mount a series of big and expensive campaigns (as in 1333, 1335 and 1336) or rebuild the destroyed network of castles. Belatedly Edward decided on the latter course, ordering the rebuilding of Roxburgh, Edinburgh, Dunottar, Stirling and Bothwell. Had he had the patience to carry this through, he would have had a much better chance of controlling Scotland. Again in 1336 the Scots declared that they fought not for any prince, but 'for the lion' – the same phrase used by the defenders of Stirling Castle in 1304. In Sir Andrew Murray the Scots had once again an able military leader. The 1336 campaign was Edward's last great campaign in Scotland, and much of what it achieved was undone by Sir Andrew Murray during the winter of 1336/7. Edward's military ventures in Scotland in 1337 were much more modest. They achieved little more than the lifting of the siege of Stirling Castle and the maintenance of the status quo in southern Scotland, but by the end of the year Sir Andrew Murray was raiding across the border.

Early in 1338 a small English army besieged Dunbar, where the defence was directed by the countess of Dunbar, 'black Agnes', who appeared on the battlements to hurl insults at the besiegers. The siege cost Edward III £6,000, but in the summer it was lifted and the English withdrew.

Meanwhile Edward III was nurturing a more grandiose scheme. His mother Isabella was sister of three French kings and daughter of Philip IV; when the male line of the Capetians died out in 1328, Edward did not press his remote claim, but the French crown passed to the house of Valois. It was not until 1337, when his interest in the conquest of Scotland was waning, that Edward persuaded Parliament to sanction a full-scale conquest of France and the assertion of his maternal claim to the French throne. In the summer of 1338 Edward crossed into Flanders. The Hundred Years' War had begun.

David II's Personal Reign, 1341–6

The chronicler Walter Bower wrote that the invasion of France came 'happily for Scotland, for if the king of England had continued his warfare in Scotland he would have gained possession of the whole land without difficulty, as far as it is humanly possible to judge'. Bower's reaction is understandable, although his conclusion is doubtful. Indeed, Edward may have seen in the invasion of France a better return on his investment, and a means of saving face when it became clear that the conquest of Scotland was impossible. The invasion of France reduced pressure on the Scots and initiated a new phase of the war in which events in France were to be of great consequence for Scotland.

The respite from sustained English attack brought recovery and more settled conditions, and in the summer of 1341 it was thought safe to bring the young king and queen back from France. Sir Andrew Murray had died in 1338, leaving William Douglas of Liddesdale as the most able Scottish captain. John Randolph earl of Moray was released from captivity in the autumn of 1340. Edinburgh Castle was recovered by Randolph and Douglas in 1341, followed by Roxburgh and Stirling the following year. Government became more regular, too: David held frequent great councils and parliaments, and issued a number of written acts.

Meanwhile Edward III was becoming increasingly embroiled in the war in France. In 1340 he destroyed the French fleet at Sluys, but he had no other successes in Flanders, and his siege of Tournai was a failure. Campaigning in Brittany also proved indecisive, so Edward accepted a two-year truce in 1343. On the expiry of the truce, Edward invaded Normandy in the summer of 1346, took Caen, and advanced almost to the gates of Paris; thence he withdrew in the face of a massive French army, turned north and crossed the Somme, and turned at bay at Crécy a few miles beyond. There on 26 August the English archers, fighting from the same type of defensive position as at Halidon Hill, destroyed the French cavalry in a terrible slaughter. Having destroyed the flower of French chivalry and revolutionised medieval warfare, Edward settled down to the siege of Calais, whose resistance was to hold up his progress for nearly a year.

By the Treaty of Corbeil (1326), the Scots and French had strengthened the 'auld alliance'. One clause of the treaty ran 'If war arises between the king of France and the king of England, the kings of Scotland are obliged to the king of France and his heirs to make war on the king of England to the utmost of their power, any truce between the kings of Scotland and England . . . to be at an end'. In October David II mustered an army to fulfil the alliance and aid the French. Sweeping through Liddesdale and Cumberland, laying waste as they went, the Scots crossed the Pennines and approached Durham. On 17 October they were met by a substantial force under William la Zouche, archbishop of York, at Neville's Cross. Once again the English archery proved its effectiveness, forcing the Scots from a defensive position to engage on disadvantageous terrain. The first Scottish battalion, under John Randolph, was driven back, and rescued from disaster by the intervention of the king with the second division. But as they were pressed hard, they required the support of the third division, led by the earl of March and Robert the Steward. But they deserted and fled; as an English writer observed, 'they led off the dance, leaving David to caper as he wished'. David, wounded by an arrow, extricated his men as best he could, but was overtaken by Sir John Coupland and captured in hand-to-hand struggle. Also captured were the earls of Fife, Menteith, Sutherland and Wigtown, and Sir William Douglas of Liddesdale; among the slain were John Randolph earl of Moray, the earl of Strathearn, the constable, marshal, and chamberlain. In 1347 Edward Balliol, who had spent little time in Scotland during the previous five years, advanced at the head of less than four thousand men as far as Falkirk, and sold an expensive truce to the Scots; then Balliol disbanded his army and withdrew to his island fortress of Hestan, to reign as 'king of Scots' over a tiny corner of Galloway.

David's Captivity, 1346–57

The government was entrusted to Robert the Steward, the heir apparent whose desertion at Neville's Cross had led to the king's capture. Although David's nephew, he was a few years his senior. His earlier career had been undistinguished; he had submitted without a fight in 1335, leaving Sir Andrew Murray to fight on almost alone. Two years before he had fled from Rothesay castle in a rowing boat as the English approached, taking with him only his family charters. Consciousness of family right may have weighed much with Robert; at Neville's Cross he may have reflected that only David Bruce's life stood between him and a throne.

The eleven years of his lieutenancy (a new title, replacing the earlier guardianship) were equally undistinguished: there was financial chaos, with examples of non-payments and remissions; in the localities, sub-lieutenants were often appointed, strong men with a powerful landed interest in the area; and the number of surviving documents which passed the royal seals declined dramatically.

David II has been described as devious, unpatriotic, and unworthy of his father. But the strategy and tactics which led to his capture at Neville's Cross do not necessarily reflect a wayward youth; the decision to invade England in the autumn of 1346, while Edward III was bogged down outside Calais, was strategically correct, while disaster could have been averted but for the desertion of the Steward and the earl of March. His rule during the years 1341 to 1346 and again after his return from captivity in 1357 display a competence absent from the intervening years.[26] The accusation of lack of patriotism rests on the negotiations for his release and ransom in 1346–57, and here David's behaviour can be explained by the growing enmity between him and the Steward, and his desire to repay Robert's disloyalty by depriving him of the succession.

Paradoxically, David's capture benefited his house and the Scottish cause. Up to 1346, Edward III had upheld the cause of Edward Balliol, who was unacceptable to the Scots; but he now had the king universally recognised in Scotland in his own hand. If he could exact suitable terms, David would be of more use to him than Balliol, who had fled three times.

Negotiations for David's release were opened in 1348. Edward III was anxious to reach an agreement, and it was hinted in 1349 that Edward Balliol was obstructing the process. In 1350 David wrote to the pope, complaining that Edward's conditions for his freedom included homage, vassal status and attendance at English councils and parliaments, military service, recognition of Edward or his successor as David's heir should he die without children; he asked for the pope's help and counsel in his misfortune, and begged him to write to the king of France urging him to make David's release a condition of any treaty with England.

In 1351 Edward sent Sir William Douglas to Scotland on parole with moderated demands: David could be ransomed for £40,000 if he agreed that if he died without children then one of Edward's younger sons would succeed him. In the following year David himself was temporarily at liberty in Scotland to persuade his parliament to accept similar terms: his release and restoration of English-occupied territory for a moderate ransom and alteration of the succession in favour of the Plantagenets. But his persuasion was in vain; an English chronicler reported that the Scottish parliament declared that they would willingly ransom their king for money, but would not become subject to the king of England. By the summer of 1352 David had returned to prison.

In the summer of 1354 a new treaty (the Treaty of Newcastle) was negotiated whereby David would be released for a ransom of 90,000 marks (£60,000) in nine annual instalments, with a truce for the duration of the payment, and no other conditions regarding the succession or homage. Edward made arrangements for David's release in exchange for hostages as surety, but by the end of the year the agreement had fallen through. The reason for this was French diplomacy; early in 1355 the French sent much gold to Scotland to persuade the Scots to break off negotiations and resume the war. They were successful insofar as they recaptured the town of Berwick and besieged the garrison in the castle; but the Scots melted away when Edward III appeared in January 1356 to relieve the defenders.

While the English king was in southern Scotland in January, he received a surprise visit from Edward Balliol. Balliol, full of bitter recriminations, took the Scottish crown from his head and handed it to Edward together with a handful of Scottish earth and stone, as a symbolic renunciation of his claim. In return for passing over his right to Edward, the English king was to pay off his debts (5,000 marks) and grant him an annual pension of £2,000. Balliol, having striven for more than twenty years to be king of Scotland, retired on this to live in quiet obscurity until his death in 1364.

Edward III now had a claim to the Scottish throne himself. It was as flimsy as his claim to the crown of France, but this was unlikely to dissuade such an opportunist. In February 1356 he sacked Haddington (the 'burnt Candlemas') and advanced to the Forth at Whitekirk. He intended to cross the Forth and advance to Scone for his 'coronation' as king of Scots; but (by the intervention of the Virgin of Whitekirk, according to Bower) his ships were stayed by contrary winds, and he was forced to withdraw having achieved only destruction. It was his last campaign in Scotland.

Meanwhile, the war in France had been renewed. Edward's son, Edward the Black Prince, launched great plundering raids into central and southern France in 1355 and 1356 in an attempt to draw the French into battle; but the French had learned the lesson of Crécy, and it was not until 19 September 1356 that King John of France and a vastly superior army engaged the forces of the Black Prince near Poitiers. The French dismounted most of their knights and tried to close on foot, using small divisions of cavalry to turn the English archers' defensive position. There was fierce fighting involving the French knights who managed to get through the hail of arrows, but in the end they were driven back with heavy losses, including the capture of King John and his younger son.

David's Personal Reign, 1357–71

After this disaster, the Scots could no longer hope for French help, and hastened to seek an agreement for David's ransom. Negotiations, nominally led by the Steward but in fact presided over by Bishop William Landallis of St Andrews, dragged on through 1357; the Treaty of Berwick was ratified on 3 October 1357. Its terms were very similar to those of the unratified Treaty of Newcastle of 1354, except that the amount of the ransom was raised from 90,000 to 100,000 marks. Given the state of the war in France, these were the best conditions the Scots could hope for; David was recognised as king of Scots, and the independence of the kingdom was not compromised. He was released on 7 October 1357, after eleven years in captivity.

David faced a number of problems. The Steward's administration had been lax in terms both of law and order and finance. David was petitioned by parliament to hold regular justice ayres 'to strike terror into wrongdoers'; he soon developed a reputation for rigour and harshness in the enforcement of justice. The chancery had all but come to a standstill: there are no great seal registers for Robert's lieutenancy, and we know of only a few charters which passed the royal seals during these years, many of them during David's brief return to Scotland in 1352. The exchequer records show arrears and laxness in accounting. If David was to have any hope of meeting the ransom payments, all this would have to change.

Parliament proposed some new measures for meeting the payments. One allowed the king to requisition the wool crop (Scotland's main export) at cost price, sell it profitably in Flanders, and direct the profit towards the ransom payments. The great custom, a levy on exported wool and hides, was doubled in 1358 and trebled in 1359. A new assessment of land values was ordained and carried out, and in a rare move direct taxation was levied for three years (1357–60). The first two instalments of the ransom were comfortably met in 1358 and 1359, and then payments ceased. It was not inability to pay which led David to default; his financial measures had been successful, and he had quickly restored the crown finances. He may have hoped that the war in France would embroil Edward so deeply that he would be prepared to renegotiate the ransom on a basis more advantageous to the Scots. Two trusted friends, Robert Erskine and Norman Leslie, were in France in 1359 persuading the Dauphin Charles to contribute 50,000 marks towards the ransom in return for which David promised to make war on England at some unspecified future time. But the French agreed to the Treaty of Brétigny in May 1360, whereby Edward gained half of France and a huge ransom for the release of King John; although they did not give up the 'auld alliance' as the treaty originally specified, they were so heavily committed financially that the 50,000 marks was never forthcoming. Still Edward III held his hand, and the Scottish defaulters were allowed to go unpunished.

This was as well for David, because in the early 1360s he faced a serious baronial conspiracy. On his return he had attempted to placate the nobility, making Robert the Steward earl of Strathearn and creating a new earldom of Douglas for Sir William Douglas; but he had come to rely on lesser men like Sir Robert Erskine and others, who managed the financial and judicial administration; to these were added two important churchmen, the bishops of St Andrews and Brechin. The great nobles, led by Robert the Steward and William earl of Douglas, resented their influence. It would be false to view them as leaders of a 'patriotic party' against an untrustworthy king; the immediate cause of the conspiracy seems to have been the Steward's dynastic ambition. The king's mistress, Catherine Mortimer, was murdered in 1360 by Thomas Stewart earl of Angus, who was arrested and died in prison; she was replaced in the king's favour by Margaret Drummond (widow of Sir John Logie), whom David proposed to marry on the death of the estranged Queen Joan in 1362.

If Margaret could give David an heir, the Steward's expectations of the succession would be frustrated. So 'a great sedition and conspiracy' was set in train by the Steward and the earls of Douglas and March, to bend the king to their will or else drive him into exile. David, who had shown courage in war in 1346, was not going to be daunted by a baronial conspiracy. As a result of his financial stringency and the non-payment of the ransom, he had a full treasury and could afford to pay his troops; and he could count on the loyalty of lesser men like Erskine and Archibald Douglas. As the king rode out to challenge the rebels, the earl of Douglas narrowly escaped capture at Lanark; the Steward, never one with a stomach for a fight, deserted and joined the king; Douglas and March had no choice but to submit. In April 1363 David triumphantly married Margaret Drummond and drew instruments of submission from the rebels; the Steward promised to be faithful to the king and to uphold him and his officials.

Negotiations between David and Edward in November 1363 resulted in two draft memoranda proposing reductions in the financial burden and a revival of the proposal that Edward or one of his sons might succeed David should the latter die without issue. The first memorandum envisaged direct succession by Edward III himself, but guaranteed the Scots constitutional safeguards which compare advantageously with those offered in the Treaty of Union of 1707. The second memorandum was similar, but offered fewer concessions in return for the succession of one of Edward's younger sons who was not his heir apparent. David put the proposals before parliament in March 1364, and they were emphatically rejected.

The rejection led to further diplomatic moves. In 1365 Edward offered to settle the ransom at £100,000, one-third as much again as the original 100,000 marks, but ignoring the two instalments (totalling 20,000 marks) which had already been paid. When the Scots refused in 1366, Edward retorted with demands for homage, cession of territory, and military aid against France as his price for a final peace. Negotiations continued for the next three years, until the prospect of the renewal of the war in France in 1369 brought genuine concessions from Edward: the treaty agreed in 1369 scrapped the demands for homage, territory, military aid, and alteration of the succession, and recognised the payment of 20,000 marks in 1357–9 as counting towards the ransom. The residue of the ransom was fixed at 56,000 marks (a total of 100,000 marks, less the 20,000 paid in 1357–9 and four instalments of 6,000 marks paid under the 1365 agreement). The new instalments of the ransom were to be 4,000 marks annually for fourteen years, the lowest ever, at a time when 'David's revenues were more flourishing than they had ever been'.

David had, by diplomacy and luck, vastly improved his position in the years since 1357. He took a great personal interest in government, attending justice ayres and exchequer audits himself, increasing his revenue from customs, and issuing more than six hundred surviving documents under his seals in the space of fourteen years. Meanwhile, he quietly encroached on the English occupied lands in southern Scotland, taking half the revenues from Annandale and appointing sheriffs and officials in other border areas and extracting some revenue from them. In the late 1360s, his position approached that which his father had enjoyed in his last years.

He was still frustrated by his inability to produce an heir. Margaret Drummond had not given him children, and in 1370 he proposed to divorce her and marry instead Agnes Dunbar. Margaret sailed to Avignon to protest to the pope about her treatment. The pope threatened the Scottish king with ecclesiastical penalties; but before he had time to act, or David to consummate his marriage to Agnes Dunbar, the king suddenly died at Edinburgh on 22 February 1371. He was forty-seven years of age.

It has been remarked that it is 'striking that David, with few assets save his own astuteness and forceful personality, made himself so completely the master of Scotland'.[27] Many of David's greater subjects, such as the Steward, the earl of Douglas and the earl of Mar, experienced his wrath, but never without justification and never with vindictiveness. His one failure lay in his apparent infertility; he could not produce an heir to rescue the kingdom from his detested nephew, and so in 1371 the house of Stewart ascended the Scottish throne.

CHAPTER 10

A Changing Society

HIGHLAND AND LOWLAND IN LATE MEDIEVAL SCOTLAND

The narrative of events in Scotland from 1296 to 1371 leaves the impression of a very eventful period, often dramatic and sometimes tragic. No one need doubt that these events had profound social consequences; it is generally agreed by historians that prolonged and widespread war brings social change in its wake.

In the Highlands changes in the nature of lordship and society accentuated a cultural divide. One curious aspect of Scottish history is the fact that while the West Highlands and Islands provided Scotland with its ruling dynasty and much of its predominating culture in the early Middle Ages, in the later Middle Ages and subsequently these areas have tended to be marginalised. Two of the greatest of Scotland's medieval kings, Alexander III (1249–86) and Robert I (1306–29) brought the islands and adjacent mainland areas into the orbit of the Scottish kingdom, and during the Wars of Independence control of the Highlands was a crucial factor. The Battle of the Pass of Brander was one of the most decisive engagements in the Bruce versus Comyn struggle; and in 1309 Bruce could claim among his adherents the earls and guardians of the Highland earldoms of Ross, Sutherland, Lennox, Mar and Caithness, Alexander of Argyll, Donald of Islay, 'the barons of the whole of Argyll and the Isles acknowledging the faith of the Lord Robert'; soon after he revived the great central Highland earldom of Moray in favour of his nephew, Thomas Randolph. Among the seals on the Declaration of Arbroath in 1320 were those of the earls of Moray, Ross, Caithness, and Sutherland, Donald Campbell of Argyll and John Cameron of Atholl.

Related to issues of the Highlands and Islands was the relationship of Scotland to Ireland. Edward I had been able to raise Irish troops to fight in Scotland, and it was partly in response to this that Robert I and his brother Edward Bruce mounted a series of campaigns against English rule in Ireland from 1315 to 1318 in an unsuccessful attempt to have Edward Bruce recognised as high king of Ireland. The death of Edward in 1318 did not end Bruce interest in Ireland; Robert was son-in-law of the earl of Ulster, by his title of earl of Carrick he had possessions in Ulster, and he was active there in 1327 and 1328, a decade after the collapse of his brother's dynastic schemes. Although the Bruces did not destroy English power in Ireland, they weakened it. During the wars against Scotland in the 1330s and the Hundred Years' War against France from 1338, Irish problems tended to be ignored by Edward III, and the English colony contracted within the 'Irish Pale', a small administrative district centred on Dublin. In the 1360s this consisted of almost all of Leinster and Meath and the north-eastern fringes of Munster, but a century later it had dwindled to a narrow coastal strip stretching from the Wicklow mountains to Dundalk, incorporating part of the plain of Meath. The rest of Ireland was left to native Gaelic Irish families and to Anglo-Irish families who adopted Gaelic and Irish culture, customs and language, and became almost indistinguishable from the native Irish. Among these families there was frequent quarrelling and struggle for supremacy, which the English of the Pale had little power to influence or prevent.

It has been said that 'the latent English retreat from a large part of Ireland in the first half of the fourteenth century opened up to Hebrideans and West Highlanders an almost limitless prospect of interference in Irish affairs and of lucrative employment in Irish wars. . . . These Irish developments, far from healing the old division between west and east, between the Isles and the mainland, in fact perpetuated it.'[1] A distinction in dress between Highland and Lowland had been noted in the mid-twelfth century. Fordun, writing c. 1370, relates this distinctiveness in dress, which was also apparent in language, to distinctness of geographical regions.[2]

An interest in Irish affairs seems to have been important for the Clan Donald from the lifetime of Robert I onwards. Angus Óg Macdonald was confirmed by Robert I in possession of Lochaber, Ardnamurchan, Morvern, Duror and Glencoe. He was with Robert I at Bannockburn (1314), and died soon after. He was married to a Connacht princess, and was succeeded by his son Alexander, who died fighting beside Edward Bruce at Dundalk in 1318. Alexander added Mull and Tiree to the Clan Donald's lands, which now comprised Islay, Gigha and Jura and the mainland possessions. His son, John Macdonald, was 'Lord of the Isles' (*rí Innse Gall, Dominus Insularum*) from c. 1325 to 1387. During the half-century of his rule, the lordship became a very powerful and independent force. John did not share his father's and grandfather's loyalty to the house of Bruce, and Edward Balliol in 1336 confirmed to him all his island and mainland possessions, now including Skye and Lewis. David II, on his return to Scotland in 1341, soon came to terms with him and confirmed him in possession of most of his island and mainland lordship. John became allied by marriage to the Stewarts, who succeeded to the Scottish throne in 1371. His son and successor, Donald, was thus a grandson of Robert II (1371–90), and a great-great-grandson of Robert I. To John's rule belongs credit for the creation of the lordship's power, and the establishment of the links and relationships which were to last for a further century and more.[3]

The Irish connection was one of the most important aspects of this. Scottish mercenaries or 'Gallowglass' (*Gall-óglaig*) fighting under noble chieftains, usually cadet sons of important Scottish clans, became a potent factor in Irish warfare, and sometimes acquired hereditary possessions in Ireland.[4] The most successful of them was John Mór Macdonald, younger son of John, lord of the Isles who died in 1387, and brother of his successor Donald. John Mór was granted Dunivaig in Islay, but dissatisfied with this he rebelled against his elder brother. On the collapse of his rebellion he fled to Ireland and took service with the O'Neill lord of Ulster. For this he was rewarded with the marriage of the heiress of the Glens of Antrim, which thereafter were held by his family along with the lands of Dunivaig in Islay. Thus by *c*. 1400 the Clan Donald held lands in Ireland, where they could take refuge and from which they could draw support.

The Lordship of the Isles which existed from *c*. 1325 until *c*. 1493 shows signs of internal stability as well as external power. It was ruled by the chief of Clan Donald, whose principal residence was at Finlaggan in Islay. On a tiny island in Loch Finlaggan, connected to Finlaggan Castle by a causeway, the Lord's 'Council of the Isles' met. The elaborate composition of this council is suggestive of stability and a well-defined social structure.

Finlaggan Castle, Islay. *(Alan Macquarrie)*

Eilean na Comhairle, Loch Finlaggan. *(Alan Macquarrie)*

Misunderstandings between Highlander and Lowlander were inflamed when their interests conflicted. The most spectacular example was the Battle of Harlaw in 1411, when Donald Lord of the Isles fought a Lowland army near Aberdeen to prosecute his claim to the earldom of Ross. Lowland sources claim this as an indecisive or drawn battle, or at worst a pyrrhic victory for the Highland army; Gaelic sources were in no such doubt, and proclaim it as a victory for the Lord of the Isles. What cannot be doubted is that in the short term the Scottish government was able to maintain garrisons in Easter Ross, but that by the 1430s at latest the Lords of the Isles were recognised as earls, having in effect gained their objectives.

No one, however, could disguise the government's further defeat by the forces of the Lordship at Inverlochy in 1431, when the Highland army was led by Donald Balloch Macdonald, son of John of Dunivaig and the Glens. This effectively shattered James I's aggressive Highland policy, and ensured the continuity of the Lordship of the Isles for a further sixty years.

The relative stability of the Lordship of the Isles contrasts with the turbulence of other Gaelic areas, such as Badenoch and Atholl. From the 1370s these were characterised as dens of lawless caterans (Gaelic *cathrain*, a light infantryman) and 'wild Scots' who raided down the Tay as far as Perth and Fife, north to Elgin and Inverness, and east into the glens of Angus. The government had no control in Moray or Atholl, and there was no local authority like the Clan Donald to quell feud and violence. The famous 'clan fight' at Perth between thirty champions on each side in 1396 appears to have been a judicial duel between two clans contesting the headship of the Clan Chattan, a great confederation of central Highland clans. After James IV's attack on the Lordship of the Isles in 1493, similar violence became common in the west as well. By the end of the medieval period, Highland and Lowland were truly two very different places.

WAR AND PLAGUE

The Impact of War

Wars were fought by socially mixed armies under aristocratic leadership. When a local muster was summoned, all able-bodied adult males were expected to turn out to join the army of their earldom, led by the earl. Peasants were expected to arm themselves in some way, with pikes or spears or bows and arrows, and the best form of body armour they could get hold of; they were expected also to bring some rations, though not for the whole notional forty days of a campaign. Knights accompanied the earl, equipped with horses and full body armour, and brought with them esquires and sergeants, also mounted but more lightly armed. Knight service was notionally for forty days a year performable on a twenty-day summons, but in practice fourteenth-century campaigns exceeded this. It is probable that in the thirteenth century 'knight service' was becoming an increasingly notional concept, with few campaigns in a long period of peace: knight's fees became increasingly subdivided and fragmented until they were little more than a legal fiction. But King Robert I had a need for a standing army of trained knights, and so we find conservatism in the charters of his reign, a return to granting of authentic knight's fees to faithful followers (common in the twelfth century, but less so in the thirteenth). His armies were feudal armies of the old kind, and there is little evidence of the use of mercenaries or indentured retainers. This practice continued during the minority of David II and up until Neville's Cross (1346), which effectively brought campaigning to an end; David built up the financial position of the crown during his personal reign and was able to pay the troops which crushed the great rebellion in 1363. When the war was resumed in the 1380s there was a greater element of local leader-ship (principally by the Douglases), though national armies were still summoned on occasion (like the great host which unsuccessfully besieged Roxburgh in 1436). Warfare in the fifteenth century tended to become more expensive and specialised (for example, with the introduction of cannon), and in consequence more infrequent. General musters and knights' summonses still occasionally took place for great campaigns (e.g. in 1436, 1460, 1482 and 1513), but the war was much more discontinuous than it had been in the fourteenth century.

The overwhelming impression of the war from 1296 to 1338 is of its unremitting nature. There were big English armies in Scotland in 1296, 1297, 1298, 1300, 1303–4, 1307, 1310, 1314 and 1322; every year from 1332 to 1338 there were English armies in Scotland, some of them very big indeed. Thereafter, as Edward III became increasingly embroiled in campaigning in France, his armies in Scotland were smaller and less frequent in their appearance; but the 'burnt Candlemas' of 1356 brought another big army and fleet into Scotland. This last campaign involved burning and pillaging on a spectacular scale; but all armies were destructive to a greater or lesser extent.

Even when great armies were not involved, there was plenty of cross-border raiding, and in the border shires violence or the threat of violence became part of everyday life. After Aeneas Silvius Piccolomini (the future Pope Pius II) visited Scotland on a papal errand in 1435, he told alarming tales about his sojourn in the border country. He lodged in a peasant house, built of drystone walls without lime or mortar, roofed with thatch and heather, and with a fire on the hearth where the people burned black stones for fuel instead of wood. During the night a man burst in to inform the household that the English were approaching, so all the able-bodied men left, leaving Aeneas alone with the women; they assured him that as a foreigner travelling under safe-conduct he would not be harmed, and neither would they. Nocturnal disturbances of this kind, he gathered, were rather routine. It seems that Aeneas used his time profitably when he was left alone with the women. His memoirs state that 'the women are fair of complexion, comely and pleasing, but not distinguished for their chastity; they give their kisses more readily than Italian women do their handshakes'. Aeneas also noted that 'Nothing pleases the Scots as much as the abuse of the English'.[5]

One consequence of frequent disturbances, coupled with the weakness of the crown in the years 1371 to 1424, was the increase in the importance of great lords in the borders, most notably the Douglases and the earls of March. There are times, indeed, when the Anglo-Scottish war takes on the appearance not of a struggle between nations, but a feud between the earls of Douglas as the greatest Scottish border family and the Percy earls of Northumberland as their English counterparts. The Douglases were a family (like others) raised up to greatness by Robert I because of their loyalty and good service to him, but who subsequently became a threat to the crown in its weakness and able almost to carry on their own private border war. It is significant that James II struck against them before he reopened the war against England.

The local importance of great lords increased; other classes were also rising in status. Robert I's war effort was aided by his ability to by-pass traditional loyalties and appeal to the patriotism of lesser men. Increasing 'freedom' – that is, removal from the bonds of thralldom or serfdom – was a phenomenon taking place in fourteenth-century Scotland, and the war was one of its causes. This is the point of Barbour's famous lines in *The Bruce*:

> A, fredome is a noble thing!
> Fredome mays man to haiff liking.
> Fredome al solace to man giffis;
> He levys at es that frely levys.[6]

How high was mortality due to war? This is a question which cannot be easily answered. We can guess only a little about the population of Scotland. Scottish armies were numbered in thousands, not in tens of thousands. The Scottish army at Bannockburn was probably King Robert's biggest, and it numbered between 5,000 and 10,000. The armies which suffered the heavy defeats of Halidon (1333), Neville's Cross (1346), and Humbleton (1404) may have approached the lower figure. At these battles, casualties among the aristocracy were high; probably the scale of the defeat was calculated more on the number of aristocratic casualties than on the total number; we cannot assume that on every battlefield vast hordes of peasants were cut down. Indeed, most peasants were archers and supporters to the knights and men at arms, and so were in less exposed positions. Certainly, we know that among the English casualties at Bannockburn those most heavily affected were the mounted knights, while many Welsh archers were rescued.

So although war obviously had its casualties, it may have increased mortality among the noble and knightly classes rather more than among other social groups; misery and uncertainty it did cause, a constant state of tension and hostility in the borders, but it may not have increased non-noble mortality by too much.

The Great Mortality and its Aftermath

From the middle of the fourteenth century another phenomenon did contribute to population decline: plague. The Black Death, a virulent epidemic of bubonic and pulmonary plague carried by the rat flea, swept Europe from east to west in 1347 and 1348, reaching England in the summer of the latter year. It did not immediately spread into Scotland; the Scots complacently called it 'the foul death of the English', and regarded it as a divine judgment on their enemies. An English writer describes how the Scots gathered an army in Ettrick Forest in 1349, hoping to take advantage of their enemies' disease-ridden state, when they found the disease breaking out in their midst.[7] The normal pattern of epidemics was for the disease to originate in its bubonic form, involving swelling of the lymph nodes, then for the pneumonic or pulmonary form (severe infection of the lungs) to become increasingly common. The latter form is very quick acting, resulting in death in the space of two or three days, and is highly contagious. A contemporary description of the symptoms of the 'first mortality' of 1349 suggests that pneumonic plague was the more common form in Scotland.

Scottish chroniclers estimated that one third of the known world's population perished. Some writers have suggested that the effects of the Black Death were less severe in Scotland than elsewhere; but there is little evidence one way or the other. Evidence from north English towns like Chester and Carlisle does not suggest any abatement in the north. Bower's comments on the death of twenty-four canons of St Andrews, mostly priests, is of interest in that priests, who had to minister to the dying, were particularly at risk, while in a closed community like St Andrews Priory the disease could spread very rapidly. Pneumonic plague was predominantly an urban disease, and one would expect mortality to have been highest in the towns of Berwick, Edinburgh, Perth, Dundee and Aberdeen.[8]

One of the most serious factors was that the plague came in successive waves. The 'first mortality' struck in 1349, the second in 1362, the third in 1379 and the fourth in 1417. By this time plague was endemic in Europe and enumeration was abandoned. Plague was not the only contagious disease which became common in the later Middle Ages; Bower mentions an epidemic called 'le qwhew', possibly whooping cough, which afflicted nobles and commoners alike in 1420.[9]

Little is known about measures taken to alleviate disease and distress. It has been suggested that some poor hospitals were converted into infirmaries for the sick in the early fifteenth century. Later we know of burgh authorities ordering the destruction of dogs and cats in urban areas, believing that this measure would prevent the spread of disease.

Nor was disease the only cause of misery and mortality. There may have been climatic deterioration in the early fourteenth century, leading to a succession of bad harvests and harsh winters; there is talk of icy winters in which mills were brought to a standstill, and corn could not be ground for months. There is reason to believe that throughout the thirteenth century the population was increasing, which suggests better weather. In the early fourteenth century, there are recorded outbreaks of swine and fowl pest, poor harvests and bitter winters, as well as the Black Death itself.

Chroniclers speak of the population being reduced by a third in the 'first mortality' alone, and this figure is comparable with known mortality rates in other countries. The subsequent epidemics were less severe, but prevented any recovery in the population until the mid-fifteenth century. Such a disaster could not fail to bring with it profound social consequences.

For the survivors, these were not all bad. Where wealth is distributed among a smaller number of people, each individual should expect a greater share of it. This is a crude statement, but it does appear that peasants and husbandmen were better off. As labourers became fewer, their services became more expensive, and landowners had to attract them with lower rents and better conditions. The *nativus*, or unfree peasant, becomes more and more infrequent in records, until he is last mentioned in 1364; 'the entire institution [of serfdom] died a quiet death in the fourteenth century'. A new assessment of rents ordered by David II shows that in 1366 these were on average about half of what they had been in Alexander III's reign. In England, landlords tried to counter this phenomenon by reimposing legal unfreedom which was tending to go out of use, and thus provoked the great Peasants' Revolt of 1381.

The French 'Jacquérie' of 1358 had similar causes. In Scotland, there was no peasants' revolt; there were no artificial attempts by the nobility to counter the natural tendency towards increasing freedom and prosperity of the surviving peasantry.

Why was this so? The nobility was not similarly affected by the Black Death, and although its numbers were thinned by mortality in war (especially between 1333 and 1346), mortality rates among Scottish noble families were relatively low by European standards. One possible explanation is that Scottish society was more close-knit than those of bigger countries, with a narrower gulf between peasants and nobles. The war effort had helped to bring society closer together; lords and men alike were committed to the same struggle to keep their country free. Whereas in the thirteenth century the 'community of the realm' had been an aristocratic body of king and nobility, in the fourteenth century the ideal of 'freedom' from bondage and oppression involved lesser men as well, and brought them increasingly to play their part in the defence of the nation to which they consciously belonged. For this reason, nobles were unable or unwilling to reimpose outmoded restrictions on a reduced but more prosperous peasantry on whom they had come to depend and with whom they shared a common interest – the freedom of the Scottish nation.[10]

LORDS, TOWNSMEN AND OTHER MEN

The question of what constituted 'lordship' or 'nobility' in fourteenth-century Scotland was not as clear as it later became. Obligations such as taxation and military service were not clear-cut, nor was the right to summons to or attendance at parliament. In theory, anyone who held his land in freehold, with security of tenure and perpetual and heritable right, was a laird, and therefore a lord. It was towards this very broad band of people that James I directed his Act of Parliament of 1426, requiring that all landholders holding direct from the king – prelates, earls, barons and freeholders – should attend parliament in person or face a fine.[11] In practice, this legislation was inoperable, but it set out the theory of what constituted the 'aristocracy', those who had a right or duty to be consulted in the governance of the kingdom. This 'baronage' was a broad band at the top of society, ranging from the earls (usually about a dozen in number, or a little over) to the lesser freeholders who might have little distinction from the wealthier husbandmen except the nature of their tenure; some of them would have been hard-pressed even to call themselves lairds.

But although it was broad, this band represented only a tiny fraction of society. Edward I's 'Ragman Rolls' of 1296 contain the names of some fifteen hundred lay 'aristocrats' whose homage was extorted; allowing that some will have evaded the summons, probably the number did not exceed two thousand lairds, or an average of about two to a parish. Counting their families, heirs, minors, females and others, the total of the 'nobility' can hardly have been much more than about 1 per cent of the population before the plague, rising perhaps to about 1.5 per cent during the period of highest mortality; the sources agree that mortality from the plague was more severe among the lower classes than among the aristocracy.[12]

The aristocracy was not a static band. We have seen that the mortality had an effect on rents and consequently on nobles' incomes after the mid-fourteenth century. Other changes were taking place as well, particularly a transformation in the nature of the earldoms and of comital wealth and power. The earldoms were ancient territorial lordships of Celtic origin, whose earliest history is in most cases lost to view. In the eleventh century there were about fourteen of them, held by *mormaer*, a rank rendered in Latin as *comites*, earls. Throughout most of the twelfth century the earls were men with Gaelic names, and few Anglo-Normans were promoted to comital rank. In the thirteenth century many of the earldoms fell by intermarriage or failure of heirs to persons with Anglo-Norman surnames, and the distinction between native and incomer was breaking down. As well as the earldoms, there was a roughly equal number of great provincial lordships which were territorially similar, but which did not carry the title of earl; examples are Lordships with such diverse origins as Annandale, Renfrew, Lauderdale, Garioch, and the Lordship of the Isles. Some of these seem to have been created out of existing (but obscure) territorial units by twelfth-century kings for the benefit of Anglo-Normans whom they wished to reward. In most respects except the name, these great provincial lordships resembled earldoms.

In the late fourteenth and fifteenth centuries, two noble families rose to the highest prominence: the Stewarts and the Douglases. Both were descendants of loyal followers of Robert Bruce (himself of baronial rather than royal origins), whose families were richly rewarded for their loyalty. The disloyalty of Robert Stewart cost him the trust of David II, but little else, as he succeeded to the throne in 1371 with his family estates intact. But Robert Stewart's accession was opposed by Lord Douglas (created 1st earl of Douglas in 1358) on the grounds that Stewart was no more royal than himself; he cobbled together a preposterous 'claim' based on supposed Balliol/Comyn relationships, then allowed Stewart to buy him off with the justiciarship of southern Scotland and the wardenship of the East March. Robert Stewart had a very large family, the number of his legitimate and illegitimate progeny extending to nearly two dozen, and these were married into the comital and upper baronial levels of society. Thus crown and nobility were coming closer together; the unbroken descent from Malcolm III was long gone, and the lustre of the mighty deeds of Robert Bruce was fading.

The earl of Douglas might well taunt Robert Stewart that he was equally 'royal', and within a few years so many other nobles had intermarried into the Stewart family that an alarming number of them could claim royal connections. Such royal connections as Alexander Stewart 'Wolf of Badenoch' could act in a high-handed and lawless fashion; more sinister were the pretensions of the archetypal wicked uncle, Robert Stewart earl of Fife, created duke of Albany in 1398. He was suspected of complicity in the death of his nephew the heir to the throne, David duke of Rothesay, in 1402, and even of connivance in the capture of his other nephew, later James I, in 1406; on Robert III's death he assumed full control of the government as heir apparent and duke of Albany (the title *dux Albaniae* being not a territorial title but a revival of the old Gaelic name for Scotland – as it were, 'leader of Scotland'); he was granted the new title of *gubernator*, governor, rather than lieutenant, and could style himself governor 'by the grace of God' and refer to the Scots as 'my subjects'.

The seemingly royal pretensions of the Albany Stewarts, and the accretions of the house of Stewart in general, were rudely shattered by the aggression of James I after his return from captivity in 1424; the Albany family were eliminated in 1425, other Stewarts were similarly destroyed and downgraded through the reign, until by the end of James I's reign almost the only noble Stewarts left were the house of Atholl, who murdered him in 1437.

The Douglases were a different problem. After the first earl's unsuccessful challenge in 1371, they had no royal pretensions; but by the mid-fifteenth century, their territorial power in south and south-west Scotland was vast, and they had important cadet branches, most notably the 'red Douglases' earls of Angus and the Douglases of Dalkeith, earls of Morton. During the reigns of Robert II and Robert III, the Douglases effectively waged their own private war on the Borders, and James I and James II could not expect to renew the war as a national enterprise without their support. James I's siege of Roxburgh in 1436 failed because of baronial dissension; probably it was with one eye to the renewal of the war that James II launched his aggressive and largely unprovoked attack on the Douglas power in the 1450s. It is noteworthy how little support the earls of Douglas received from their fellow nobles; the king was able to isolate them and pick them off at will.

Throughout the fifteenth century, the theme of cooperation between crown and nobility runs much more consistently than that of occasional 'overmighty' pretensions. Without a developed executive administration for police, revenue raising and local government, the crown had little choice but to cooperate with the baronage, with their local control and patronage. The nobles, on the other hand, could see no alternative to the Stewart monarchy, and were horrified by the frequent violent changes of dynasty in England. Even the murderers of James I were a small isolated group gathered around the Atholl Stewarts, and appear to have been motivated by personal grievances rather than any wish to alter the succession.

The greatest families in late fourteenth- and fifteenth-century Scotland were those which had risen under Robert I: Stewarts, Douglases, Dunbars, Macdonalds, and others. But social mobility brought some new families to prominence at different times. David II, distrustful of his nephew the Steward and his allies, promoted such lairdly families as Leslie and Erskine, so that the Leslies acquired the earldom of Ross by marriage, and the Erskines married into the comital family of Mar. The Drummonds increased their importance due to the marriage of Annabella Drummond to King Robert III. During the royal minorities which followed the deaths of James I and James II, the lesser families of Livingston, Crichton and Boyd used their household position to exercise political influence, without having a territorial power-base to support them; royal attacks on the nobility probably facilitated their brief ascendancies, but crown and nobility were easily able to reduce them when kings came of age and shook off their tutelage.

It is easy to document upward social mobility. Downward social mobility has left less trace, but it must have been happening at all levels of society. Probably it was a more gradual but more widespread process.

With so much fluidity in the personnel at the top of society, and the social change one would expect in the wake of war and plague, one expects to find new institutions governing interrelationships between men. The most typical and interesting of these is the 'bond of manrent', a written document specifying a lord–man relationship not based on landholding; the term 'bastard feudalism' does not do justice to the complexities of these relationships.[13]

The nobility is a tiny, if well documented, fragment of society. For the vast majority, the husbandmen, cottars and landless labourers, we are much less well informed. We have seen that mortality led to a fall in rents and a general amelioration in the condition of the peasantry; the *nativus* or serf disappears, and although labour service continues it appears to be lighter than before.

The nobility was a small but very important section of society; equally small, but of great economic significance, was the urban population. In the fourteenth century, burghs became even more important to kings as a source of finance, since Robert I needed money to pay for the war, and David II needed it to pay for his ransom. Burghs thus were brought into the consultative process of parliament. The development of a fully defined constitutional status for the burghs in the fourteenth century reflects their changing importance in society as a whole, and is characteristic of the many social changes which came about in fourteenth-century Scotland, brought about by mortality from war and disease. For a variety of reasons and in a rich variety of ways, Scottish society was very different in the late fourteenth century from what it had been a hundred years before.[14]

CHAPTER 11

The Scottish Church in the Later Middle Ages

CHURCH AND STATE IN SCOTLAND, 1329–1469

Scotland and the Avignon Popes

During the Wars of Independence, most popes, with the exception of Boniface VIII, had been broadly pro-Plantagenet. After 1309, the popes resided at Avignon in southern France, and were increasingly subservient to the wishes of the kings of France. This did not prevent John XXII from continuing to support Edward II against Robert Bruce, though this was due more to the doubtful legality of Bruce's position than to any pro-English bias, and during the 1320s the pope genuinely strove for an acceptable peace between England and Scotland. After the outbreak of the Hundred Years' War in 1338, the Avignon popes, themselves Frenchmen, supported the house of Valois against Edward III. During the latter stages of the Avignon papacy Scotland, as France's ally, was always likely to have favourable relations with the popes.

At home, the Scottish Church 'ay stude in dowte and in peryle' during the early years of Edward III's renewal of war. The See of St Andrews, the premier bishopric of the kingdom, was vacant between the death of Lamberton in 1331 and 1342, when David II, newly returned from France, persuaded Benedict XII to appoint William Landallis to the vacant see. Landallis was bishop for over forty years. He 'began his long diplomatic career as a leader of the missions to England for the release of the king' after Neville's Cross (1346). Under the influence of Landallis 'the Scottish kirk was to show a bold face to Edward III when he renewed the policy of ecclesiastical intrusion'.[1]

David II was conventionally pious, going on pilgrimages, rewarding and encouraging Scottish crusaders, and building a church dedicated to St Monan. He staffed his household and administration with clerics, and 'the Scottish episcopate included persons who were closely associated with the king: bishop Landallis had served him year after year as a diplomatist, so also had Master Walter Wardlaw, who had been the king's secretary before being rewarded with the bishopric of Glasgow in 1368'. Appointment to a bishopric was the ultimate reward for loyal service to the king.

The Great Schism

This appearance of order was thrown into confusion a few years after David's death in 1371. As early as 1365 there had been moves to return the papacy to Rome, and this was done in 1377. Gregory XI's return to Rome was not a success, however, and there was disturbance in Rome. The pope's plans to return to Avignon were prevented by his death in 1378. The cardinals, under acute pressure from the Roman mob, felt obliged to elect an Italian as pope, and chose Bartolomeo Prignano, archbishop of Bari, as the most suitable Italian candidate.

Prignano took the name of Urban VI and was crowned as pope; but 'his outbursts of temper became so violent and uncontrolled that most historians agree that he took leave of his senses upon election to the papacy'. The same group of cardinals who had elected Urban left Rome, denounced his election as invalid, declared him deposed, and elected Cardinal Robert de Génève as pope. He took the name of Clement VII and returned to Avignon. The 'Great Schism' had begun.[2]

Clement was supported in France, Urban in Italy; and by chain reaction Clement soon gained the obedience of Castille, Aragon, Navarre, Portugal, Naples, Savoy, Sicily, Rhodes, and Scotland, while the German empire, Scandinavia, northern and central Italy, England and Ireland mostly followed Urban. In Scotland, as elsewhere, there was an increasing tendency towards litigiousness among churchmen seeking after benefices, and the papacy, anxious not to lose support in any country where it had adherents, was keen to show itself as the fount of ecclesiastical justice. Thus the practice of petitioning the pope for provision to benefices became increasingly common.

In spite of these problems, some attempts were made to preserve standards within the Scottish Church. To this end in 1383 Clement VII appointed for Scotland its first cardinal, Walter Wardlaw Bishop of Glasgow. Wardlaw died in 1387. The role of enforcing church discipline was carried on most notably by bishop Walter Trail of St Andrews (1385–1401) 'a man of distinguished academic and ecclesiastical background'. As well as his attempts to reform abuses such as clerical concubinage and the use of churches and churchyards for dancing, bear-baiting and wrestling, he also strove for political stability by associating himself with Archibald 'the Grim', earl of Douglas, and Queen Annabella in supporting Rothesay during his lieutenancy (1399–1402). Subsequently there was a dispute over the bishopric of St Andrews, but the bishops of Glasgow during the period were men of ability. Matthew Glendinning (1387–1408), was conservator of the Marches and ambassador to England. In 1401 he was one of the commissioners appointed to negotiate a peace with England, and showed his spirit when an Englishman suggested that the right of the king of England to homage by the king of Scots should be put to arbitration; Glendinning replied that Henry IV's right to the throne of England should be put to arbitration as well. His successor William Lauder (1404–25) served as chancellor and 'was frequently employed in affairs of state'. Other Scottish bishops had similar long careers of public service at a time when the crown most needed them.[3]

Men like these provided continuity and stability during the period of the early Stewarts and the Albany governorship. The Church was also troubled, for the Great Schism continued unresolved upon the death of Clement VII in 1394, with the election of Peter de Luna (Benedict XIII, 1394–1422) as Avignon pope. Scotland was to be unswervingly loyal to Benedict for twenty-four years. The principal act of his pontificate regarding Scotland was the foundation of St Andrews University in 1411–13, necessitated by the withdrawal of France from Benedict's allegiance in 1409. The University repaid its founder in 1418 by recommending to the Governor that he abandon Benedict, already deserted by almost everyone else, and profess obedience to Martin V, recently elected as a compromise candidate by the Council of Constance. The Governor was reluctant, but in October 1418 Scotland recognised Martin and ended the Great Schism.[4]

The resolution of the Great Schism should have brought an end to religious controversy in Scotland. All those who had held benefices under Benedict XIII retained them. A few institutions which had become independent of English superiority during the Schism returned to subjection, such as the diocese of Galloway and the Knights Hospitallers; in other cases, such as the diocese of the Isles, which had been divided up between English bishops in the Isle of Man and Scottish bishops in Skye, the division became permanent. The diocese of Orkney presented a different situation, being neither within the Scottish kingdom nor part of the Scottish province of the Church; but after the acquisition of the earldom of Orkney by the Sinclairs of Roslin in the 1370s, a series of Scottish bishops was provided by the Avignon popes, and thereafter 'the bishops of Orkney were all Scotsmen'.[5]

Scotland and the Conciliar Movement

Although the Western Church was reunited in the recognition of a single pope, there was disagreement about the extent of his authority. The Council of Constance (1414–17) had resolved the Schism, but had also decreed that 'this council holds its authority direct from Christ; everyone, no matter his rank or office, even if it be papal, is bound to obey it'. Further, it laid down that general councils should be held at frequent intervals. Thereafter the council dissolved itself, leaving Martin V free to undo its work.

Under Martin and his successor Eugenius IV (1431–47), the old system of provisions and reservation continued as if nothing at all had happened. From 1418, a flood of Scottish supplications reached Martin, requesting provisions to benefices and other graces. The Council had not checked the flood of wealth into the papal curia. James I, on his return to Scotland in 1424, determined to interfere in church matters as in every other aspect of his kingdom. Through parliament James attempted to restrict this practice, known as 'barratry', but his legislation proved ineffective and the flood of petitions continued.[6]

James used the papacy to further the career of John Cameron, his secretary, keeper of the privy seal, and chancellor from 1427. When the see of Glasgow became vacant in 1425, the chapter of Glasgow were prevailed upon to elect Cameron, and the pope, after initial reluctance, provided him. Cameron was then denounced before the pope by William Croyser, archdeacon of Teviotdale, as the originator of the barratry legislation. The personalities of the post-Schism popes and James I made conflict inevitable, and this was complicated in 1431 by the convening of the Council of Basle, called under the terms laid down at Constance.

James I and Cameron became conciliarists, Croyser a papalist. Basle reaffirmed the superiority of council over pope, whereupon the new pope, Eugenius IV, dissolved it; but the council took no notice and continued to sit. Eugenius, under pressure from the emperor, recognised the council again in 1433, but it 'continued in its anti-papal attitude, reasserted once again the decrees of Constance, imposed many restrictions on the papal legates, and prescribed an oath to be taken by the pope after his election'. For these and other reasons Eugenius again denounced the council and transferred it to Ferrara (1438) and then to Florence (1439), where it would be closer to papal control. But the councillors who had ignored Eugenius in 1431 were not now going to be coerced, and so continued in session at Basle, electing an anti-pope (Felix V) in 1439.

Cameron attended the Council of Basle for a time in 1434–5, and numbers of other Scots were also present, some of whom took a prominent part. Croyser denounced Cameron before the council, and for his pains was denounced as a traitor and rebel before parliament in 1435. A cardinal's secretary, Aeneas Sylvius Piccolomini (the future Pope Pius II), visited Scotland in 1435 to prepare a legatine visit, and in 1436 the bishop of Urbino was sent to Scotland as papal legate. He was still in Scotland with the issues unresolved when James was murdered early in 1437.[7]

Curiously, while James I supported conciliarism in Scotland, his son and successor James II was a papalist; while the Douglases, who dominated the years immediately following James I's death, fell heir to conciliarism. This was due to the continuity shown in the early years of James II's minority, and due also to the influence of the papalist James Kennedy, a nephew of James I who was appointed bishop of Dunkeld in 1437 and transferred to St Andrews in 1440. He was to be the most influential churchman of James II's reign.[8]

Despite Kennedy's papalism, and the papacy's eventual victory over the council in 1449, James II had 'remarkable success in securing bishops after his own heart', and extensions of his control over ecclesiastical appointments. He had a right to appoint to vacancies within a bishop's gift during an episcopal vacancy, and after 1457 a provincial council of the Scottish Church allowed him also appointment to major elective dignities. But the king's increasing powers over appointments were not abused at this time. William Turnbull, bishop of Glasgow (1447–53), persuaded Pope Nicholas V to found Scotland's second university in Glasgow in 1451, and was succeeded by one of its first teachers, Andrew de Durisdeer (bishop 1455–73), who had worked in the household of the cardinal who reformed the University of Paris.[9]

The Aftermath: Scottish Archbishops

The foundation of Glasgow University by Turnbull was a result of rivalry between Glasgow and St Andrews, in response to Kennedy's foundation of a new college, St Salvator's, in St Andrews University in 1450. The rivalry between the two dioceses was to continue in the second half of the century, sometimes in less beneficial ways. Patrick Graham, Kennedy's nephew and successor at St Andrews, was elected in 1465, having previously been bishop of Brechin. In 1472, possibly on his own initiative and heavily in debt, he persuaded Pope Sixtus IV to elevate St Andrews into a metropolitan archbishopric with authority over all the other Scottish sees, including Galloway, Orkney and the Isles. This antagonised the other bishops and the crown, which had not been consulted. The bishops complained to the king about Graham, and in 1475 he was excommunicated for non-payment of his debts. His sanity seems to have crumbled under pressure, and it was reported in 1476 that he had lost his reason. Upon investigation he was deprived of his bishopric and died in confinement. Graham was succeeded by William Scheves, a humbly born but distinguished academic with medical training. Scheves owed his position to royal favour and was loyal to James III. Several long-serving diocesans were passed over, and the bishops resented the metropolitan's rank.[10]

In 1487 James III secured an Indult or privilege promising that the pope would take account of royal nominations to bishoprics and senior dignities. In spite of this, episcopal appointments during the fifteenth century were usually men with good ecclesiastical careers and academic records. Scandalous appointments were a feature of the sixteenth century, not the fifteenth.[11]

The last major landmark in Church–state developments in late medieval Scotland was the erection of Glasgow as a second archbishopric in 1492. This was a reward for Robert Blackadder, a supporter of the 1488 revolution which overthrew James III, and a rebuff for Scheves, James's loyal creature. 'Wasteful controversy between the two archbishops ensued, and the leadership that might have come from an effective primacy of St Andrews was undermined.'[12]

THE CONDITION OF THE SCOTTISH CHURCH IN THE LATER MIDDLE AGES

In the Middle Ages the influence of the Christian Church penetrated into every aspect of life and society. Christenings, marriages and funerals were performed in churches; clerks (*clerici*, members of the clergy) acted as notaries in legal transactions; schools, hospitals and almshouses were run by churchmen. The level of Sunday churchgoing was very much higher than in Scotland today. The country was divided into parishes, each of which had a kirk served by a parson or vicar; and although parishes varied in size, it would probably be true to say that except in the west and north Highland areas, few villages were more than four or five of miles from a parish church. Scotland differed, however, from England, where almost every village had a parish church.

Glasgow Cathedral's Blackadder aisle was built by Glasgow's first archbishop. *(Historic Scotland)*

Problems of the Late Medieval Church in Scotland

Evidence for apathy and hostility on the part of the laity is difficult to find, since it was not in the clergy's interest to publicise such problems. But a problem did exist:

> In the parish church of Strageith in Dunblane diocese, many of the parishioners are distant from the church . . . so they take no pains to come to the church, indeed, some of them come scarcely once in the year, namely at Easter, and moreover many of them come like beasts and are utterly ignorant of the divine offices and the commandments of the church.[13]

We can never know how extensive religious apathy was in late medieval Scotland; but perhaps the vicar of Strageith was not the only clergyman in Scotland who had difficulty in getting his parishioners to attend church regularly. There are examples of churches being described as ruined in roof or walls, without vestments, service-books or ornaments, and reduced to a condition which made the conduct of divine service difficult or impossible. Under such circumstances it is hard to see the faithful pouring out to mass in their hordes every Sunday morning. There was, however, little questioning by laymen of the whole theological structure of salvation by good works, which included, as well as mass, pilgrimages, indulgences, and other devotional acts.

Since many aspects of religious observance were a valuable source of income to the clergy, they were much encouraged. Devotion to saints, pilgrimages, and regular churchgoing were encouraged by clergy such as Walter Bower, abbot of Inchcolm, whose massive *Scotichronicon* is full of salutary moral lessons, including discussions of the perils of excommunication and of the many advantages to be gained from going to mass.[14]

Lollardy in Scotland

It would be wrong, however, to see this moralising as going totally unquestioned by the laity. There was little of the apathy to religious questions which dominates present-day society, though the indifference and ignorance of the parishioners of Strageith suggest that it did exist; and many moralistic tales include stock wicked characters, who mock the clergy and sacraments and are invariably duly punished for their evil way of life. If they had not existed in fact, there might have been no need to invent them. Perhaps also had respect for the mass been universal, there would have been no need to list its beneficial properties.

Disrespect for the mass – where it existed – can be attributed to the ideas of the Lollards, followers of the English academic John Wycliffe (d. 1384). Evidence for Lollardy in Scotland is slender, but recurring. There were very few burnings of Lollards in Scotland: the Englishman John Resby was burned at St Andrews in 1407 and the Bohemian Paul Crawar in 1433, and an unnamed heretic was burned in the diocese of Glasgow in 1422.[15] But the threat was taken seriously; in 1399 the duke of Rothesay swore to restrain Lollards, and it was said of the duke of Albany (d. 1420) that 'All Lollard he hatyt and heretyke'. Bower wrote that Resby gained 'great fame by preaching to the simple folk' and 'his conclusions are still held by some Lollards in Scotland'. The only Scottish Lollard writings which survive from this period are the outpourings of the esquire Quentin Flockhart (Folkehyrde), in a letter written to his parish priest in 1410:

> . . . I have warned the three estates of the church as a whole [i.e., bishops, priests and clerks] what their condition should be and for what purpose they were established until they leave this world by the authority of God's will. And I warn you in particular, on behalf of God and for the dangers which may follow in this life and the next, that you should dispose yourself with all zeal to the correcting of your errors; so that you should not be seen to uphold error, but that you should become perfect in the following, namely, that you should give up all worldly

concerns, and live your life in your home which is the church, and study only the divine Law, the Lord's Prayer and the Creed, and teach all of God's ordinances to your parishioners in the mother tongue.[16]

The priest is further urged to keep only what is necessary and secretly to give the rest of his goods to God, by giving liberally to the poor; if he does not do so, the Lollards will make war on him with greater vehemence than against Jews and Saracens, because his works are more evil than theirs.

Even more radical were the views of a group of Ayrshire Lollards who were brought before the bishop of Glasgow in 1494:

> That images are not to be had, nor yet to be worshipped. That the relics of the saints are not to be worshipped. . . . That Christ ordained no priests to consecrate. That after the consecration in the mass there remains bread; and there is not the natural body of Christ. . . . That every faithful man or woman is a priest. . . . That the Pope deceives the people by his Bulls and his Indulgences. That the mass profiteth not the souls that are in purgatory. That the Pope and his bishops deceive the people by their pardons. . . . That faith should not be given to miracles. That we should not pray to the glorious Virgin Mary, but to God only.[17]

Many of the same concerns are evident in both writings: the need for virtuous clergy, the invalidity of ceremonies performed by sinful priests, the worthlessness of crusading and pilgrimages, the need for vernacular scriptures. There is little theological refinement, and no anticipation of the Protestant doctrine of justification by faith.

The continued existence of a Lollard problem is still hinted at in the poems of William Dunbar, who describes how 'The schip of faith tempestuous wind and rane / Dryvis in the see of Lollerdy that blawis.' And who, in the good-humoured 'Flyting of Dunbar and Kennedy', cheerfully trades accusations of Lollardy with his opponent, which would have had no point if Lollardy had been extinct.[18]

Although the evidence is limited, it shows that some sort of Lollard underground existed throughout the fifteenth century, posing a problem of which the established Church was aware, but which it was anxious to keep as quiet as possible. Lollardy never seems to have been as extensive in Scotland as it was in England, but there are hints of its existence, and it is in the context of these that we must view Bower's moralising, aimed to keep the simple folk on the straight and narrow way.

Criticism of the Church and Clergy

It is clear that the lives of many clergy were not such as to inspire respect from their lay neighbours. The statutes of the Church set down certain standards of dress and behaviour, which were not always strictly observed. The papal registers have plenty of examples which show both secular clergy and religious living in a way which deserved condemnation, but it must be remembered that many of these accusations are *ex parte* statements made by men who were anxious to secure the benefices of those whom they accused. We also possess the confessions of Scots clergy who were involved in crimes which required absolution from the papal penitentiary. Heresy, apathy and hostility are very poorly documented, but clerical bad behaviour must have gone some way towards fuelling them.[19]

Education

One way of combating heresy, other than moralising, was by education and the fifteenth century saw the foundation of universities at St Andrews, Glasgow and Aberdeen. However, even though better educated than they had ever been before, the clergy were now more litigious and acquisitive. Many of them sought training in canon law as a way of obtaining benefices through litigation. A bishop would have 'mensal churches' whose revenues were attached to his household, likewise deans and archdeacons had parsonages appropriated to them; simple canons had parsonages which they seldom visited; and religious houses, Cistercians, Benedictines and Augustinians, also had appropriated parish churches. Vicarages often became appropriated too, and those that were not were often held in plurality by careerists, members of the household of the king, or of a great noble or ecclesiastic. At Rome, where more and more benefices were acquired, there was a staff of Scottish canon lawyers, attached to the households of cardinals, who acted as procurators for Scottish benefice-hunters. Unsuccessful applicants for a benefice were frequently compensated with a pension from the revenues. Thus the parochial structure increasingly came to pay not for the spiritual care of parishioners, but for the comforts of higher ecclesiastics, institutions, and legal fees.

Attempts to remedy this situation by burgh running of town kirks at Edinburgh, Dundee, Aberdeen and elsewhere tended to be along conservative lines, with a proliferation of altars, chapels and mass-priests. Religious orders came in for increasing criticism from the time of James I's denunciation of the religious houses in Parliament in 1425:

> The downhill condition and most threatening ruin of holy religion, now declining from day to day . . . fill us with apprehension. . . . Wherefore we require and warn you, laying aside excuses for all your faults and slackness, to apply yourselves . . . to the reformation of this your holy religion.[20]

There are plenty of examples of accusations against the immorality of religious men, of dilapidation, alienation, concubinage and secularisation.

At the same time, there was a general increase in lay literacy and lay education. An Education Act of 1496, requiring noblemen's eldest sons to attend grammar schools and universities, reflects social changes which were already taking place; it has been estimated that by *c.* 1500 some 60 per cent of the nobility were able to sign their names.[21] Education had come too late to make the nobility Lollards in the fifteenth century, but in the sixteenth it made them receptive to new ideas coming into Scotland. With the increase in literacy and education among the gentry it was going to be much more difficult than before for the religious establishment to contain criticism and heresy.

CHAPTER 12

Nadir and Recovery:
the House of Stewart, 1371–1460

THE EARLY STEWARTS AND GOVERNOR ALBANY

The Reign of Robert II, 1371–90

Robert Stewart was fifty-five when he became king on David II's death. According to Bower, he was impressive-looking, humble, mild, affable, cheerful and honourable. His career during David II's lifetime had showed little of the last quality, and humility and mildness were not attributes required of medieval kings. His most extraordinary quality seems to have been his enormous fertility; during his long life he fathered some two dozen children, many of them illegitimate. By the 1420s, Robert Stewart's large family had married extensively into the Scottish aristocracy; more than half the earldoms were held by royal Stewarts, including Fife, Menteith, Buchan, Mar, Strathearn and Atholl.

Their connections with royalty meant that many of the nobility were more closely related to the crown than ever before, and some acted in a way that took their kinship with the king as setting them above the law. The most notorious example was Alexander Stewart lord of Badenoch and earl of Buchan, the 'wolf of Badenoch'; as justiciar of the north he had extorted protection money from the bishop of Moray for a number of years before 1390; when in that year the bishop stopped paying, Stewart burned the cathedral of Elgin with its burgh, parish church, hospital and eighteen manses of canons. The instigator of the deed, the son of one king and brother of another, went unpunished.[1]

Indeed, the Stewarts were regarded as more baronial than royal in their lineage. Robert Stewart as heir apparent must have been alarmed when, immediately on his uncle's death in February 1371, his position was challenged by William earl of Douglas, who claimed that he was just as 'royal' as any Stewart, and concocted a preposterous claim to the throne based on a supposed connection with the Balliols and Comyns. He was prevailed on by Sir Robert Erskine and the Earl of March to forego his pretensions, and as a reward the new king made him justiciar in the south and warden of the East March, while his son and heir received a lump sum, an annuity, and the hand of the king's daughter in marriage. Erskine and Dunbar were also rewarded for their help in securing the crown for the Stewart. Robert was crowned with ceremony at Scone on 26 March 1371.[2]

In Robert II's early years, there is evidence of continuity with the administration built up by David II. Sir Robert Erskine lived into the 1380s, and others of David II's household continued in office. The exchequer receipts remain at a level comparable with David's later years into the mid-1370s, showing a healthy surplus in 1373–4. But direct taxation was discontinued after 1373 and other problems followed. The boom in the wool trade which had inflated the customs revenue in the 1350s and '60s began to peter out, until by 1390 receipts from this source had nearly halved. Less and less money was actually reaching the chamberlain, and by 1390 it was reported that sheriffs were not appearing in person or through their legal representative for the exchequer audit. The ransom continued to be paid until Edward III's death in 1377, when it lapsed because the Scots regarded it as a personal payment to him; so a stimulus for good financial management was removed. By Robert II's death in 1390, the crown finances had degenerated to virtual chaos.[3]

The maintenance of law and order also declined. One of the most glaring examples came in 1382, when John Lyon thane of Glamis was murdered by Sir James Lindsay of Crawford; the crime went unpunished, and in 1384 parliament complained that 'offences and outrageous crimes have been wont to be committed against the law for no short time'. Parliament went on to issue a commission to John earl of Carrick, the heir apparent, to maintain law and justice throughout the kingdom, and passed statutes relating to shrieval assizes. John was already forty-seven, and showed little energy or ability for his new task; there is evidence that crimes continued to go unpunished. In 1388 Earl John was lamed by a kick from a horse, so the estates took the excuse to remove him and to entrust the position of guardian (*custos*) to the king's second son, Robert earl of Fife and Menteith. He was also given the title of Governor (*gubernator*), the 'helmsman' of Scotland during Robert II's declining years. Robert was to show more ability than his father or brother when he became sole Governor of Scotland in 1406; for now, however, the problems of justice and administration remained.

The most impressive achievement of Robert II's reign came in the field of the renewed war against England. While David II lived, relations with England had been almost cordial; there had been no real fighting since Neville's Cross (1346), and the truce was not due to expire until 1384. The ransom continued to be paid until Edward III's death in 1377, but thereafter was stopped with 20,000 marks left unpaid, although the truce was still observed after a fashion. The greatest border families, however, began to engage in warfare of their own, while Robert II claimed that he had no desire to see the truce broken but could not restrain his nobles. In 1379 George Dunbar earl of March arrived as an unwelcome guest at Roxburgh fair (the burgh and castle were in English hands) and sacked and burned the town. In 1380 John of Gaunt, King Richard II's uncle, was on the Marches with a force of 2,000 men accusing the Scots of repeated encroachments on English-occupied territory in Berwickshire and Roxburghshire, but could obtain no satisfaction; in the following year he was again on the borders negotiating with the Scots when news arrived of the Peasants' Revolt, causing him to seek refuge in Scotland. He was hospitably entertained at Holyrood Abbey.

Despite John of Gaunt's generous treatment in Scotland, both sides prepared for a renewal of war as the expiry of the treaty approached. In 1383 the English government demanded the return of all 'English' land in Scotland which had been recovered over the last few years, and the balance of David II's ransom; in 1384 they proposed to punish the Scots for 'rebellion' against England. As a precaution, Robert II concluded a new agreement with the French whereby the French king agreed to send money, troops and arms to Scotland in the event of war, and the Scottish castles were made ready, with guns and powder making their first appearance in the exchequer records.

The first foray came immediately on the expiry of the truce at Candlemas 1384, when the earl of March and Archibald 'the Grim' lord of Galloway seized Lochmaben Castle and swept the English out of Annandale. John of Gaunt retaliated by marching to Edinburgh, but the castle was too strong for him; he was disposed to spare the town and Holyrood Abbey because of his earlier hospitable treatment there, and allowed himself to be bought off. After his withdrawal the Scots raided into the north of England, joined by a small band of French knights who had arrived in advance of the force promised under the 1383 agreement. This force arrived in the Firth of Forth in May 1385. In July a well-equipped and disciplined Franco-Scottish army set out for the border and stormed Wark Castle. The French were eager for battle when they learned of the approach of a massive army under the young Richard II and John of Gaunt, and were dismayed when the Scots decided to retreat and lay waste their own countryside; but however unchivalrous the French might have thought this, the tactic was effective. The English advanced through the borders as far as Edinburgh, burning Melrose, Dryburgh and Newbattle Abbeys as nests of 'schismatic' adherents of Clement VII; Holyrood was again spared on John of Gaunt's orders, but the burgh of Edinburgh was put to the flames. By the end of a fortnight the massive English army was starving and forced into retreat. Meanwhile the Franco-Scottish army had invaded the English West March, devastating Cumberland and appearing before the walls of Carlisle; the French believed that they burned and plundered more in the dioceses of Durham and Carlisle than was to be found in all the towns of Scotland put together. As they returned to Edinburgh through the border country, the French were amazed to see the Scottish countrymen returning to their homes with goods and livestock which they had driven into hiding as the English had approached.

The Scots had had the better of the hostilities of 1385; but the use of French troops in Scotland was not a success. They were unpopular, plundering the countryside and despising the Scottish tactic of retreating in the face of the enemy. Furthermore, a planned French invasion of southern England did not materialise, so the force in Scotland was left isolated. It departed amid bitter recriminations, leaving the admiral behind as surety for the payment of damages allegedly inflicted during their stay.

The frantic military activity of 1385 left both sides exhausted and disposed to accept a series of short truces until 1388. Meanwhile, Richard II's authority was increasingly threatened during the constitutional crisis led by the 'lords appellant' in 1387–8, and in the latter year the Scots sought to exploit the difficulties faced by the English, which included also rivalry between the border families of Percy and Neville.

The three-pronged attack of the summer of 1388 was one of the most ambitious Scottish campaigns since 1327. There was a diversionary thrust into Ireland, a land whose reannexation was dear to Richard's heart, followed by a raid across the Solway to Cockermouth. Then the main Scottish army marched south through the West March, devastating as far as Stainmore Forest on the Yorkshire border. A smaller force under the earls of March, Moray and Douglas advanced through the East March as far as Newcastle and then withdrew. Henry Percy, called 'Hotspur', son of the earl of Northumberland, having decided not to attack the main Scottish army in the west, crossed the Pennines and caught up with the small force at Otterburn in Redesdale. It was nearly nightfall on 5 August when the Scots realised that they were under attack and rushed to arms; the earl of Douglas took the field only partially armed and was mortally wounded. As darkness fell and the battle raged his death went unnoticed, and the dying earl commanded his attendants to conceal his body from friend and foe, 'for if my enemies knew it they would rejoice'. When dawn broke the next day, it was on a Scottish victory; Hotspur was captured and many of his knights were dead. Douglas was the most considerable of the Scottish casualties, but the victory was attributed to him, and thus 'a dead man won a fight'.

Otterburn was a significant victory for the Scots. It was not simply a skirmish between two border families, but part of a concerted campaign involving the earls of Fife, Douglas, March and Moray and Archibald 'the Grim' lord of Galloway, with the approval of the king and the earl of Carrick. In England, the repercussions of the Scottish victory were immediate, with the fall of the government of the 'lords appellant' and the return to power of Richard II. Richard favoured a policy of peace with France and warfare within the British Isles, and was reluctant to include the Scots in a truce agreed with France in 1389; but French pressure persuaded him not to risk repeating the failures of 1385 and 1388, and Robert II quickly agreed to be included in the truce in 1389.

By the end of Robert II's reign the English were left only with precarious garrisons at Roxburgh, Jedburgh and Berwick; Annandale, Teviotdale and Tweeddale had been recovered by the Scots. The elusive final peace had still not been achieved, but at least the Scots were included in a long truce. It has been justly remarked that 'as far as success in foreign affairs is concerned, Robert II's reign was second only to Robert I's in late medieval Scottish history'. Bower states that he left his kingdom in great tranquillity as a lover of peace, in full freedom and bountiful peace. A different assessment is that of John Mair: 'Whatever our writers [of history] may contend, I cannot hold this aged king, Robert II I mean, to have been a skillful warrior or wise in council'.[4] Robert II was seventy-four years old at his death, and had for some years shown little inclination for personal government. Fortunately, the diplomats and military commanders of his last years were men of greater ability.

Robert III, 1390–1406

Robert II's son and successor, John earl of Carrick, was not among these. His period as commissioner for law and justice (1384–8) had not been a success, and when in the latter year he was lamed the opportunity was taken to remove him and promote his more ambitious brother, Robert earl of Fife.[5]

On his father's death in 1390, John, with consent of parliament, took the name Robert after his father and great-grandfather, since the name John was held to be unlucky for a king; it was hoped that the name Robert would bring good luck. It did not. The laxness of law and order and administrative chaos prevalent in Robert II's later years continued and intensified. During the four months which elapsed between the death of Robert II and the coronation of Robert III, the burghs of Forres and Elgin were burned. In 1391 or 1392 there was an outrage at Glen Brerachan near Pitlochry, when Sir Walter Ogilvie sheriff of Angus and his brother were slain by Highland 'caterans' led by Duncan Stewart, a bastard son of the Wolf of Badenoch. In 1395 there was a judicial combat on the borders between an English and a Scottish knight, presided over by the wardens of the Marches, Douglas and Percy. A more notorious judicial combat was held in the following year at Perth between thirty 'caterans' on each side, watched by the king and the foreign dignitaries who were attending his court.

Although this kind of disorder was largely absent from the Lordship of the Isles under Macdonald rule, the lord of the Isles did allow his brother, Alasdair Carrach, to make depredations into Moray and extort protection money from the earl of Moray; attempts to persuade the Lord to restrain his brother were unavailing. In 1398 a Moray chronicler wrote: 'In those days there was no law in Scotland, but he who was stronger oppressed him who was weaker, and the whole realm was a den of thieves; murders, herschips [pillaging], arson and all other misdeeds went unpunished, and justice, as if outlawed, lay in exile beyond the bounds of the realm'. In some localities great nobles such as the Lord of the Isles or the earls of Douglas and March could maintain order; but central control was lacking.

In 1398 the king's elder son, David earl of Carrick, was knighted with ceremony at Edinburgh and created duke of Rothesay; he was the first Scottish royal duke (the title had been introduced in England in 1337), and was immediately followed by his uncle Robert earl of Fife, who was created duke of Albany. The titles were honorific rather than territorial; Rothesay was Robert III's favourite residence, and Albany was a revival of the Gaelic name of Scotland, *Alba*. The earl of Fife had been effective ruler of Scotland since 1388, and did not take kindly to the promotion of the nineteen-year-old Rothesay, soon quarrelling with him. Meanwhile Rothesay, who seems to have been headstrong, first betrothed and then repudiated a daughter of George Dunbar, earl of March, marrying instead a daughter of Archibald earl of Douglas. Dunbar, outraged, sought reparation from the king, but could not even get the repayment of his daughter's dowry; so he fled to England, while earl Archibald seized his castle of Dunbar. One of the most powerful border lords, as well as one of the heroes of Otterburn, had been estranged by the crown and driven to seek English help.

Rothesay Castle, Bute, the favourite residence of Robert III. *(Historic Scotland)*

Rothesay alienated others by his behaviour as well. His uncle Albany stood aloof during a major English invasion in 1400, while the new English king Henry IV accused Rothesay of sending libellous letters to France accusing him of treasonable crimes. Rothesay was ambitious to supplant his uncle as the power behind the throne, and Albany's failures to maintain law and order and the chaotic state of the crown finances provided grounds for his removal. A general council at Perth in January 1399 hinted at the maladministration of the king's officers and appointed Rothesay as lieutenant at the head of a council of twenty-one, to enjoy the emoluments formerly paid to Albany. The chief instigators of this palace revolution were the queen, Annabella Drummond, Walter Trail bishop of St Andrews, and Archibald 'the Grim' earl of Douglas; they probably hoped to control Rothesay. Their hopes were misplaced, for Rothesay was volatile and fickle; but in any case the three of them all died in 1400–1, leaving Rothesay isolated. It was said, wrote Bower, that with their deaths 'dignity departed, honour withdrew and decency died' in Scotland.[6] Albany began to ingratiate himself once more with the king, and to spread rumours against Rothesay's administration.

Suddenly in March 1402, shortly after Rothesay had observed a bright comet above Edinburgh, 'signifying the death or removal of a prince', he was arrested by Albany on the king's orders. Despite the portent, Rothesay apparently suspected nothing. He was imprisoned at Falkland and decently confined, but died of dysentery, 'or as some would have it, of hunger' on the night of 25/26 March. Albany's accomplice in Rothesay's overthrow was the new earl of Douglas, Archibald son of Archibald the Grim; the two of them were summoned before a general council at Edinburgh in May 1402 and questioned about the circumstances of the duke's death. The estates declared that he had 'departed this life by divine providence and not otherwise'. The king publicly declared their innocence in his son's death, and forbade murmurings and rumours.

One reason for concluding matters quickly was the threat of renewed war. The Welsh had risen against Henry IV, who had deposed Richard II in 1399; an imposter calling himself 'Richard II' appeared in Scotland, and was honourably entertained by Albany until his death in 1419, when he was buried at Stirling with full royal honours.

But the main cause of renewed war was the feud between the Douglases and Dunbars. When the earl of March sought to reoccupy his earldom he had some local support, but was opposed by the lairds of Lothian, whom he met in battle and defeated at Nisbet Moor in the Merse on 22 July 1402. Albany's over-confidence in trying to exact retribution resulted in a more serious Scottish defeat at Humbleton Hill in Northumberland on 14 September 1402.

Although Humbleton negated many of the Scottish gains of recent years, Percy was unable to follow it up. He besieged but failed to capture Cocklaws in Teviotdale, whose commander agreed to surrender it if not relieved by 1 August 1403. Albany gathered an army and marched to its relief, only to find that the opposition did not turn up; Percy had been killed in rebellion at Shrewsbury on 21 July. Scots fought on both sides at Shrewsbury: Archibald Douglas, a captive of Humbleton, fought in Percy's army and

Linlithgow Palace and St Michael's Kirk were rebuilt by James I.
(Historic Scotland)

Dauphin Louis until 1436. In 1433 an English embassy arrived in Scotland to try to dissuade James from the French alliance, and offering the restoration of Roxburgh and Berwick. The French also sent ambassadors in 1435 in the hope of persuading James to make war on the Borders, indicating that this would be more useful than the 6,000 men who were still promised for France. It was the forfeiture of the earl of March which may have decided James; the earl's brother was openly siding with the English garrison in Berwick Castle, and the two of them raided southern Scotland in September 1435, only to be routed by the Scots at Piperdean. Soon after James's daughter set out for France to marry the Dauphin, and in the summer of 1436 James projected the first ambitious military venture of his reign, the siege of Roxburgh.

According to Bower, James's host numbered 200,000 armed men with at least the same number of footsoldiers and carts. This is an exaggeration, but indicates that it was an ambitious venture. The army broke up and raised the siege at the end of a fortnight, having achieved nothing. No source expressly states the reason for failure, but they hint at dissension and disagreement among the host. Perhaps the Scottish nobility when joined together arrayed for war put up a more united, coherent and threatening opposition to the king than when he was browbeating them individually or in parliament. Whatever the reason, it was the first serious setback which James had suffered, the first demonstration that his powerful personality was fallible. A general council was summoned to Perth for 1 October, which by the end of the month had been transformed into a full parliament (which suggests that James was trying to raise taxation for the war). Sources are scanty and inferential, but there is enough to suppose that 'there was a first-class row between the king and the estates' when, by one reconstruction of events, the opposition was voiced by Sir Robert Graham as 'speaker' and the king only secured his will by surrounding the assembly with troops; Graham, having threatened the king with arrest, had to flee.

A fresh general council was summoned to meet in February 1437, at which James was confident that he would get his way. Not suspecting any trouble, he spent Christmas at the Dominican friary in Perth with the papal legate, the bishop of Urbino, who was in Scotland on behalf of Pope Eugenius IV to woo the king away from conciliarism and opposition to 'barratry'. On 20 February, James was suddenly assassinated in the Dominican friary by a small conspiracy of nobles.

Most of them had a personal grievance. Sir Robert Graham, as well as political idealism, had the motive that he was uncle of Malise Graham earl of Menteith, deprived earl of Strathearn and a hostage in England; Sir Robert Stewart, grandson of the earl of Atholl, had seen James leave his father as a hostage in England where he had died; two burgesses of Perth who were involved may have been the victims of James's extortionate 'benevolences'. But the sources agree that the ringleader in the conspiracy was Walter earl of Atholl, the king's aged uncle, who sought to become regent for the child James II. There seems to have been no attempt to alter the succession. Atholl's son had died as a hostage in England, but it is clear that James did not suspect Atholl or his grandson, who was chamberlain of the royal household and who admitted the assassins to the Blackfriars and laid the ground for the murder.

Sir Robert Graham had miscalculated when he led parliamentary opposition to James, probably in 1436; the estates deserted him and he had to flee in isolation. He and his fellow assassins had miscalculated even more seriously in their expectation that the murder of the king would be universally welcomed. In fact even James's many enemies united in revulsion at the deed. A brother of the dispossessed earl of March tried to arrest the assassins as they fled and was wounded by them; the earl of Douglas, who had experienced the king's capricious wrath in 1431, and who was now made lieutenant, helped round up the conspirators and had them put to death, amid reports of fiendish tortures. Before his execution Graham is reported to have said that his executioners would one day pray for his soul because of the good he had done them in ridding the realm of so cruel a tyrant.[12]

James I has been described as 'an angry young man in a hurry'. He certainly was in a hurry, and his haste and disregard for the safety, rights and feelings of others contributed to his death; but he was no longer young (in his forty-third year), and had become fat, greedy and avaricious. It is difficult to reconcile the thoughtful and amorous author of the *Kingis Quair* with the aggressive politician who could be ruthless, arbitrary and totalitarian. Part of James's problem was that he had no sense of what was practically possible as distinct from what he wished; he passed legislation which would have required a police force to enforce it, and treated the nobility in a way which eventually drove a small faction of them into a desperate act of murder, while many others 'may have given a private sigh of relief when they heard of it'. James is difficult to assess; he faced many of the same problems as David II, but was very much less successful in solving them; and his achievements compare unfavourably with those of his son, whose objectives were similar.

The Minority of James II, 1437–49

But the boy James was only six, and twelve years were to pass before he began to exercise power himself, years among the most disorderly in Scottish history – perhaps a reflection on James I's repression as much as anything. If the problems of other royal minorities in Scotland have been grossly exaggerated, those of James II's youth were certainly serious. In the short term, power was to be exercised by Archibald, 5th earl of Douglas, supported by the queen mother as custodian of the young king, and James's chancellor, Bishop Cameron, who retained office. But the 5th earl seems not to have had the determination and ability of many of his Douglas predecessors, and by 1439 the estates in general council felt it necessary to exhort him to 'raise the country' and proceed against 'rebels and unruleful men'.

His death in June of the same year removed the last vestiges of restraint on the nobility. In the following year his teenage son William was judicially murdered at the 'Black Dinner' at Edinburgh by Sir Alexander Livingston and Sir William Crichton. The chief beneficiary of the earl's murder was his great-uncle James 'the Gross' who succeeded to the earldom but died less than three years later. The years

1443 to 1449 were a period of feuding between Crichtons and Livingstons, Crawfords and Kennedys, Stewarts and Ruthvens, Ogilvies and Lindsays. Murders of great and lesser men alike went unpunished.

It is clear that the Douglases, howsoever powerful, were no substitute for royal authority, and did not seek to be. Only Albany among the nobility had come close to fulfilling that role. Further, the Douglases, like the royal house of Stewart, were subject to their own internal feuds, and the 'Black Dinner' shows this erupting into violence. Families like Crichton and Livingston came to power because they were able to control the boy-king's person; they had risen to prominence in James I's household, where he had used men of their rank in the same way David II had done. Now they retained and increased their influence because the greater nobility had been so cowed by James I. There were very few earls to oppose them; many comital titles had fallen into James I's hand, the Graham earl of Menteith was hostage in England, and the Atholl Stewarts had been destroyed for their part in James's murder. In a way the crisis of the 1440s was of James I's own making.[13]

UNSUNG HERO: JAMES II AND HIS LEGACY

The Crown and the Douglases

In 1449 James married Marie de Gueldres, a daughter of the duke of Gueldres and niece of the duke of Burgundy; four of his sisters were married to husbands who were French or friends of the French. James's bride was escorted to Scotland by a Netherlandish fleet in June 1449, and the couple were married at Holyrood on 3 July. His marriage marked the end of James's minority, and he acted quickly to shake off the dominance of the Livingstons. In September the chief members of the family were arrested and brought to trial before parliament in January 1450. There were only two executions, of Sir Robert Livingston of Linlithgow, a cousin of Alexander Livingston of Callander, who had been comptroller, and the younger Alexander Livingston, son of the laird of Callander; the laird himself and his eldest son James were forfeited and temporarily imprisoned for having detained the king's person and embezzled monies from the customs. The earl of Douglas and his supporters stood by and let the king punish their former allies; the Livingstons no longer served any useful purpose for them.[14]

The Douglases certainly had no fear or suspicion of the king. Some time in 1449–50 Earl William loaned the king £100; in the autumn of 1450 he set out on pilgrimage to Rome to take advantage of the jubilee indulgence proclaimed by Pope Nicholas V. The earl cut a magnificent figure in the city during his stay, so that he was 'commended by the supreme pontiff above all pilgrims', and was hospitably received on his return journey at the Lancastrian court in London.

During his absence, King James launched a sudden attack on his lands, seizing his castles and killing his tenants, sparing only those who gave oaths of allegiance; in this act he is said to have been incited by Bishop Turnbull of Glasgow and by the Crichtons. When the earl returned in the spring of 1451 it was to find the king besieging his fortress of Craig Douglas on the Yarrow. There was a suspension of hostilities until a compromise arrangement was prepared for parliament which was to meet at Edinburgh at the end of June 1451. At this the earl submitted and resigned all his lands into the king's hands, whereupon James regranted them to him 'notwithstanding any crimes committed . . . or of treason, treachery or otherwise'. Between 6 and 8 July the king issued charters confirming to Douglas most of his lands and offices. The most important Douglas possession retained by the king at this time was the earldom of Wigtown; but the compromise was a relief to most of the nobility: 'all gud Scottis men war rycht blyth of that accordance', wrote a contemporary. In October 1451 the king restored the earldom of Wigtown as well, together with the lands of Stewarton and Dunlop in Ayrshire.

Despite this apparent reconciliation, tension continued between king and earl. Allies of Douglas slew Sir John Sandilands of Calder; stories of the murder of James's faithful servant John Herries of Terregles and others are less reliable, but may have a basis in truth. There seems to have been some sort of incident at Edinburgh in January 1452 in which Douglas narrowly escaped capture by the

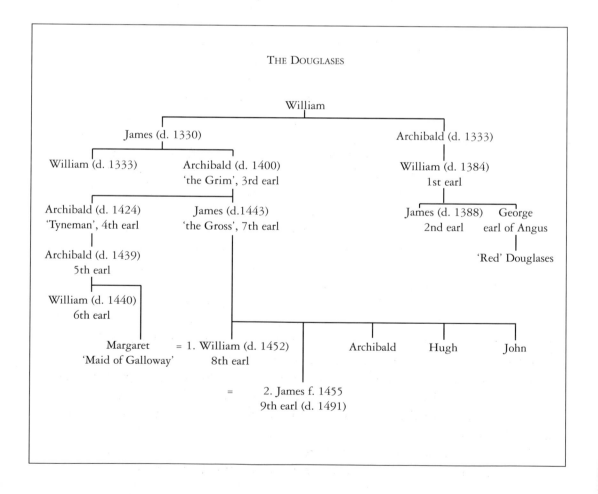

THE DOUGLASES

Crichtons. When he arranged to meet the king at Stirling in February, Earl William took the precaution of demanding a royal safeconduct, which was readily granted. The king then murdered Earl William over dinner in hot blood, allegedly because he would not break a bond which he had made with the earls of Crawford and Ross. Perhaps things might have ended differently if the two men had not wined and dined so well that night (22 February 1452). Douglas had already spent one night as the king's guest before the fatal banquet, and the king had previously drawn back from a confrontation, and was to do so again. James may not have intended to do more than frighten Douglas, and it was probably not he who struck the final blow, but a court-ier who 'strak him next eftir the king with ane poleax on the heid and strak out his brains'; what is fairly certain is that the incident was unpremeditated.

Earl William's heir was his brother James. A month after the murder he marched with power on Stirling; the violated letter of safeconduct was symbolically pilloried and drawn at the tail of a horse, the burgh of Stirling was sacked, and the new earl issued a formal defiance of the king. James too gathered his forces, and was aided by support and finance from the two chief bishops of the kingdom, Kennedy of St Andrews and Turnbull of Glasgow. The earl of Huntly defeated Douglas's ally Crawford at Brechin (May 1452). James summoned a parliament of his supporters to Edinburgh in June and was duly exculpated for Douglas's death on the grounds that the latter had refused to break with the king's enemies; then in July he marched through the border country wasting the Douglas lands. In August negotiations began between the king and the earl, which resulted in an 'appointment' agreed at the end of August. The chief points were these: Douglas forgave the king and his adherents for the murder of his brother; he agreed to revoke all bonds with the king's enemies made in the past, and promised to enter into none in the future; he would give sureties for his future safety, would honour the king and defend the borders; he would not seek to obtain unentailed Douglas lands without royal permission. In January 1453 their reconciliation was completed when James promised the earl that he would seek a papal dispensation to enable him to marry his brother's widow, the 'fair maid of Galloway', thus enabling the earl to reunite the Douglas earldom (which was entailed to heirs male) with the unentailed territories accumulated mainly by Archibald the Grim before he became earl.

Much of the basis of Douglas power lay in the unentailed lands with their concentration in Galloway and the fortress of Threave Castle, rather than in the rich but scattered lands of the earldom itself. So the king's agreement to the reunification of the Douglas inheritance seems to indicate that he expected good relations with Earl James to last. In 1453 Douglas's ally Crawford was also restored. At about the same time the king lost some loyal supporters: the leaders of the Crichton family died in 1453, and Bishop Turnbull in 1454, having seen his new university at Glasgow established.

If King James hoped for better relations in future, his suspicions were soon rekindled. He sent Earl James to the Lancastrian court to renegotiate the truce in the spring of 1453; while in England, Douglas secured the release of Malise Graham earl of Menteith, the deprived earl of Strathearn who had been sent south as a surety for James I's ransom in 1427 and neglected for a quarter of a century. He was a great-grandson of Robert II by his second marriage and a relative of the Atholl Stewarts who had murdered James I. But Malise, although he lived until 1490, was never very active politically; the release of Malise Graham was not one of the accusations brought against the earl at the time of his forfeiture two years later. It is surely right that 'it is unlikely that the earl's transactions in England furnished the motive for the Scottish king's third attack on the Black Douglases'.

So why did King James turn on the Black Douglases again in 1455? There was little of substance in the accusations at the parliament which assented to their forfeiture, yet the king forced his way without opposition. Some aspects of the king's dealings in 1455 were unscrupulous: he began his attack on Douglas castles in March 1455, but not until 24 April did he summon the earl to answer charges of treason. By this time he had taken Inveravon and Abercorn castles and wasted the Douglas estates in Clydesdale, Avondale and Douglasdale. The earl was much slower to react than he had been in 1452, and seems to have shrunk from a direct confrontation with the king; when he found desertion in his own ranks he decided to slip away to seek English help. His three brothers were left behind to be routed in a skirmish with the border lairds at Arkinholm near Langholm at the end of April 1455; Archibald was killed, Hugh was wounded, captured and executed, and John fled to join his brother in exile.

The collapse of the Douglases was sudden. Threave Castle withstood James's bombardment until July, but it fell before English help approached. By the time parliament reconvened in August 1455 to pass sentence of forfeiture on the Douglases, all fighting was over. The sentence was passed on the technical grounds that the earl, having been summoned to answer charges of treason, had failed to appear and was therefore contumacious. James's success was due to his military skill: his possession of artillery and grasp of its importance, his rapid strikes against enemy castles, and his ability to neutralise one enemy while attacking another.

Renewal of the War with England

The parliament of August 1455 confirmed to the king the acquisition of lands worth some £2,000 annually, and passed statutes which would make it difficult for James's successors to alienate certain crown lands in future. There was a military as well as a financial side to this transaction, for key castles were among the expressly 'annexed' lands; and finance and war were becoming inextricably linked as warfare became more expensive, with James dragging his huge bombards (of which Mons Meg is the most famous) round the country. Guns gave the king an irresistible advantage over the nobles which his predecessors had not had; but James needed an increased income with which to pay for them.

One motive which may have prompted James to destroy the Douglases was his desire to renew the war against England; and he rightly saw the Douglas power and doubtful loyalty as an obstacle to this. As early as May 1455 he made an unsuccessful sortie against Berwick; in October 1455 he made provision for a standing garrison in the Marches and for observation of the narrow corridor which the English maintained linking Roxburgh and Berwick. In May 1456 he renounced the truce with England, and in July harried the English-held lands around Roxburgh; in July he raided deep into Northumberland, looting and destroying fortalices in his way. In February 1457 he took advantage of the deepening York–Lancaster crisis to launch another attack on Berwick, which was again abortive. A series of truces was arranged, while James bided his time.

Meanwhile his domestic policies, as set out in the parliament of 1455, went ahead; there was unwonted cooperation between crown and nobility. In 1458 parliament voted special praise to the king, who had removed all breakers of the king's justice, 'no masterful party remaining'; the king was exhorted to maintain the statutes which he had taken in hand, to be pleasing to God, so that 'all his lieges may pray for him to God and give thanks to Him that sends them such a prince to be their governor and defender'.[15] They had not had such a military genius since Robert I, nor such a shrewd manipulator of domestic and foreign politics since David II. James II, however unscrupulous, was every inch a successful king. Both in strategy and politics, he was single-minded in pursuit of an objective, seizing boldly on any advantage his opponents left him; this differed from his father's seemingly directionless violence against all the nobility in general. Once the Douglases had been curbed, crown and nobility operated in apparent harmony for the improvement of justice and administration; even seemingly unpopular acts like a revocation of grants made during the minority, a curbing of regality jurisdictions, and an ending of hereditary crown offices, were offset by the prospect of a time without civil war or feud, and of a successful war against England.

The Battle of Northampton in July 1460 gave James his chance; Henry VI was captured by the Yorkists, but his queen remained in the field, and the Wars of the Roses flared up again. James quickly mobilised the great military resources which he had been amassing over a number of years and marched on Roxburgh; this mighty fortress was garrisoned at a cost of £2,000 a year in wartime and had frustrated James I's army in a matter of days. Now, at the end of July 1460, James settled his army before its walls while his guns went to work on them. James was so confident of success that he summoned the queen and royal ladies to come and witness the fall of Roxburgh; and when they arrived on 3 August he ordered a special salvo to be fired from all his guns. One of these exploded as he stood nearby, and a fragment struck the king in the thigh, killing him.[16]

Postscript: The Legacy of James II

The death of the brilliant young king, just short of his thirtieth birthday, did not deter the besiegers, who carried on his work until Roxburgh was battered into submission on 8 August. Having taken Roxburgh, the queen and magnates took the ten-year-old James III to Kelso Abbey for his coronation on 10 August. James II's

The site of Roxburgh Castle. *(Historic Scotland)*

The walls, Berwick-on-Tweed. *(Historic Scotland)*

ability is reflected in the fact that his son's minority was not nearly as troubled as his own or his father's had been. A prophecy had declared that a dead king would capture Roxburgh Castle, and this had come true; but it was also due to James's planning and forethought that the Scots were able to recover Berwick from the beleaguered Lancastrians in 1461. The acquisition of Orkney and Shetland in 1469–70 brought Scotland to its greatest extent, before James III's incompetence lost Berwick again, for the last time, in 1482. There is evidence that Berwick had quickly recovered its economic importance for Scotland, becoming a centre of foreign exchange.

James II was successful in almost everything he attempted. So why is he something of an unsung hero? His personality was not unattractive, he was bluff and popular with nobles and common soldiers alike, his attack on the Douglases was not resented in the way his father's treatment of the nobility had been, and he seems to have been trusted by the rest of the nobles. The recoveries of Roxburgh and Berwick, the last vestiges of the 'English Pale' established by Edward III, were significant military achievements, the greatest since Otterburn, and of considerable economic value. Physically, James was handsome and athletic, but the one contemporary portrait shows him disfigured by the red birthmark which gave him his nickname 'the fiery face'.

After the reign of James II Scottish kings moved towards a *rapprochement* with England, leading to the first peace treaty of 1503. The expulsion of the English from France in 1453 and the end of the Hundred Years' War were in the long term to dictate a change in international relationships in which England and Scotland would find new roles.

What is most striking about these two centuries (1286–1469) is not institutional developments, but the way in which Scotland fought a long and ultimately successful defensive war without a developed constitutional and administrative edifice such as existed in England. Much more depended on individuals, nobles and non-nobles, doing what they conceived to be their national duty in their own sphere or locality. When a small faction (like the murderers of James I) or a great magnate dynasty (like the Douglases) acted against that concept they were abandoned by the rest. In the face of the foreign threat, the Scottish community showed remarkable loyalty and *esprit de corps*. It is the threat and reality of war which gives Scottish history a unique flavour of robust individualism linked to a common national purpose in this period – fighting for the preservation of the kingdom.

Notes

Chapter 1: The Romans in Scotland and their Legacy

1. Claudius Ptolemaeus, *Geographia*, ed. K. Müller, vol. i (Paris, A.F. Didot, 1883)
2. Tacitus, *Agricola*, ed. R.M. Ogilvie and I.A. Richmond (Oxford, Oxford University Press, 1967)
3. L. Keppie, *Scotland's Roman Remains* (Edinburgh, John Donald, 1986), esp. ch. 11
4. Sources collected and translated in J.C. Mann and R.G. Penman, eds, *Literary Sources for Roman Britain* (London, LACTOR, 1985)
5. E.A. Thompson, *St Germanus of Auxerre and the End of Roman Britain* (Woodbridge, Boydell, 1968)
6. A.O. Curle, *The Treasure of Traprain: a Scottish Hoard of Roman Silver Plate* (Glasgow, Maclehose, 1923); National Museums of Scotland, *The Treasure of Traprain* (Edinburgh, National Museums of Scotland, 1980)

Chapter 2: Early Kingdoms and Peoples

1. Walter Bower, *Scotichronicon*, ed. D.E.R. Watt (Aberdeen, Aberdeen University Press, 1987–98), v, 291–7
2. Most of the sources are collected and translated in A.O. Anderson, *Early Sources of Scottish History AD 500–1286* (Edinburgh, Oliver & Boyd, 1922), i. See also J.W.M. Bannerman, *Studies in the History of Dalriada*, (Edinburgh, Scottish Academic Press, 1974); Adomnán, *Life of Columba*, ed. A.O. and M.O. Anderson (2nd edn Oxford, Oxford University Press, 1991); the most important Annals are *Annals of Ulster*, ed. S. Mac Airt and G. Mac Niocaill (Dublin, Dublin Institute for Advanced Studies, 1983), and *Annals of Tigernach*, ed. W. Stokes, in *Revue Celtique* 1895–7 (reprinted Llanerch, 1993)
3. *Life of Columba*, 188–9
4. *Ibid.*, 189–91
5. John of Fordun, *Chronica Gentis Scottorum*, ed. W.F. Skene (Edinburgh, Historians of Scotland, 1871), book 3, cap. 46
6. Henry of Huntingdon, quoted in A.O. Anderson, *Scottish Annals from English Chroniclers, AD 500–1286* (London, David Nutt, 1908), 18
7. Edited in M.O. Anderson, *Kings and Kingship in Early Scotland* (2nd edn Edinburgh, Scottish Academic Press, 1980)
8. Bede, *Ecclesiastical History of the English People*, ed. B. Colgrave and R.A.B. Mynors (Oxford, Oxford University Press, 1969)
9. W.F.H. Nicolaisen, *Scottish Place-Names* (London, B.T. Batsford, 1976), ch. 8
10. G.W.S. Barrow, 'Pre-feudal Scotland: Shires and Thanes', in G.W.S. Barrow, *The Kingdom of the Scots* (London, Edward Arnold, 1973)
11. I. Henderson, *The Picts* (London, Thames & Hudson, 1967); F.T. Wainwright, ed., *The Problem of the Picts* (London, Thomas Nelson, 1955)
12. J.R. Allen and J. Anderson, *The Early Christian Monuments of Scotland* (Edinburgh, Society of Antiquaries of Scotland, 1903)
13. Maps in P.G.B. McNeill and H. MacQueen, eds, *Atlas of Scottish History to 1707* (Edinburgh, Scottish Medievalists and Department of Geography, 1996), 53–6
14. K.H. Jackson, 'The Pictish Language', in Wainwright, *Problem*, ch. 6; K. Forsyth, 'Language in Pictland, Spoken and Written', in E.H. Nicoll, ed., *A Pictish Panorama* (Balgavies, Pinkfoot Press, 1995)
15. Bede, *Ecclesiastical History*, 18–19; for arguments against the matrilineal hypothesis, see A.P. Smith, *Warlords and Holy Men: Scotland AD 80–1000* (London, Edward Arnold, 1984), 57ff., and A. Woolf, 'Pictish Matriliny Reconsidered', *Innes Review*, xlix (1998),147–67; in favour, see Anderson, *Kings and Kingship*, ch. 4; and W.D.H. Sellar, 'Warlords, Holy Men and Matrilineal Succession', *Innes Review*, xxxvi (1981), 29–43
16. *Life of Columba*, 140–5
17. Anderson, *Early Sources*, i, 201
18. W.J. Watson, *History of the Celtic Place-Names of Scotland* (London, W. Blackwood & Sons, 1926), 28

19. *Ibid.*, 15, 208
20. Gildas, *The Ruin of Britain and other Works*, ed. M. Winterbottom (Chichester, Phillimore, 1978), 23
21. St Patrick, *His Writings and Muirchu's Life*, ed. A.B.E. Hood (Chichester, Phillimore, 1978), 55–9
22. Gildas, *Ruin of Britain*, 29
23. K.H. Jackson, *The Gododdin* (Edinburgh, Edinburgh University Press, 1969)
24. Anderson, *Early Sources*, i, 163–5
25. *Life of Columba*, 38–41
26. R. Bromwich, *Trioedd Ynis Prydein: the Welsh Triads* (Cardiff, University of Wales Press, 1978), 147–9; P. Mac Cana, *The Learned Tales of Medieval Ireland* (Dublin, Dublin Institute for Advanced Studies, 1980), 47
27. A.P. Forbes, *Lives of SS Ninian and Kentigern* (Edinburgh, Historians of Scotland, 1874); K.H. Jackson, 'The Sources for the Life of St Kentigern', in N.K. Chadwick *et al.*, *Studies in the early British Church* (Cambridge, Cambridge University Press, 1958); A. Macquarrie, *The Saints of Scotland* (Edinburgh, John Donald, 1997), ch. 5
28. Anderson, *Early Sources*, i, 150, 166–7
29. Jackson, *Gododdin*, 98–9, 147
30. Sources mostly gathered in Anderson, *Early Sources*, i, and *Scottish Annals*
31. Bede, *Ecclesiastical History*, 116–7
32. Adomnán, *De Locis Sanctis*, ed. D. Meehan (Dublin, Dublin Institute for Advanced Studies, 1958)
33. Bede, *Ecclesiastical History*, 576–7

Chapter 3: The Coming of Christianity

1. W.H.C. Frend, 'The Christianising of Roman Britain', in M.W. Barley and R.P.C. Hanson, eds, *Christianity in Britain, 300–700* (Leicester, Leicester University Press, 1968)
2. Allen and Anderson, *Early Christian Monuments*, iii, 494–7
3. Jackson, *Gododdin*, 37
4. Stones mostly described in Allen and Anderson, *Early Christian Monuments*; J. Close-Brooks, 'Pictish and other Burials', in J.G.P. Friell and W.G. Watson, eds, *Pictish Studies*, BAR 125 (Oxford, BAR, 1984)
5. St Patrick, *His Writings and Muirchu's Life*, Confessio
6. Bede, *Ecclesiastical History*, 222–3
7. A.A.M. Duncan, 'Bede, Iona and the Picts',

in R.H.C. Davies and J.M. Wallace-Hadrill, eds, *The Writing of History in the Middle Ages: Essays presented to R.W. Southern* (Oxford, Clarendon Press, 1981). See, however, T.O. Clancy, 'The Real St Ninian', *Innes Review*, lii (2001), 1–28, arguing that Ninian and Finnian are identical but dissimilated by scribal confusion; also my *Saints of Scotland*, ch. 3, esp. p. 73
8. *Monumenta Germaniae Historica: Epistolae iii: Epistolae Merowingici et Karolini Aevi*, i (Berlin, 1892), 282–3; *MGH Poetae Latini Medii Aevi*, iv: *Poetae Latini Aevi Carolini*, iv, ed. K. Strecker (Berlin, 1923), 942–62
9. J. MacQueen, *St Nynia*, 2nd edn (Edinburgh, Polygon, 1990), 88–101
10. *Lives of SS Ninian and Kentigern*; translated in MacQueen, *St Nynia*, 102–24
11. Gildas, *Ruin of Britain*, 79, 80–6
12. *Lives of SS Ninian and Kentigern*; Jackson, 'Sources for the Life of St Kentigern'; Macquarrie, *Saints of Scotland*, ch. 5
13. Adomnán, *Life of Columba*; Bede, *Ecclesiastical History*, esp. 220–5; *Annals of Ulster*; Anderson, *Early Sources*, i, 22–117 *passim*.
14. *Ibid.*, i, 142–5
15. A. Macquarrie, '*Vita Sancti Servani*: the Life of St Serf', *Innes Review*, xliv (1993), 122–52
16. Bede, *Ecclesiastical History*, 222–5
17. Adomnán, *Life of Columba*, 80–1
18. *Die irische Kanonensammlung*, ed. H. Wasserchleben, 2nd edn (Leipzig, 1885)
19. Bede, *Ecclesiastical History*, 224–5
20. *Ibid.*, 566–7
21. Eddius Stephanus, *Life of Bishop Wilfrid*, ed. B. Colgrave (Cambridge, Cambridge University Press, 1927), ch. 10; Bede, *Ecclesiastical History*, 294–309
22. Cummian, *Letter 'De controversia paschali' and 'De ratione computandi'*, ed. M. Walsh and D.Ó. Cróinín, Studies and Texts 86 (Toronto, Pontifical Institute, 1988)
23. Bede, *Ecclesiastical History*, 552–5
24. *Two Lives of St Cuthbert*, ed. B. Colgrave (Cambridge, Cambridge University Press, 1940)
25. Bede, *Ecclesiastical History*, 552–3

Chapter 4: The Making of Scotland

1. Anderson, *Early Sources*, i, under the dates cited
2. B.E. Crawford, *Scandinavian Scotland* (Leicester, Leicester University Press, 1987)
3. D.A. Binchy, 'The Passing of the Old Order' in B.Ó Cuív, ed. *The Impact of the Scandinavian*

Invasions (Dublin, Dublin Institute for Advanced Studies, 1962)

4. Anderson, *Early Sources*, i, 263–5

5. *Ibid.*, 389–90

6. Adomnán, *Cáin Adomnáin*, ed. K. Meyer (Oxford, Clarendon Press, 1905)

7. Nicolaisen, *Scottish Place-Names*, ch. 6

8. Anderson, *Early Sources*, i, 277

9. Nicolaisen, *Scottish Place-Names*, 108–11

10. Anderson, *Early Sources*, i, 302–4; A. Macquarrie, 'The Kings of Strathclyde, *c.* 400–1018', in A. Grant and K.J. Stringer, eds, *Medieval Scotland: Crown, Lordship and Community: Essays presented to G.W.S. Barrow* (Edinburgh, Edinburgh University Press, 1993), 1–19

11. Anderson, *Early Sources*, i, 509

12. Crawford, *Scandinavian Scotland*, 161–3; A.A.M. Duncan, *Scotland: the Making of the Kingdom* (Edinburgh, Oliver & Boyd, 1975), 83

13. A. Macquarrie, *Cille Bharra* (Droitwich, Grant Books, 1984), 11–12, 17

14. K. Forsyth, 'The Inscriptions on the Dupplin Cross' in *From the Isles of the North: Medieval Art In Ireland and Britain*, ed. C. Bourke (Belfast, HMSO, 1995), 237–44

15. Anderson, *Early Sources*, i, 268–9, 270–1

16. *Ibid.*, 273, 288–9

17. *Ibid.*, 273–4; Mac Cana, *Learned Tales of Medieval Ireland*, 47, 142–5

18. K.H. Jackson, *The Gaelic Notes in the* Book of Deer (Cambridge, Cambridge University Press, 1972)

19. See below, pp. 85–6

20. Macquarrie, 'The Kings of Strathclyde, *c.* 400–1018'

21. Anderson, *Early Sources*, i, 368; Smyth, *Warlords and Holy Men*, 215–18. Probably the destruction of the British dynasty was not as permanent as Dr Smyth argues.

22. M. Herbert, *Iona, Kells and Derry* (Oxford, Oxford University Press, 1988); J.W.M. Bannerman, '*Comarbe Coluim Chille* and the Relics of Columba', *Innes Review*, xliv (1993), 14–47

23. Anderson, *Early Sources*, i, 431–43, esp. 432, 434

24. A. Macquarrie, 'Early Christian Religious Houses in Scotland: Foundation and Function', in J. Blair and R. Sharpe, eds, *Pastoral Care before the Parish* (Leicester, Leicester University Press, 1992), 110–33

25. D. Broun, 'The Origin of Scottish Identity in its European Context', in B.E. Crawford, ed.,

Scotland in Dark Age Europe (St Andrews, Committee for Dark Age Studies, 1994)

26. Anderson, *Scottish Annals*, 66–7

27. Anderson, *Early Sources*, i, 429; *Scottish Annals*, 69–73

28. Anderson, *Early Sources*, i, 444–8

29. *Ibid.*, 473–5. For the possibility that 'Sueno's Stone' by Forres is Dub's funerary monument, see A.A.M. Duncan, 'The Kingdom of the Scots', in L.M. Smith (ed.), *The Making of Britain: the Dark Ages* (Basingstoke, Macmillan, 1984), 131–44, esp. 139–40.

30. Anderson, *Scottish Annals*, 76–7

31. Anderson, *Early Sources*, i, 511–16

32. Smyth, *Warlords and Holy Men*, 233–7; articles on the Battle of Carham in *Scottish Historical Review*, lv (1976), 1–19, 20–8

33. Anderson, *Early Sources*, i, 569–77

34. *Ibid.*, 581–2, 588, 593–604

35. *Early Sources*, ii, 1–58

36. Thurgot's Life of Queen Margaret is translated in Anderson, *Early Sources*, ii, 59–88. See also D. Baker, '"A Nursery of Saints": St Margaret of Scotland reconsidered', in D. Baker, ed., *Medieval Women: Studies presented to Rosalind M.T. Hill* (Oxford, Blackwell, 1978), 119–41; Macquarrie, *Saints of Scotland*, ch. 10

37. K.H. Jackson, 'Duan Albanach', *Scottish Historical Review*, xxxvi (1957), 125–37

Chapter 5: The Twelfth Century

1. Anderson, *Scottish Annals*, 117–19

2. As shown in their earliest charters; A.C. Lawrie, *Early Scottish Charters prior to 1153* (Glasgow, Maclehose, 1905); A.A.M. Duncan, 'The Earliest Scottish Charters', *Scottish Historical Review*, xxxvii (1958), 103–35

3. Fordun, *Chronica*, i, 224–5

4. Androw of Wyntoun, *Orygynale Cronykil of Scotland*, ed. D. Laing (Scottish Text Society, 1872–9), ii, 176

5. Anderson, *Early Sources*, ii, 144–5

6. Cf. the witness-lists of David's charters. G.W.S. Barrow, *The Charters of King David I* (Woodbridge, Boydell, 1999)

7. Anderson, *Early Sources*, ii, 99–100, 119; 173–4; 183

8. G.W.S. Barrow, *The Acts of Malcolm IV King of Scots* (Edinburgh, Edinburgh University Press, 1960), 166

9. P. McNeill and R. Nicholson, eds, *An Historical Atlas of Scotland* (St Andrews, Conference of Scottish Medievalists, 1975), 30–2, 129–34

10. For the Western Isles in this period, see R.A.

McDonald, *The Kingdom of the Isles* (East Linton, Tuckwell Press, 1997)

11. Anderson, *Scottish Annals*, 202
12. Anglo-Saxon Chronicle, ed. G.N. Garmonsway (London, J.M. Dent, 1954), 264–5
13. Anderson, *Scottish Annals*, 221–2
14. Fordun, *Chronica*, i, 222
15. Anderson, *Early Sources*, ii, 221–2; *Scottish Annals*, 228
16. The sources are mostly collected in A.C. Lawrie, *Annals of the Reigns of Malcolm and William, Kings of Scots*, (Glasgow, Maclehose, 1910) and also in Anderson, *Early Sources*, ii, and *Scottish Annals*.
17. Anderson, *Scottish Annals*, 239
18. So called in the title of the poem on his death, Anderson, *Early Sources*, ii, 256–8; Barrow, *Acts of Malcolm IV*, 220
19. Duncan, *Making of the Kingdom*, 226
20. Barrow, *Acts of Malcolm IV*, 20–1
21. Anderson, *Scottish Annals*, 254–5
22. Text in E.L.G. Stones, *Anglo-Scottish Relations, 1174–1328* (Oxford, Clarendon Press, 1970), 2–11
23. Anderson, *Scottish Annals*, 268
24. *Ibid.*, 278
25. *Ibid.*, 287–8, 294–5
26. A. Macquarrie, *Scotland and the Crusades* (Edinburgh, John Donald, 1985), 30–1; K.J. Stringer, *Earl David of Huntingdon, 1152–1219* (Edinburgh, Edinburgh University Press, 1985), 38–40
27. Text in Stones, *Anglo-Scottish Relations*, 12–17
28. Anderson, *Early Sources*, ii, 346, 356
29. Duncan, *Making*, 240–55
30. Anderson, *Scottish Annals*, 330

Chapter 6: Reforms of the Church

1. Macquarrie, *Saints of Scotland*, 2–3
2. Lawrie, *Early Scottish Charters*, no. 50
3. Duncan, *Making*, 260
4. The Glasgow-York dispute is documented in A.W. Haddan and W. Stubbs, *Councils and Ecclesiastical Documents relating to Great Britain and Ireland* (Oxford, 1869–78), ii, pt 1.
5. Anderson, *Scottish Annals*, 159–60
6. *Ibid.*, 243
7. Wyntoun, *Cronykil*, s.a. 1165
8. Anderson, *Scottish Annals*, 264–5
9. *Ibid.*, 280–2; *Early Sources*, ii, 305
10. Duncan, *Making*, 274
11. Translated in Anderson, *Scottish Annals*, 299–300; see *ibid.*, 310
12. A.I. Dunlop, ed., 'Bagimond's Roll', *Miscellany*

of the Scottish History Society, vi (Edinburgh, Scottish History Society, 1939), 3–77

13. I.B. Cowan, *The Parishes of Medieval Scotland* (Edinburgh, Scottish Records Society, 1967)
14. 'Life of Queen Margaret', quoted in Anderson, *Early Sources*, ii, 76
15. Macquarrie, 'Early Christian Religious Houses'; I.B. Cowan and D.E. Easson, *Medieval Religious Houses: Scotland* (2nd edn London, Longman, 1976), 46–54, is useful but incomplete.
16. *Early Sources*, ii, 31–2
17. The evidence for the foundation of monasteries in Scotland is set out in Cowan and Easson, *Medieval Religious Houses: Scotland*, with some additional information in D.E.R. Watt and N.F. Shead, *The Heads of Religious Houses in Scotland* (Edinburgh, Scottish Record Society, 2001).

Chapter 7: Economy and Society in Medieval Scotland

1. Bannerman, *Studies in the History of Dalriada*; Jackson, *Gaelic Notes in the Book of Deer*
2. Anderson, *Scottish Annals*, 84, 86
3. *Ibid.*, 118
4. Macquarrie, *Scotland and the Crusades*, 9–10
5. Up to 1153 the sources are mostly gathered in Lawrie, *Early Scottish Charters*; thereafter royal grants are in Barrow, *Acts of Malcolm IV* and in G.W.S. Barrow with W.W. Scott, *Acts of William I King of Scots, 1165–1214* (Edinburgh, Edinburgh University Press, 1971)
6. For Earl David's colonisation of Garioch, see Stringer, *Earl David*
7. Duncan, *Making*, 448, 530
8. Macquarrie, *Scotland and the Crusades*, chs 2 and 3
9. Information on foundation of burghs is gathered in G.S. Pryde, *The Burghs of Scotland: a Critical List* (London, Oxford University Press, 1965), and in *Historical Atlas of Scotland*, 31–2, 132–4.

Chapter 8: The Thirteenth Century: the Alexandrian Age

1. Anderson, *Early Sources*, ii, 398–400
2. *Ibid.*, 404
3. *Ibid.*, 406–13
4. Anderson, *Scottish Annals*, 334–5
5. Fordun, *Chronica*, Gesta Annalia, ch. 42; Anderson, *Early Sources*, ii, 471
6. *Ibid.*, 492–5, 496–8; *Scottish Annals*, 358–9
7. Stones, *Anglo-Scottish Relations*, 34–7, 38–53
8. Anderson, *Scottish Annals*, 348–58

9. Anderson, *Early Sources*, ii, 539–40
10. *Ibid.*, 555–7
11. *Ibid.*, 539
12. J. MacQueen and T. Scott, *The Oxford Book of Scottish Verse* (London, Oxford University Press, 1966), 4
13. See above, pp. 9, 11; Bower, *Scotichronicon*, v, 291–7
14. Anderson, *Early Sources*, ii, 562–91, *passim*; *Scottish Annals*, 362–76, *passim*
15. Anderson, *Early Sources*, ii, 607–42
16. *Ibid.*, 647–9
17. *Ibid.*, 655–7
18. Stones, *Anglo-Scottish Relations*, 76–83
19. Anderson, *Early Sources*, ii, 686, 688–92
20. Stones, *Anglo-Scottish Relations*, 84–7

Chapter 9: Scotland's Great War

1. Stones, *Anglo-Scottish Relations*, 84–7
2. E.L.G. Stones and G.G. Simpson, *Edward I and the Throne of Scotland, 1290–1296* (Oxford, Oxford University Press, 1978), ii, 144–5
3. For what follows, see also F. Watson, *Under the Hammer: Edward I and Scotland, 1286–1307* (East Linton, Tuckwell Press, 1998)
4. Bower, *Scotichronicon*, vi, 2–5
5. J. Stevenson, *Documents Illustrative of the History of Scotland* (Edinburgh, H M General Register House, 1870), i, no. 21
6. G.W.S. Barrow, *Robert Bruce and the Community of the Realm of Scotland* (2nd edn, Edinburgh, Edinburgh University Press, 1976), 25–6
7. Stevenson, *Documents*, i, no. 108
8. Stones, *Anglo-Scottish Relations*, 88–101
9. The texts are in Stones and Simpson, *Edward I and the Throne of Scotland*, ii; commentary in Barrow, *Bruce*, chs. 1–3, and R. Nicholson, *Scotland: the Later Middle Ages* (Edinburgh, Oliver & Boyd, 1974), ch. 2
10. Barrow, *Bruce*, 81–3; Nicholson, *Later Middle Ages*, 45–6
11. *Acts of the Parliament of Scotland*, ed. T. Thanson and C. Innes (Record Commission, 1814–75), i, 451–3
12. Stones, *Anglo-Scottish Relations*, 140–5
13. Barrow, *Bruce*, ch. 4; Nicholson, *Later Middle Ages*, ch. 3
14. J. Bain, ed., *Calendar of Documents relating to Scotland* (Edinburgh, H.M. General Register House, 1881–8), ii, no. 823
15. Barrow, *Bruce*, ch. 5; Nicholson, *Later Middle Ages*, 52ff.
16. *Ibid.*, 55–6
17. Barrow, *Bruce*, chs 6–8; Nicholson, *Later Middle Ages*, ch. 3
18. Stones, *Anglo-Scottish Relations*, no. 33, at 254–5
19. Barrow, *Bruce*, 205–8
20. Stones, *Anglo-Scottish Relations*, no. 34, at 266–7 For narratives of this period, see Barrow, *Bruce*, chs 10–15; Nicholson, *Later Middle Ages*, chs 4–5; C. McNamee, *The Wars of the Bruces* (East Linton, Tuckwell Press, 1997)
21. A near-contemporary account of Bruce's campaigns is John Barbour, *The Bruce*, ed. M.P. McDiarmid and J.A.C. Stevenson (Edinburgh, Scottish Text Society, 1980–5)
22. *Acts of the Parliament of Scotland*, i, 459
23. A good translation is in A.A.M. Duncan, *The Nation of Scots and the Declaration of Arbroath* (London, Historical Association, 1970)
24. Macquarrie, *Scotland and the Crusades*, 69–80
25. Narrative of this period in Nicholson, *Later Middle Ages*, chs 6–7; R. Nicholson, *Edward III and the Scots* (London, Oxford University Press, 1965); Grant, *Independence and Nationhood: Scotland 1306–1469* (London, Edward Arnold, 1984), is less favourable to David II.
26. For David's personal government, see B. Webster, *The Acts of David II, King of Scots 1329–1371* (Edinburgh, Edinburgh University Press, 1982)
27. Nicholson, *Later Middle Ages*, 182

Chapter 10: A Changing Society

1. G.W.S. Barrow, 'The Highlands in the Lifetime of Robert Bruce', in his *The Kingdom of the Scots*, 362–83, at 377
2. Fordun, *Chronica*, book 2, chs 8, 9
3. J.W.M. Bannerman, 'The Lordship of the Isles', in J.M. Brown, ed., *Scottish Society in the Fifteenth Century* (London, Edward Arnold, 1977), 209–40; J. Munro and R.W. Munro, *Acts of the Lords of the Isles, 1336–1493* (Scottish History Society, 1986)
4. K. Nicholls, *Gaelic and Gaelicised Ireland in the Middle Ages* (Dublin, Gill and Macmillan, 1972), 87–90
5. P. Hume Brown, *Early Travellers in Scotland* (Edinburgh, D. Douglas, 1891), 25–38
6. Quoted in MacQueen and Scott, *Oxford Book of Scottish Verse*, 10
7. Nicholson, *Later Middle Ages*, 148–9
8. A. Grant, *Independence and Nationhood*: 73–5
9. Bower, *Scotichronicon*, 8, 114–7
10. Duncan, *The Nation of Scots and the Declaration of Arbroath*
11. *Acts of the Parliament of Scotland*, ii, 9, ch. 8

12. Grant, *Independence and Nationhood*, ch. 5
13. J.M. Brown, 'The Exercise of Power' in Brown, *Scottish Society in the Fifteenth Century*, ch. 3
14. Grant, *Independence and Nationhood*, ch. 3

Chapter 11: The Scottish Church in the Later Middle Ages

1. Nicholson, *Later Middle Ages*, 142, 150
2. *Ibid.*, 190–1
3. *Ibid.*, 192, 220, 237–8
4. *Ibid.*, 245–6
5. *Ibid.*, 192, 414–5
6. *Acts of the Parliament of Scotland*, ii, 16, ch. 9
7. Nicholson, *Later Middle Ages*, 294–7, 332–8
8. A.I. Dunlop, *The Life and Times of James Kennedy, Bishop of St Andrews* (Edinburgh, Oliver & Boyd, 1950)
9. Nicholson, *Later Middle Ages*, 387
10. *Ibid*, 461–5
11. J. Herkless and R.K. Hannay, *The Archbishops of St Andrews* (Edinburgh, Blackwood, 1907–15), 1, 157–8
12. Nicholson, *Later Middle Ages*, 557–8
13. E.R. Lindsay and A.I. Cameron, *Calendar of Scottish Supplications to Rome, 1418–1422* (Scottish History Society, 1934), 122
14. Bower, *Scotichronicon*, 8, 139–47
15. Nicholson, *Later Middle Ages*, 239–41, 299–300
16. J.H. Baxter, ed., *Copiale Prioratus Sanctiandree* (London, Oxford University Press, 1930), 230–6
17. John Knox, *History of the Reformation in Scotland*, ed. W.C. Dickinson (London, Nelson, 1949), 1, 8–9
18. Nicholson, *Later Middle Ages*, 561
19. Register of the Sacred Penitentiary, Vatican Archives, Rome. Most of these records remain unpublished.
20. *Acts of the Parliament of Scotland*, ii, 25
21. G.G. Simpson, *Scottish Handwriting, 1150–1650* (Edinburgh, Bratton, 1973), 10–12; J. Wormald, *Court, Kirk and Community: Scotland, 1470–1625* (London, Edward Arnold, 1981), 68ff.

Chapter 12: Nadir and Recovery: The House of Stewart, 1371–1460

1. Bower, *Scotichronicon*, 7, 446–7
2. *Ibid.*, 364–7; for Robert II's reign, see *ibid.*, 7, book 14; Wyntoun, *Cronykil*, 3, 9–44
3. Nicholson, *Later Middle Ages*, 187–8
4. Grant, *Independence and Nationhood*, 42; John Major (Mair), *A History of Greater Britain* (Scottish History Society, 1892), 329
5. Bower, *Scotichronicon*, 8, book 15, chs 1–19; Wyntoun, *Cronykil*, 3, 44–98
6. Bower, *Scotichronicon*, 8, 36–7
7. See in general S. Boardman, *The Early Stewart Kings: Robert II and Robert III, 1371–1406* (East Linton, Tuckwell Press, 1996); Nicholson, *Later Middle Ages*, chs. 8–9
8. Bower, *Scotichronicon*, 8, book 15, chs 21–37; Wyntoun, *Cronykil*, 3, 98–101
9. Bower, *Scotichronicon*, 8, 122–5
10. *The Kingis Quair of James Stewart*, ed. M.P. Macdiarmid (London, Heinemann, 1973)
11. Bower, *Scotichronicon*, 8, book 16, is the main contemporary source. James's legislation is in *Acts of the Parliament of Scotland*, 2. E.M.W. Balfour-Melville, *James I King of Scots* (London, Methuen, 1936), Nicholson, *Later Middle Ages*, ch. 11, A.A.M. Duncan, *James I King of Scots, 1424–1437* (Glasgow, Department of Scottish History, University of Glasgow, 1984), M. Brown, *James I* (Edinburgh, Canongate Academic, 1994), are the most important secondary works.
12. *The Life and Death of James I of Scotland* (Maitland Club, 1837); M. Connolly, 'The Dethe of the Kynge of Scotis: a New Edition', *Scottish Historical Review*, 71 (1992), 46–69
13. Nicholson, *Later Middle Ages*, ch. 12
14. There are few narrative sources for the reign of James II. Chief is the 'Auchinleck Chronicle', unreliably edited in C. McGladdery, *James II* (Edinburgh, John Donald, 1990), 160–73. The best modern accounts are still Nicholson, *Later Middle Ages*, ch. 13, and Dunlop, *Life and Times of James Kennedy*.
15. *Acts of the Parliament of Scotland*, ii, 52
16. Nicholson, *Later Middle Ages*, 396

A Note on Further Reading

Most of the important primary sources and secondary works used in the preparation of this book are referred to in the notes. Among more general works, see also Michael Lynch, *Scotland: a New History* (London, Pimlico, 1991), the best one-volume history of Scotland now available. Among multi-volume histories, *The Edinburgh History of Scotland*, ed. G. Donaldson (Edinburgh, Oliver & Boyd, 1965–75) and *The New History of Scotland*, ed. J. Wormald (London, Edward Arnold, 1981–84) are still the best, though a new multi-volume history, *The New Edinburgh History of Scotland*, ed. R. Mason, is in preparation at the time of writing. Historic Scotland produce lavishly illustrated books on the Dark Ages, of which Anna Ritchie, *Picts* (Edinburgh, HMSO, 1989) and Sally M. Foster, *Picts, Gaels and Scots* (London, B.T. Batsford & Historic Scotland, 1996) are especially good. A.D.M. Barrell, *Medieval Scotland* (Cambridge, Cambridge University Press, 2000) is stronger for the later Middle Ages than for earlier periods. A.A.M. Duncan, *The Kingship of the Scots, 842–1292: Succession and Independence* (Edinburgh, Edinburgh University Press, 2002), has appeared too recently to be taken account of in the present work. For the later Middle Ages, the series of biographies *The Stewart Dynasty in Scotland* (various publishers), ed. N. Macdougall, is very valuable. W. Ferguson, *The Identity of the Scottish Nation* (Edinburgh, Edinburgh University Press, 1998) is a fascinating essay on national identity.

Index

(Page numbers in bold indicate entries for black and white pictures in the text.)